D0868708

Mastering Hadoop

Go beyond the basics and master the next generation
of Hadoop data processing platforms

Sandeep Karanth

PUBLISHING

BIRMINGHAM - MUMBAI

Mastering Hadoop

Copyright © 2014 Packt Publishing

All rights reserved. No part of this book may be reproduced, stored in a retrieval system, or transmitted in any form or by any means, without the prior written permission of the publisher, except in the case of brief quotations embedded in critical articles or reviews.

Every effort has been made in the preparation of this book to ensure the accuracy of the information presented. However, the information contained in this book is sold without warranty, either express or implied. Neither the author, nor Packt Publishing, and its dealers and distributors will be held liable for any damages caused or alleged to be caused directly or indirectly by this book.

Packt Publishing has endeavored to provide trademark information about all of the companies and products mentioned in this book by the appropriate use of capitals. However, Packt Publishing cannot guarantee the accuracy of this information.

First published: December 2014

Production reference: 1221214

Published by Packt Publishing Ltd.
Livery Place
35 Livery Street
Birmingham B3 2PB, UK.

ISBN 978-1-78398-364-3

www.packtpub.com

Cover image by Poonam Nayak (pooh.graphics@gmail.com)

Credits

Author
Sandeep Karanth

Reviewers
Shiva Achari
Pavan Kumar Polineni
Uchit Vyas
Yohan Wadia

Commissioning Editor
Edward Gordon

Acquisition Editor
Rebecca Youé

Content Development Editor
Ruchita Bhansali

Technical Editors
Bharat Patil
Rohit Kumar Singh
Parag Topre

Copy Editors
Sayanee Mukherjee
Vikrant Phadkay

Project Coordinator
Kranti Berde

Proofreaders
Simran Bhogal
Maria Gould
Ameesha Green
Paul Hindle

Indexer
Mariammal Chettiyar

Graphics
Abhinash Sahu
Valentina Dsilva

Production Coordinator
Arvindkumar Gupta

Cover Work
Arvindkumar Gupta

About the Author

Sandeep Karanth is a technical architect who specializes in building and operationalizing software systems. He has more than 14 years of experience in the software industry, working on a gamut of products ranging from enterprise data applications to newer-generation mobile applications. He has primarily worked at Microsoft Corporation in Redmond, Microsoft Research in India, and is currently a cofounder at Scibler, architecting data intelligence products.

Sandeep has special interest in data modeling and architecting data applications. In his area of interest, he has successfully built and deployed applications, catering to a variety of business use cases such as vulnerability detection from machine logs, churn analysis from subscription data, and sentiment analyses from chat logs. These applications were built using next generation big data technologies such as Hadoop, Spark, and Microsoft StreamInsight and deployed on cloud platforms such as Amazon AWS and Microsoft Azure.

Sandeep is also experienced and interested in areas such as green computing and the emerging Internet of Things. He frequently trains professionals and gives talks on topics such as big data and cloud computing. Sandeep believes in inculcating skill-oriented and industry-related topics in the undergraduate engineering curriculum, and his talks are geared with this in mind. Sandeep has a Master's degree in Computer and Information Sciences from the University of Minnesota, Twin Cities.

Sandeep's twitter handle is @karanths. His GitHub profile is https://github.com/Karanth, and he writes technical snippets at https://gist.github.com/Karanth.

Acknowledgments

I would like to dedicate this book to my loving daughter, Avani, who has taught me many a lesson in effective time management. I would like to thank my wife and parents for their constant support that has helped me complete this book on time. Packt Publishing have been gracious enough to give me this opportunity, and I would like to thank all individuals who were involved in editing, reviewing, and publishing this book. Questions and feedback from curious audiences at my lectures have driven much of the content of this book. Some of the subtopics are from experiences I gained working on a wide variety of projects throughout my career. I would like to thank my audience and also my employers for indirectly helping me write this book.

About the Reviewers

Shiva Achari has over 8 years of extensive industry experience and is currently working as a Big Data architect in Teradata. Over the years, he has architected, designed, and developed multiple innovative and high-performing large-scale solutions such as distributed systems, data center, Big Data management, SaaS cloud applications, Internet applications, and data analytics solutions.

He is currently writing a book on Hadoop essentials, which is based on Hadoop, its ecosystem components, and how we can leverage the components in different phases of the Hadoop project life cycle.

Achari has experience in designing Big Data and analytics applications, ingestion, cleansing, transformation, correlating different sources, data mining, and user experience using Hadoop, Cassandra, Solr, Storm, R, and Tableau.

He specializes in developing solutions for the Big Data domain and possesses a sound hands-on experience on projects migrating to the Hadoop world, new development, product consulting, and POC. He also has hands-on expertise on technologies such as Hadoop, Yarn, Sqoop, Hive, Pig, Flume, Solr, Lucene, Elasticsearch, Zookeeper, Storm, Redis, Cassandra, HBase, MongoDB, Talend, R, Mahout, Tableau, Java, and J2EE.

Shiva has expertise in requirement analysis, estimations, technology evaluation, and system architecture, with domain experience of telecom, Internet applications, document management, healthcare, and media.

Currently, he supports presales activities such as writing technical proposals (RFP), providing technical consultation to customers, and managing deliveries of Big Data practice group in Teradata.

He is active on LinkedIn at http://in.linkedin.com/in/shivaachari/.

> I would like to thank Packt Publishing for helping me out with the reviewing process and the opportunity to review this book, which was a great opportunity and experience. I will wish the publication and author best of luck for the success of the book.

Pavan Kumar Polineni is working as Analytics Manager at Fantain Sports. He has experience in the fields of information retrieval and recommendation engines. He is a Cloudera certified Hadoop administrator. His is interested in machine learning, data mining, and visualization.

He has a Bachelor's degree in Computer Science from Koneru Lakshmaiah College of Engineering and is about to complete his Master's degree in Software Systems from BITS, Pilani. He has worked at organizations such as IBM and Ctrls Datacenter. He can be found on Twitter as @polinenipavan.

Uchit Vyas is an open source specialist and a hands-on lead DevOps of Clogeny Technologies. He is responsible for the delivery of solutions, services, and product development. He explores new enterprise open source and defining architecture, roadmaps, and best practices. He has consulted and provided training on various open source technologies, including cloud computing (AWS Cloud, Rackspace, Azure, CloudStack, Openstack, and Eucalyptus), Mule ESB, Chef, Puppet and Liferay Portal, Alfresco ECM, and JBoss, to corporations around the world.

He has a degree in Engineering in Computer Science from the Gujarat University. He worked in the education and research team of Infosys Limited as senior associate, during which time he worked on SaaS, private clouds, virtualization, and now, cloud system automation.

He has also published book on Mule ESB, and is writing various books on open source technologies and AWS.

He hosts a blog named Cloud Magic World, `cloudbyuchit.blogspot.com`, where he posts tips and phenomena about open source technologies, mostly cloud technologies. He can also be found on Twitter as `@uchit_vyas`.

I am thankful to Riddhi Thaker (my colleague) for helping me a lot in reviewing this book.

Yohan Wadia is a client-focused virtualization and cloud expert with 5 years of experience in the IT industry.

He has been involved in conceptualizing, designing, and implementing large-scale solutions for a variety of enterprise customers based on VMware vCloud, Amazon Web Services, and Eucalyptus Private Cloud.

His community-focused involvement enables him to share his passion for virtualization and cloud technologies with peers through social media engagements, public speaking at industry events, and through his personal blog at `yoyoclouds.com`.

He is currently working with Virtela Technology Services, an NTT communications company, as a cloud solutions engineer, and is involved in managing the company's in-house cloud platform. He works on various open source and enterprise-level cloud solutions for internal as well as external customers. He is also a VMware Certified Professional and vExpert (2012, 2013).

www.PacktPub.com

Support files, eBooks, discount offers, and more

For support files and downloads related to your book, please visit www.PacktPub.com.

Did you know that Packt offers eBook versions of every book published, with PDF and ePub files available? You can upgrade to the eBook version at www.PacktPub.com and as a print book customer, you are entitled to a discount on the eBook copy. Get in touch with us at service@packtpub.com for more details.

At www.PacktPub.com, you can also read a collection of free technical articles, sign up for a range of free newsletters and receive exclusive discounts and offers on Packt books and eBooks.

http://PacktLib.PacktPub.com

Do you need instant solutions to your IT questions? PacktLib is Packt's online digital book library. Here, you can search, access, and read Packt's entire library of books.

Why subscribe?

- Fully searchable across every book published by Packt
- Copy and paste, print, and bookmark content
- On demand and accessible via a web browser

Free access for Packt account holders

If you have an account with Packt at www.PacktPub.com, you can use this to access PacktLib today and view 9 entirely free books. Simply use your login credentials for immediate access.

Table of Contents

Preface

We are in an age where data is the primary driver in decision-making. With storage costs declining, network speeds increasing, and everything around us becoming digital, we do not hesitate a bit to download, store, or share data with others around us. About 20 years back, a camera was a device used to capture pictures on film. Every photograph had to be captured almost perfectly. The storage of film negatives was done carefully lest they get damaged. There was a higher cost associated with taking prints of these photographs. The time taken between a picture click and to view it was almost a day. This meant that less data was being captured as these factors presented a cliff for people from recording each and every moment of their life, unless it was very significant.

However, with cameras becoming digital, this has changed. We do not hesitate to click a photograph of almost anything anytime. We do not worry about storage as our externals disks of a terabyte capacity always provide a reliable backup. We seldom take our cameras anywhere as we have mobile devices that we can use to take photographs. We have applications such as Instagram that can be used to add effects to our pictures and share them. We gather opinions and information about the pictures, and we click and base some of our decisions on them. We capture almost every moment, of great significance or not, and push it into our memory books. The era of big data has arrived!

This era of Big Data has similar changes in businesses as well. Almost everything in a business is logged. Every action taken by a user on the page of an e-commerce page is recorded to improve quality of service and every item bought by the user are recorded to cross-sell or up-sell other items. Businesses want to understand the DNA of their customers and try to infer it by pinching out every possible data they can get about these customers. Businesses are not worried about the format of the data. They are ready to accept speech, images, natural language text, or structured data. These data points are used to drive business decisions and personalize experiences for the user. The more data, the higher the degree of personalization and better the experience for the user.

We saw that we are ready, in some aspects, to take on this Big Data challenge. However, what about the tools used to analyze this data? Can they handle the volume, velocity, and variety of the incoming data? Theoretically, all this data can reside on a single machine, but what is the cost of such a machine? Will it be able to cater to the variations in loads? We know that supercomputers are available, but there are only a handful of them in the world. Supercomputers don't scale. The alternative is to build a team of machines, a cluster, or individual computing units that work in tandem to achieve a task. A team of machines are interconnected via a very fast network and provide better scaling and elasticity, but that is not enough. These clusters have to be programmed. A greater number of machines, just like a team of human beings, require more coordination and synchronization. The higher the number of machines, the greater the possibility of failures in the cluster. How do we handle synchronization and fault tolerance in a simple way easing the burden on the programmer? The answer is systems such as Hadoop.

Hadoop is synonymous with Big Data processing. Its simple programming model, "code once and deploy at any scale" paradigm, and an ever-growing ecosystem make Hadoop an inclusive platform for programmers with different levels of expertise and breadth of knowledge. Today, it is the number-one sought after job skill in the data sciences space. To handle and analyze Big Data, Hadoop has become the go-to tool. Hadoop 2.0 is spreading its wings to cover a variety of application paradigms and solve a wider range of data problems. It is rapidly becoming a general-purpose cluster platform for all data processing needs, and will soon become a mandatory skill for every engineer across verticals.

This book covers optimizations and advanced features of MapReduce, Pig, and Hive. It also covers Hadoop 2.0 and illustrates how it can be used to extend the capabilities of Hadoop.

Hadoop, in its 2.0 release, has evolved to become a general-purpose cluster-computing platform. The book will explain the platform-level changes that enable this. Industry guidelines to optimize MapReduce jobs and higher-level abstractions such as Pig and Hive in Hadoop 2.0 are covered. Some advanced job patterns and their applications are also discussed. These topics will empower the Hadoop user to optimize existing jobs and migrate them to Hadoop 2.0. Subsequently, it will dive deeper into Hadoop 2.0-specific features such as **YARN (Yet Another Resource Negotiator)** and HDFS Federation, along with examples. Replacing HDFS with other filesystems is another topic that will be covered in the latter half of the book. Understanding these topics will enable Hadoop users to extend Hadoop to other application paradigms and data stores, making efficient use of the available cluster resources.

This book is a guide focusing on advanced concepts and features in Hadoop. Foundations of every concept are explained with code fragments or schematic illustrations. The data processing flow dictates the order of the concepts in each chapter.

What this book covers

Chapter 1, Hadoop 2.X, discusses the improvements in Hadoop 2.X in comparison to its predecessor generation.

Chapter 2, Advanced MapReduce, helps you understand the best practices and patterns for Hadoop MapReduce, with examples.

Chapter 3, Advanced Pig, discusses the advanced features of Pig, a framework to script MapReduce jobs on Hadoop.

Chapter 4, Advanced Hive, discusses the advanced features of a higher-level SQL abstraction on Hadoop MapReduce called Hive.

Chapter 5, Serialization and Hadoop I/O, discusses the IO capabilities in Hadoop. Specifically, this chapter covers the concepts of serialization and deserialization support and their necessity within Hadoop; Avro, an external serialization framework; data compression codecs available within Hadoop; their tradeoffs; and finally, the special file formats in Hadoop.

Chapter 6, YARN – Bringing Other Paradigms to Hadoop, discusses YARN (Yet Another Resource Negotiator), a new resource manager that has been included in Hadoop 2.X, and how it is generalizing the Hadoop platform to include other computing paradigms.

Chapter 7, Storm on YARN – Low Latency Processing in Hadoop, discusses the opposite paradigm, that is, moving data to the compute, and compares and contrasts it with batch processing systems such as MapReduce. It also discusses the Apache Storm framework and how to develop applications in Storm. Finally, you will learn how to install Storm on Hadoop 2.X with YARN.

Chapter 8, Hadoop on the Cloud, discusses the characteristics of cloud computing and Hadoop's Platform as a Service offering across cloud computing service providers. Further, it delves into Amazon's managed Hadoop services, also known as Elastic MapReduce (EMR) and looks into how to provision and run jobs on a Hadoop EMR cluster.

Chapter 9, HDFS Replacements, discusses the strengths and drawbacks of HDFS when compared to other file systems. The chapter also draws attention to Hadoop's support for Amazon's S3 cloud storage service. At the end, the chapter illustrates Hadoop HDFS extensibility features by implementing Hadoop's support for S3's native file system to extend Hadoop.

Chapter 10, HDFS Federation, discusses the advantages of HDFS Federation and its architecture. Block placement strategies, which are central to the success of HDFS in the MapReduce environment, are also discussed in the chapter.

Chapter 11, Hadoop Security, focuses on the security aspects of a Hadoop cluster. The main pillars of security are authentication, authorization, auditing, and data protection. We will look at Hadoop's features in each of these pillars.

Chapter 12, Analytics Using Hadoop, discusses higher-level analytic workflows, techniques such as machine learning, and their support in Hadoop. We take document analysis as an example to illustrate analytics using Pig on Hadoop.

Appendix, Hadoop for Microsoft Windows, explores Microsoft Window Operating System's native support for Hadoop that has been introduced in Hadoop 2.0. In this chapter, we look at how to build and deploy Hadoop on Microsoft Windows natively.

What you need for this book?

The following software suites are required to try out the examples in the book:

- **Java Development Kit (JDK 1.7 or later)**: This is free software from Oracle that provides a **JRE (Java Runtime Environment)** and additional tools for developers. It can be downloaded from `http://www.oracle.com/technetwork/java/javase/downloads/index.html`.

- **The IDE for editing Java code**: IntelliJ IDEA is the IDE that has been used to develop the examples. Any other IDE of your choice can also be used. The community edition of the IntelliJ IDE can be downloaded from `https://www.jetbrains.com/idea/download/`.

- **Maven**: Maven is a build tool that has been used to build the samples in the book. Maven can be used to automatically pull-build dependencies and specify configurations via XML files. The code samples in the chapters can be built into a JAR using two simple Maven commands:

```
mvn compile
mvn assembly:single
```

These commands compile the code into a JAR file. These commands create a consolidated JAR with the program along with all its dependencies. It is important to change the mainClass references in the pom.xml to the driver class name when building the consolidated JAR file.

Hadoop-related consolidated JAR files can be run using the command:

```
hadoop jar <jar file> args
```

This command directly picks the driver program from the mainClass that was specified in the pom.xml. Maven can be downloaded and installed from http://maven.apache.org/download.cgi. The Maven XML template file used to build the samples in this book is as follows:

```xml
<?xml version="1.0" encoding="UTF-8"?>
<project xmlns="http://maven.apache.org/POM/4.0.0"
xmlns:xsi="http://www.w3.org/2001/XMLSchema-instance"
xsi:schemaLocation="http://maven.apache.org/POM/4.0.0 http://
maven.apache.org/xsd/maven-4.0.0.xsd">
  <modelVersion>4.0.0</modelVersion>
  <groupId>MasteringHadoop</groupId>
  <artifactId>MasteringHadoop</artifactId>
  <version>1.0-SNAPSHOT</version>
  <build>
    <plugins>
      <plugin>
        <groupId>org.apache.maven.plugins</groupId>
        <artifactId>maven-compiler-plugin</artifactId>
        <version>3.0</version>
        <configuration>
          <source>1.7</source>
          <target>1.7</target>
        </configuration>
      </plugin>
      <plugin>
        <version>3.1</version>
        <groupId>org.apache.maven.plugins</groupId>
        <artifactId>maven-jar-plugin</artifactId>
        <configuration>
          <archive>
            <manifest>
              <mainClass>MasteringHadoop.MasteringHadoopTest</
mainClass>
            </manifest>
          </archive>
        </configuration>
      </plugin>
```

```xml
        <plugin>
          <artifactId>maven-assembly-plugin</artifactId>
          <configuration>
            <archive>
              <manifest>
                <mainClass>MasteringHadoop.MasteringHadoopTest</
mainClass>
              </manifest>
            </archive>
            <descriptorRefs>
              <descriptorRef>jar-with-dependencies</descriptorRef>
            </descriptorRefs>
          </configuration>
        </plugin>
      </plugins>
      <pluginManagement>
        <plugins>
          <!--This plugin's configuration is used to store Eclipse
m2e settings
                   only. It has no influence on the Maven build
itself. -->
          <plugin>
            <groupId>org.eclipse.m2e</groupId>
            <artifactId>lifecycle-mapping</artifactId>
            <version>1.0.0</version>
            <configuration>
              <lifecycleMappingMetadata>
                <pluginExecutions>
                  <pluginExecution>
                    <pluginExecutionFilter>
                      <groupId>org.apache.maven.plugins</groupId>
                      <artifactId>maven-dependency-plugin</
artifactId>
                      <versionRange>[2.1,)</versionRange>
                      <goals>
                        <goal>copy-dependencies</goal>
                      </goals>
                    </pluginExecutionFilter>
                    <action>
                      <ignore />
                    </action>
                  </pluginExecution>
                </pluginExecutions>
              </lifecycleMappingMetadata>
            </configuration>
```

```
        </plugin>
      </plugins>
    </pluginManagement>
  </build>
  <dependencies>
    <!-- Specify dependencies in this section -->
  </dependencies>
</project>
```

- **Hadoop 2.2.0**: Apache Hadoop is required to try out the examples in general. *Appendix, Hadoop for Microsoft Windows*, has the details on Hadoop's single-node installation on a Microsoft Windows machine. The steps are similar and easier for other operating systems such as Linux or Mac, and they can be found at `http://hadoop.apache.org/docs/r2.2.0/hadoop-project-dist/hadoop-common/SingleNodeSetup.html`

Who this book is for

This book is meant for a gamut of readers. A novice user of Hadoop can use this book to upgrade his skill level in the technology. People with existing experience in Hadoop can enhance their knowledge about Hadoop to solve challenging data processing problems they might be encountering in their profession. People who are using Hadoop, Pig, or Hive at their workplace can use the tips provided in this book to help make their jobs faster and more efficient. A curious Big Data professional can use this book to understand the expanding horizons of Hadoop and how it is broadening its scope by embracing other paradigms, not just MapReduce. Finally, a Hadoop 1.X user can get insights into the repercussions of upgrading to Hadoop 2.X. The book assumes familiarity with Hadoop, but the reader need not be an expert. Access to a Hadoop installation, either in your organization, on the cloud, or on your desktop/notebook is recommended to try some of the concepts.

Conventions

In this book, you will find a number of styles of text that distinguish between different kinds of information. Here are some examples of these styles, and an explanation of their meaning.

Code words in text are shown as follows: "The `FileInputFormat` subclass and associated classes are commonly used for jobs taking inputs from HFDS."

A block of code is set as follows:

```
return new CombineFileRecordReader<LongWritable,
Text>((CombineFileSplit) inputSplit, taskAttemptContext,
MasteringHadoopCombineFileRecordReader.class);
}
```

Any command-line input or output is written as follows:

```
14/04/10 07:50:03 INFO input.FileInputFormat: Total input paths to
process : 441
```

New terms and **important words** are shown in bold. Words that you see on the screen, in menus or dialog boxes for example, appear in the text like this: "The former is called a **Map-side join** and the latter is called a **Reduce-side join**."

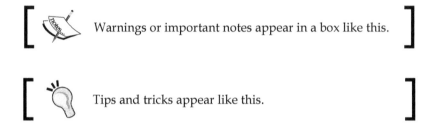

Warnings or important notes appear in a box like this.

Tips and tricks appear like this.

Reader feedback

Feedback from our readers is always welcome. Let us know what you think about this book—what you liked or may have disliked. Reader feedback is important for us to develop titles that you really get the most out of.

To send us general feedback, simply send an e-mail to feedback@packtpub.com, and mention the book title through the subject of your message.

If there is a topic that you have expertise in and you are interested in either writing or contributing to a book, see our author guide on www.packtpub.com/authors.

Customer support

Now that you are the proud owner of a Packt book, we have a number of things to help you to get the most from your purchase.

Downloading the example code

You can download the example code files for all Packt books you have purchased from your account at `http://www.packtpub.com`. If you purchased this book elsewhere, you can visit `http://www.packtpub.com/support` and register to have the files e-mailed directly to you.

You can also download latest code bundles and sample files from `https://github.com/karanth/MasteringHadoop`.

Errata

Although we have taken every care to ensure the accuracy of our content, mistakes do happen. If you find a mistake in one of our books—maybe a mistake in the text or the code—we would be grateful if you would report this to us. By doing so, you can save other readers from frustration and help us improve subsequent versions of this book. If you find any errata, please report them by visiting `http://www.packtpub.com/support`, selecting your book, clicking on the **errata submission form** link, and entering the details of your errata. Once your errata are verified, your submission will be accepted and the errata will be uploaded to our website, or added to any list of existing errata, under the Errata section of that title.

Piracy

Piracy of copyright material on the Internet is an ongoing problem across all media. At Packt, we take the protection of our copyright and licenses very seriously. If you come across any illegal copies of our works, in any form, on the Internet, please provide us with the location address or website name immediately so that we can pursue a remedy.

Please contact us at `copyright@packtpub.com` with a link to the suspected pirated material.

We appreciate your help in protecting our authors, and our ability to bring you valuable content.

Questions

You can contact us at `questions@packtpub.com` if you are having a problem with any aspect of the book, and we will do our best to address it.

1
Hadoop 2.X

"There's nothing that cannot be found through some search engine or on the Internet somewhere."

-Eric Schmidt, Executive Chairman, Google

Hadoop is the de facto open source framework used in the industry for large scale, massively parallel, and distributed data processing. It provides a computation layer for parallel and distributed computation processing. Closely associated with the computation layer is a highly fault-tolerant data storage layer, the **Hadoop Distributed File System** (HDFS). Both the computation and data layers run on commodity hardware, which is inexpensive, easily available, and compatible with other similar hardware.

In this chapter, we will look at the journey of Hadoop, with a focus on the features that make it enterprise-ready. Hadoop, with 6 years of development and deployment under its belt, has moved from a framework that supports the MapReduce paradigm exclusively to a more generic cluster-computing framework. This chapter covers the following topics:

- An outline of Hadoop's code evolution, with major milestones highlighted
- An introduction to the changes that Hadoop has undergone as it has moved from 1.X releases to 2.X releases, and how it is evolving into a generic cluster-computing framework
- An introduction to the options available for enterprise-grade Hadoop, and the parameters for their evaluation
- An overview of a few popular enterprise-ready Hadoop distributions

The inception of Hadoop

The birth and evolution of the Internet led to **World Wide Web (WWW)**, a huge set of documents written in the markup language, HTML, and linked with one another via hyperlinks. Clients, known as browsers, became the user's window to WWW. Ease of creation, editing, and publishing of these web documents meant an explosion of document volume on the Web.

In the latter half of the 90s, the huge volume of web documents led to discoverability problems. Users found it hard to discover and locate the right document for their information needs, leading to a gold rush among web companies in the space of web discovery and search. Search engines and directory services for the Web, such as Lycos, Altavista, Yahoo!, and Ask Jeeves, became commonplace.

These search engines started ingesting and summarizing the Web. The process of traversing the Web and ingesting the documents is known as **crawling**. Smart crawlers, those that can download documents quickly, avoid link cycles, and detect document updates, have been developed.

In the early part of this century, Google emerged as the torchbearer of the search technology. Its success was attributed not only to the introduction of robust, spam-defiant relevance technology, but also its minimalistic approach, speed, and quick data processing. It achieved the former goals by developing novel concepts such as **PageRank**, and the latter goals by innovative tweaking and applying existing techniques, such as MapReduce, for large-scale parallel and distributed data processing.

PageRank is an algorithm named after Google's founder Larry Page. It is one of the algorithms used to rank web search results for a user. Search engines use keyword matching on websites to determine relevance corresponding to a search query. This prompts spammers to include many keywords, relevant or irrelevant, on websites to trick these search engines and appear in almost all queries. For example, a car dealer can include keywords related to shopping or movies and appear in a wider range of search queries. The user experience suffers because of irrelevant results.

PageRank thwarted this kind of fraud by analyzing the quality and quantity of links to a particular web page. The intention was that important pages have more inbound links.

In Circa 2004, Google published and disclosed its MapReduce technique and implementation to the world. It introduced **Google File System** (**GFS**) that accompanies the MapReduce engine. Since then, the MapReduce paradigm has become the most popular technique to process massive datasets in parallel and distributed settings across many other companies. Hadoop is an open source implementation of the MapReduce framework, and Hadoop and its associated filesystem, HDFS, are inspired by Google's MapReduce and GFS, respectively.

Since its inception, Hadoop and other MapReduce-based systems run a diverse set of workloads from different verticals, web search being one of them. As an example, Hadoop is extensively used in `http://www.last.fm/` to generate charts and track usage statistics. It is used for log processing in the cloud provider, Rackspace. Yahoo!, one of the biggest proponents of Hadoop, uses Hadoop clusters not only to build web indexes for search, but also to run sophisticated advertisement placement and content optimization algorithms.

The evolution of Hadoop

Around the year 2003, Doug Cutting and Mike Cafarella started work on a project called **Nutch**, a highly extensible, feature-rich, and open source crawler and indexer project. The goal was to provide an off-the-shelf crawler to meet the demands of document discovery. Nutch can work in a distributed fashion on a handful of machines and be polite by respecting the `robots.txt` file on websites. It is highly extensible by providing the plugin architecture for developers to add custom components, for example, third-party plugins, to read different media types from the Web.

 Robot Exclusion Standard or the **robots.txt** protocol is an advisory protocol that suggests crawling behavior. It is a file placed on website roots that suggest the public pages and directories that can or cannot be crawled. One characteristic of a polite crawler is its respect for the advisory instructions placed within the `robots.txt` file.

Nutch, together with indexing technologies such as Lucene and Solr, provided the necessary components to build search engines, but this project was not at web scale. The initial demonstration of Nutch involved crawling 100 million web pages using four machines. Moreover, debugging and maintaining it was tedious. In 2004, concepts from the seminal MapReduce and GFS publications from Google addressed some of Nutch's scaling issues. The Nutch contributors started integrating distributed filesystem features and the MapReduce programming model into the project. The scalability of Nutch improved by 2006, but it was not yet web scale. A few 100 million web documents could be crawled and indexed using 20 machines. Programming, debugging, and maintaining these search engines became easier.

In 2006, Yahoo hired Doug Cutting, and Hadoop was born. The Hadoop project was part of **Apache Software Foundation (ASF)**, but was factored out of the existing Nutch project and allowed to evolve independently. A number of minor releases were done between 2006 and 2008, at the end of which Hadoop became a stable and web-scale data-processing MapReduce framework. In 2008, Hadoop won the terabyte sort benchmark competition, announcing its suitability for large-scale, reliable cluster-computing using MapReduce.

Hadoop's genealogy

The Hadoop project has a long genealogy, starting from the early releases in 2007 and 2008. This project that is part of Apache Software Foundation (ASF) will be termed **Apache Hadoop** throughout this book. The Apache Hadoop project is the parent project for subsequent releases of Hadoop and its distribution. It is analogous to the main stem of a river, while branches or distributions can be compared to the distributaries of a river.

The following figure shows the Hadoop lineage with respect to Apache Hadoop. In the figure, the black squares represent the major Apache Hadoop releases, and the ovals represent the distributions of Hadoop. Other releases of Hadoop are represented by dotted black squares.

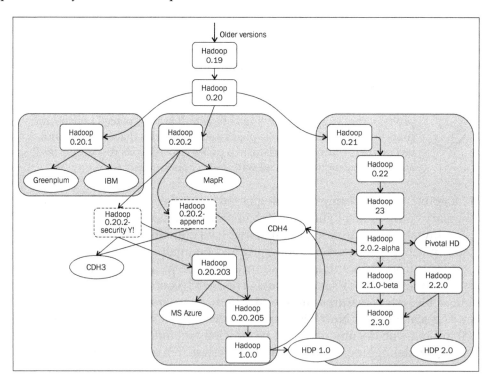

Apache Hadoop has three important branches that are very relevant. They are:

- The 0.20.1 branch
- The 0.20.2 branch
- The 0.21 branch

The Apache Hadoop releases followed a straight line till 0.20. It always had a single major release, and there was no forking of the code into other branches. At release 0.20, there was a fan out of the project into three major branches. The 0.20.2 branch is often termed MapReduce v1.0, MRv1, or simply Hadoop 1.0.0. The 0.21 branch is termed MapReduce v2.0, MRv2, or Hadoop 2.0. A few older distributions are derived from 0.20.1. The year 2011 marked a record number of releases across different branches.

There are two other releases of significance, though they are not considered major releases. They are the Hadoop-0.20-append and Hadoop-0.20-Security releases. These releases introduced the HDFS append and security-related features into Hadoop, respectively. With these enhancements, Apache Hadoop came closer to becoming enterprise-ready.

Hadoop-0.20-append

Append is the primary feature of the Hadoop-0.20-append release. It allows users to run HBase without the risk of data loss. HBase is a popular column-family store that runs on HDFS, providing an online data store in a batch-oriented Hadoop environment. Specifically, the append feature helps write durability of HBase logs, ensuring data safety. Traditionally, HDFS supported input-output for MapReduce batch jobs. The requirement for these jobs was to open a file once, write a lot of data into it, and close the file. The closed file was immutable and read many times. The semantics supported were write-once-read-many-times. No one could read the file when a write was in progress.

Any process that failed or crashed during a write had to rewrite the file. In MapReduce, a user always reran tasks to generate the file. However, this is not true for transaction logs for online systems such as HBase. If the log-writing process fails, it can lead to data loss as the transaction cannot be reproduced. Reproducibility of a transaction, and in turn data safety, comes from log writing. The append feature in HDFS mitigates this risk by enabling HBase and other transactional operations on HDFS.

Hadoop-0.20-security

The Hadoop team at Yahoo took the initiative to add security-related features in the Hadoop-0.20-Security release. Enterprises have different teams, with each team working on different kinds of data. For compliance, client privacy, and security, isolation, authentication, and authorization of Hadoop jobs and data is important. The security release is feature-rich to provide these three pillars of enterprise security.

The full Kerberos authentication system is integrated with Hadoop in this release. **Access Control Lists (ACLs)** were introduced on MapReduce jobs to ensure proper authority in exercising jobs and using resources. Authentication and authorization put together provided the isolation necessary between both jobs and data of the different users of the system.

Hadoop's timeline

The following figure gives a timeline view of the major releases and milestones of Apache Hadoop. The project has been there for 8 years, but the last 4 years has seen Hadoop make giant strides in big data processing. In January 2010, Google was awarded a patent for the MapReduce technology. This technology was licensed to the Apache Software Foundation 4 months later, a shot in the arm for Hadoop. With legal complications out of the way, enterprises—small, medium, and large— were ready to embrace Hadoop. Since then, Hadoop has come up with a number of major enhancements and releases. It has given rise to businesses selling Hadoop distributions, support, training, and other services.

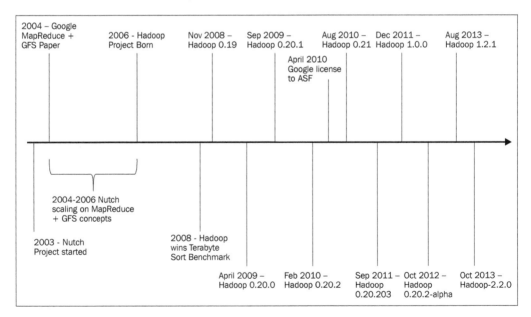

Hadoop 1.0 releases, referred to as 1.X in this book, saw the inception and evolution of Hadoop as a pure MapReduce job-processing framework. It has exceeded its expectations with a wide adoption of massive data processing. The stable 1.X release at this point of time is 1.2.1, which includes features such as append and security. Hadoop 1.X tried to stay flexible by making changes, such as HDFS append, to support online systems such as HBase. Meanwhile, big data applications evolved in range beyond MapReduce computation models. The flexibility of Hadoop 1.X releases had been stretched; it was no longer possible to widen its net to cater to the variety of applications without architectural changes.

Hadoop 2.0 releases, referred to as 2.X in this book, came into existence in 2013. This release family has major changes to widen the range of applications Hadoop can solve. These releases can even increase efficiencies and mileage derived from existing Hadoop clusters in enterprises. Clearly, Hadoop is moving fast beyond MapReduce to stay as the leader in massive scale data processing with the challenge of being backward compatible. It is becoming a generic cluster-computing and storage platform from being only a MapReduce-specific framework.

Hadoop 2.X

The extensive success of Hadoop 1.X in organizations also led to the understanding of its limitations, which are as follows:

- Hadoop gives unprecedented access to cluster computational resources to every individual in an organization. The MapReduce programming model is simple and supports a *develop once deploy at any scale* paradigm. This leads to users exploiting Hadoop for data processing jobs where MapReduce is not a good fit, for example, web servers being deployed in long-running *map* jobs. MapReduce is not known to be affable for iterative algorithms. Hacks were developed to make Hadoop run iterative algorithms. These hacks posed severe challenges to cluster resource utilization and capacity planning.

- Hadoop 1.X has a centralized job flow control. Centralized systems are hard to scale as they are the single point of load lifting. JobTracker failure means that all the jobs in the system have to be restarted, exerting extreme pressure on a centralized component. Integration of Hadoop with other kinds of clusters is difficult with this model.

- The early releases in Hadoop 1.X had a single NameNode that stored all the metadata about the HDFS directories and files. The data on the entire cluster hinged on this single point of failure. Subsequent releases had a cold standby in the form of a secondary NameNode. The secondary NameNode merged the edit logs and NameNode image files, periodically bringing in two benefits. One, the primary NameNode startup time was reduced as the NameNode did not have to do the entire merge on startup. Two, the secondary NameNode acted as a replica that could minimize data loss on NameNode disasters. However, the secondary NameNode (secondary NameNode is not a backup node for NameNode) was still not a hot standby, leading to high failover and recovery times and affecting cluster availability.

- Hadoop 1.X is mainly a Unix-based massive data processing framework. Native support on machines running Microsoft Windows Server is not possible. With Microsoft entering cloud computing and big data analytics in a big way, coupled with existing heavy Windows Server investments in the industry, it's very important for Hadoop to enter the Microsoft Windows landscape as well.

- Hadoop's success comes mainly from enterprise play. Adoption of Hadoop mainly comes from the availability of enterprise features. Though Hadoop 1.X tries to support some of them, such as security, there is a list of other features that are badly needed by the enterprise.

Yet Another Resource Negotiator (YARN)

In Hadoop 1.X, resource allocation and job execution were the responsibilities of JobTracker. Since the computing model was closely tied to the resources in the cluster, MapReduce was the only supported model. This tight coupling led to developers force-fitting other paradigms, leading to unintended use of MapReduce.

The primary goal of YARN is to separate concerns relating to resource management and application execution. By separating these functions, other application paradigms can be added onboard a Hadoop computing cluster. Improvements in interoperability and support for diverse applications lead to efficient and effective utilization of resources. It integrates well with the existing infrastructure in an enterprise.

Achieving loose coupling between resource management and job management should not be at the cost of loss in backward compatibility. For almost 6 years, Hadoop has been the leading software to crunch massive datasets in a parallel and distributed fashion. This means huge investments in development; testing and deployment were already in place.

YARN maintains backward compatibility with Hadoop 1.X (hadoop-0.20.205+) APIs. An older MapReduce program can continue execution in YARN with no code changes. However, recompiling the older code is mandatory.

Architecture overview

The following figure lays out the architecture of YARN. YARN abstracts out resource management functions to a platform layer called **ResourceManager (RM)**. There is a per-cluster RM that primarily keeps track of cluster resource usage and activity. It is also responsible for allocation of resources and resolving contentions among resource seekers in the cluster. RM uses a generalized resource model and is agnostic to application-specific resource needs. For example, RM need not know the resources corresponding to a single Map or Reduce slot.

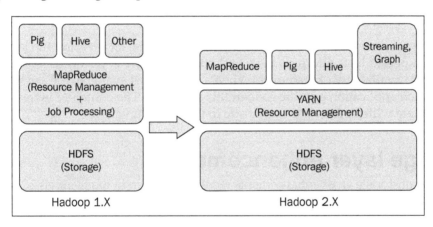

Planning and executing a single job is the responsibility of **Application Master (AM)**. There is an AM instance per running application. For example, there is an AM for each MapReduce job. It has to request for resources from the RM, use them to execute the job, and work around failures, if any.

The general cluster layout has RM running as a daemon on a dedicated machine with a global view of the cluster and its resources. Being a global entity, RM can ensure fairness depending on the resource utilization of the cluster resources. When requested for resources, RM allocates them dynamically as a node-specific bundle called a **container**. For example, 2 CPUs and 4 GB of RAM on a particular node can be specified as a container.

Every node in the cluster runs a daemon called **NodeManager** (**NM**). RM uses NM as its node local assistant. NMs are used for container management functions, such as starting and releasing containers, tracking local resource usage, and fault reporting. NMs send heartbeats to RM. The RM view of the system is the aggregate of the views reported by each NM.

Jobs are submitted directly to RMs. Based on resource availability, jobs are scheduled to run by RMs. The metadata of the jobs are stored in persistent storage to recover from RM crashes. When a job is scheduled, RM allocates a container for the AM of the job on a node in the cluster.

AM then takes over orchestrating the specifics of the job. These specifics include requesting resources, managing task execution, optimizations, and handling tasks or job failures. AM can be written in any language, and different versions of AM can execute independently on a cluster.

An AM resource request contains specifications about the locality and the kind of resource expected by it. RM puts in its best effort to satisfy AM's needs based on policies and availability of resources. When a container is available for use by AM, it can launch application-specific code in this container. The container is free to communicate with its AM. RM is agnostic to this communication.

Storage layer enhancements

A number of storage layer enhancements were undertaken in the Hadoop 2.X releases. The number one goal of the enhancements was to make Hadoop enterprise ready.

High availability

NameNode is a directory service for Hadoop and contains metadata pertaining to the files within cluster storage. Hadoop 1.X had a secondary Namenode, a cold standby that needed minutes to come up. Hadoop 2.X provides features to have a hot standby of NameNode. On the failure of an active NameNode, the standby can become the active Namenode in a matter of minutes. There is no data loss or loss of NameNode service availability. With hot standbys, automated failover becomes easier too.

The key to keep the standby in a hot state is to keep its data as current as possible with respect to the active Namenode. This is achieved by reading the edit logs of the active NameNode and applying it onto itself with very low latency. The sharing of edit logs can be done using the following two methods:

- A shared NFS storage directory between the active and standby NameNodes: the active writes the logs to the shared location. The standby monitors the shared directory and pulls in the changes.

- A quorum of Journal Nodes: the active NameNode presents its edits to a subset of journal daemons that record this information. The standby node constantly monitors these journal daemons for updates and syncs the state with itself.

The following figure shows the high availability architecture using a quorum of Journal Nodes. The data nodes themselves send block reports directly to both the active and standby NameNodes:

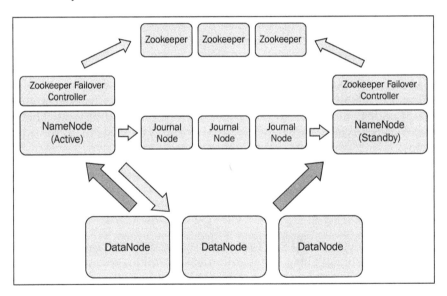

Zookeeper or any other High Availability monitoring service can be used to track NameNode failures. With the assistance of Zookeeper, failover procedures to promote the hot standby as the active NameNode can be triggered.

HDFS Federation

Similar to what YARN did to Hadoop's computation layer, a more generalized storage model has been implemented in Hadoop 2.X. The block storage layer has been generalized and separated out from the filesystem layer. This separation has given an opening for other storage services to be integrated into a Hadoop cluster. Previously, HDFS and the block storage layer were tightly coupled.

One use case that has come forth from this generalized storage model is **HDFS Federation**. Federation allows multiple HDFS namespaces to use the same underlying storage. Federated NameNodes provide isolation at the filesystem level. In *Chapter 10, HDFS Federation*, we will delve into the details of this feature.

HDFS snapshots

Snapshots are point-in-time, read-only images of the entire or a particular subset of a filesystem. Snapshots are taken for three general reasons:

*   Protection against user errors
*   Backup
*   Disaster recovery

Snapshotting is implemented only on NameNode. It does not involve copying data from the data nodes. It is a persistent copy of the block list and file size. The process of taking a snapshot is almost instantaneous and does not affect the performance of NameNode.

Other enhancements

There are a number of other enhancements in Hadoop 2.X, which are as follows:

*   The wire protocol for RPCs within Hadoop is now based on **Protocol Buffers**. Previously, Java serialization via Writables was used. This improvement not only eases maintaining backward compatibility, but also aids in *rolling the upgrades* of different cluster components. RPCs allow for client-side retries as well.

*   HDFS in Hadoop 1.X was agnostic about the type of storage being used. Mechanical or SSD drives were treated uniformly. The user did not have any control on data placement. Hadoop 2.X releases in 2014 are aware of the type of storage and expose this information to applications as well. Applications can use this to optimize their data fetch and placement strategies.

*   HDFS append support has been brought into Hadoop 2.X.

- HDFS access in Hadoop 1.X releases has been through HDFS clients. In Hadoop 2.X, support for NFSv3 has been brought into the NFS gateway component. Clients can now mount HDFS onto their compatible local filesystem, allowing them to download and upload files directly to and from HDFS. Appends to files are allowed, but random writes are not.

- A number of I/O improvements have been brought into Hadoop. For example, in Hadoop 1.X, clients collocated with data nodes had to read data via TCP sockets. However, with *short-circuit local reads*, clients can directly read off the data nodes. This particular interface also supports zero-copy reads. The CRC checksum that is calculated for reads and writes of data has been optimized using the Intel SSE4.2 CRC32 instruction.

Support enhancements

Hadoop is also widening its application net by supporting other platforms and frameworks. One dimension we saw was onboarding of other computational models with YARN or other storage systems with the Block Storage layer. The other enhancements are as follows:

- Hadoop 2.X supports Microsoft Windows natively. This translates to a huge opportunity to penetrate the Microsoft Windows server land for massive data processing. This was partially possible because of the use of the highly portable Java programming language for Hadoop development. The other critical enhancement was the generalization of compute and storage management to include Microsoft Windows.

- As part of Platform-as-a-Service offerings, cloud vendors give out on-demand Hadoop as a service. OpenStack support in Hadoop 2.X makes it conducive for deployment in elastic and virtualized cloud environments.

Hadoop distributions

In the present day, Hadoop and its individual ecosystem components are complex projects. As we saw earlier in this chapter, Hadoop has a number of different forks or code branches over a large number of releases. There are also a lot of different distributions of Hadoop. The distribution with the most activity and community involvement is the one that resides as part of Apache Software Foundation. This distribution is free and has a very large community behind it. The community contributions to the Apache Hadoop distribution shape the general direction taken by Hadoop. Support in the Apache Hadoop distribution is via online forums, where questions are addressed to the community and answered by its members.

Deployment and management of the Apache Hadoop distribution within an enterprise is tedious and nontrivial. Apache Hadoop is written in Java and optimized to run on Linux filesystems. This can lead to impedance mismatch between Hadoop and existing enterprise applications and infrastructures. Integration between the Hadoop ecosystem components is buggy and not straightforward.

To bridge these issues, a few companies came up with distribution models for Hadoop. There are three primary kinds of Hadoop distribution flavors. One flavor is to provide commercial or paid support and training for the Apache Hadoop distribution. Secondly, there are companies that provide a set of supporting tools for deployment and management of Apache Hadoop as an alternative flavor. These companies also provide robust integration layers between the different Hadoop ecosystem components. The third model is for companies to supplement Apache Hadoop with proprietary features and code. These features are paid enhancements, many of which solve certain use cases.

The parent of all these distributions is Apache Software Foundation's Hadoop sources. Users of these other distributions, particularly from companies following the third distribution model, might integrate proprietary code into Apache Hadoop. However, these distributions will always stay in touching distance with Apache Hadoop and follow its trends. Distributions are generally well tested and supported in a deep and timely manner, saving administration and management costs for an organization. The downside of using a distribution other than Apache Hadoop is vendor lock-in. The tools and proprietary features provided by one vendor might not be available in another distribution or be noncompatible with other third-party tools, bringing in a cost of migration. The cost of migration is not limited to technology shifts alone. It also involves training, capacity planning, and rearchitecting costs for the organization.

Which Hadoop distribution?

There are a number of Hadoop distributions offered by companies since 2008. Distributions excel in some or the other attribute. Decisions on the right distribution for an enterprise or organization should be made on a case-by-case basis. There are different criteria to evaluate distributions. We will inspect a few important ones.

Performance

The ability of the Hadoop distribution running on a cluster to process data quickly is obviously a desired feature. Traditionally, this has been the cornerstone for all performance benchmarks. This particular performance measure is termed as "throughput". A wide range of analysis workloads that are being processed on Hadoop, coupled with the diversity of use cases supported by analytics, brings in "latency" as an important performance criterion as well. The ability of the cluster to ingest input data and emit output data at a quick rate becomes very important for low-latency analytics. This input-output cost forms an integral part of the data processing workflow.

Latency is the time required to perform an action. It is measured in time units such as milliseconds, seconds, minutes, or hours.

Throughput is the number of actions that can be performed in unit time. It gives a sense of the amount of work done for every time unit.

Scaling up hardware is one way to achieve low latency independent of the Hadoop distribution. However, this approach will be expensive and saturate out quickly. Architecturally, low I/O latency can be achieved in different ways; one will be able to reduce the number of intermediate data-staging layers between the data source or the data sink and Hadoop cluster. Some distributions provide streaming writes into the Hadoop cluster in an attempt to reduce intermediate staging layers. Operators used for filtering, compressing, and lightweight data processing can be plugged into the streaming layer to preprocess the data before it flows into storage.

The Apache Hadoop distribution is written in Java, a language that runs in its own virtual machine. Though this increases application portability, it comes with overheads such as an extra layer of indirection during execution by means of byte-code interpretation and background garbage collection. It is not as fast as an application directly compiled for target hardware. Some vendors optimize their distributions for particular hardware, increasing job performance per node. Features such as compression and decompression can also be optimized for certain hardware types.

Scalability

Over time, data outgrows the physical capacity of the compute and storage resources provisioned by an organization. This will require expansion of resources in both the compute and storage dimensions. Scaling can be done vertically or horizontally. Vertical scaling or scaling up is expensive and tightly bound to hardware advancements. Lack of elasticity is another downside with vertical scaling. Horizontal scaling or scaling out is a preferred mode of scaling compute and storage.

Ideally, scaling out should be limited to addition of more nodes and disks to the cluster network, with minimal configuration changes. However, distributions might impose different degrees of difficulty, both in terms of effort and cost on scaling a Hadoop cluster. Scaling out might mean heavy administrative and deployment costs, rewriting a lot of the application's code, or a combination of both. Scaling costs will depend on the existing architecture and how it complements and complies with the Hadoop distribution that is being evaluated.

> **Vertical scaling** or **scaling up** is the process of adding more resources to a single node in a system. For example, adding additional CPUs, memory, or storage to a single computer comes under this bucket of scaling. Vertical scaling increases capacity, but does not decrease system load.
>
> **Horizontal scaling** or **scaling out** is the process of adding additional nodes to a system. For example, adding another computer to a distributed system by connecting it to the network comes under this category of scaling. Horizontal scaling decreases the load on a system as the new node takes a part of the load. The capacity of individual nodes does not increase.

Reliability

Any distributed system is subject to partial failures. Failures can stem from hardware, software, or network issues, and have a smaller mean time when running on commodity hardware. Dealing with these failures without disrupting services or compromising data integrity is the primary goal of any highly available and consistent system.

A distribution that treats reliability seriously provides high availability of its components out of the box. Eliminating **Single Point of Failures (SPOF)** ensures availability. The means of eliminating SPOFs is to increase the redundancy of components. For a long time, Apache Hadoop had a single NameNode. Any failure to the NameNode's hardware meant the entire cluster becoming unusable. Now, there is the concept of a secondary NameNode and hot standbys that can be used to restore the name node in the event of NameNode failure.

Distributions that reduce manual tasks for cluster administrators are more reliable. Human intervention is directly correlated to higher error rates. An example of this is handling failovers. Failovers are critical periods for systems as they operate with lower degrees of redundancy. Any error during these periods can be disastrous for the application. Also, automated failover handling means the system can recover and run in a short amount of time. Lower the recovery time from failure better is the availability of the system.

The integrity of data needs to be maintained during normal operations and when failures are encountered. Data checksums for error detection and possible recovery, data replication, data mirroring, and snapshots are some ways to ensure data safety. Replication follows the redundancy theme to ensure data availability. Rack-aware smart placement of data and handling under or over replication are parameters to watch out for. Mirroring helps recovery from site failures by asynchronous replication across the Internet. Snapshotting is a desirable feature in any distribution; not only do they aid disaster recovery but also facilitate offline access to data. Data analytics involves experimentation and evaluation of rich data. Snapshots can be a way to facilitate this to a data scientist without disrupting production.

Manageability

Deploying and managing the Apache Hadoop open source distribution requires internal understanding of the source code and configuration. This is not a widely available skill in IT administration. Also, administrators in enterprises are caretakers of a wide range of systems, Hadoop being one of them.

Versions of Hadoop and its ecosystem components that are supported by a distribution might need to be evaluated for suitability. Newer versions of Hadoop support paradigms other than MapReduce within clusters. Depending on the plans of the enterprise, newer versions can increase the efficiency of enterprise-provisioned hardware.

Capabilities of Hadoop management tools are key differentiators when choosing an appropriate distribution for an enterprise. Management tools need to provide centralized cluster administration, resource management, configuration management, and user management. Job scheduling, automatic software upgrades, user quotas, and centralized troubleshooting are other desirable features.

Monitoring cluster health is also a key feature in the manageability function. Dashboards for visualization of cluster health and integration points for other tools are good features to have in distribution. Ease of data access is another parameter that needs to be evaluated; for example, support for POSIX filesystems on Hadoop will make browsing and accessing data convenient for engineers and scientists within any enterprise. On the flip side, this makes mutability of data possible, which can prove to be risky in certain situations.

Evaluation of options for data security of a distribution is extremely important as well. Data security entails authentication of a Hadoop user and authorization to datasets and data confidentiality. Every organization or enterprise might have its authentication systems such as Kerberos or LDAP already in place. Hadoop distribution, with capabilities to integrate with existing authentication systems, is a big plus in terms of lower costs and higher compliance. Fine-grained authorization might help control access to datasets and jobs at different levels. When data is moving in and out of an organization, encryption of the bits travelling over the wire becomes important to protect against data snooping.

Distributions offer integration with development and debugging tools. Developers and scientists in an enterprise will already be using a set of tools. The more overlap between the toolset used by the organization and distribution, the better it is. The advantage of overlap not only comes in the form of licensing costs, but also in a lesser need for training and orientation. It might also increase productivity within the organization as people are already accustomed to certain tools.

Available distributions

There are a number of distributions of Hadoop. A comprehensive list can be found at `http://wiki.apache.org/hadoop/Distributions%20and%20Commercial%20 Support`. We will be examining four of them:

- Cloudera Distribution of Hadoop (CDH)
- Hortonworks Data Platform (HDP)
- MapR
- Pivotal HD

Cloudera Distribution of Hadoop (CDH)

Cloudera was formed in March 2009 with a primary objective of providing Apache Hadoop software, support, services, and training for enterprise-class deployment of Hadoop and its ecosystem components. The software suite is branded as **Cloudera Distribution of Hadoop** (CDH). The company being one of the Apache Software Foundation sponsors, pushes most enhancements it makes during support and servicing of Hadoop deployments upstream back into Apache Hadoop.

CDH is in its fifth major version right now and is considered a mature Hadoop distribution. The paid version of CDH comes with a proprietary management software, Cloudera Manager.

Hortonworks Data Platform (HDP)

The Yahoo Hadoop team spurned off to form Hortonworks in June, 2011, a company with objectives similar to Cloudera. Their distribution is branded as **Hortonworks Data Platform** (HDP). The HDP suite's Hadoop and other software are completely free, with paid support and training. Hortonworks also pushes enhancements upstream, back to Apache Hadoop.

HDP is in its second major version currently and is considered the rising star in Hadoop distributions. It comes with a free and open source management software called Ambari.

MapR

MapR was founded in 2009 with a mission to bring enterprise-grade Hadoop. The Hadoop distribution they provide has significant proprietary code when compared to Apache Hadoop. There are a handful of components where they guarantee compatibility with existing Apache Hadoop projects. Key proprietary code for the MapR distribution is the replacement of HDFS with a POSIX-compatible NFS. Another key feature is the capability of taking snapshots.

MapR comes with its own management console. The different grades of the product are named as M3, M5, and M7. M5 is a standard commercial distribution from the company, M3 is a free version without high availability, and M7 is a paid version with a rewritten HBase API.

Pivotal HD

Greenplum is a marquee parallel data store from EMC. EMC integrated Greenplum within Hadoop, giving way to an advanced Hadoop distribution called Pivotal HD. This move alleviated the need to import and export data between stores such as Greenplum and HDFS, bringing down both costs and latency.

The HAWQ technology provided by Pivotal HD allows efficient and low-latency query execution on data stored in HDFS. The HAWQ technology has been found to give 100 times more improvement on certain MapReduce workloads when compared to Apache Hadoop. HAWQ also provides SQL processing in Hadoop, increasing its popularity among users who are familiar with SQL.

Summary

In this chapter, we saw the evolution of Hadoop and some of its milestones and releases. We went into depth on Hadoop 2.X and the changes it brings into Hadoop. The key takeaways from this chapter are:

- MapReduce was born out of the necessity to gather, process, and index data at web scale. Apache Hadoop is an open source distribution of the MapReduce computational model.

- In over 6 years of its existence, Hadoop has become the number one choice as a framework for massively parallel and distributed computing. The community has been shaping Hadoop to gear up for enterprise use. In 1.X releases, HDFS append and security, were the key features that made Hadoop enterprise-friendly.

- MapReduce supports a limited set of use cases. Onboarding other paradigms into Hadoop enables support for a wider range of analytics and can also increase cluster resource utilization. In Hadoop 2.X, the JobTracker functions are separated and YARN handles cluster resource management and scheduling. MapReduce is one of the applications that can run on YARN.

- Hadoop's storage layer was enhanced in 2.X to separate the filesystem from the block storage service. This enables features such as supporting multiple namespaces and integration with other filesystems. 2.X shows improvements in Hadoop storage availability and snapshotting.

- Distributions of Hadoop provide enterprise-grade management software, tools, support, training, and services. Most distributions shadow Apache Hadoop in their capabilities.

MapReduce is still an integral part of Hadoop's DNA. In the next chapter, we will explore MapReduce optimizations and best practices.

2
Advanced MapReduce

MapReduce is a programming model for parallel and distributed processing of data. It consists of two steps: **Map** and **Reduce**. These steps are inspired from functional programming, a branch of computer science that deals with mathematical functions as computational units. Properties of functions such as immutability and statelessness are attractive for parallel and distributed processing. They provide a high degree of parallelism and fault tolerance at lower costs and semantic complexity.

In this chapter, we will look at advanced optimizations when running MapReduce jobs on Hadoop clusters. Every MapReduce job has input data and a Map task per split of this data. The Map task calls a map function repeatedly on every record, represented as a key-value pair. The map is a function that transforms data from one domain to another. The intermediate output records of each Map task are shuffled and sorted before transferring it downstream to the Reduce tasks. Intermediate data with the same keys go to the same Reduce task. The Reduce task calls the reduce function for a key and all its associated values. Outputs are then collected and stored.

The Map step has the greatest degree of parallelism. It is used to implement operations such as filtering, sorting, and transformations on data. The Reduce step is used to implement summarization operations on data. Hadoop also provides features such as **DistributedCache** as a side channel to distribute data and **Counters** to collect job-related global statistics. We will be looking at their utility in processing MapReduce jobs.

The advanced features and optimizations will be explained with the help of examples of code. Hadoop 2.2.0 will be used throughout this chapter. It is assumed that you have access to the Java development environment and a Hadoop cluster, either in your organization, the cloud, or as a standalone/pseudo-distributed mode installation on your personal computers. You need to have knowledge on how to compile Java programs and run Hadoop jobs to try out the examples.

In this chapter, we will look at the following topics:

- The different phases of a MapReduce job and the optimizations that can be applied at each phase. The input, Map, Shuffle/Sort, Reduce, and the output phases will be covered in depth with relevant examples.

- The application of useful Hadoop features such as DistributedCache and Counters.

- The types of data joins that can be achieved in a MapReduce job and the patterns to achieve them.

MapReduce input

The Map step of a MapReduce job hinges on the nature of the input provided to the job. The Map step provides maximum parallelism gains, and crafting this step smartly is important for job speedup. Data is split into chunks, and Map tasks operate on each of these chunks of data. Each chunk is called `InputSplit`. A Map task is asked to operate on each `InputSplit` class. There are two other classes, `InputFormat` and `RecordReader`, which are significant in handling inputs to Hadoop jobs.

The InputFormat class

The input data specification for a MapReduce Hadoop job is given via the `InputFormat` hierarchy of classes. The `InputFormat` class family has the following main functions:

- Validating the input data. For example, checking for the presence of the file in the given path.

- Splitting the input data into logical chunks (`InputSplit`) and assigning each of the splits to a Map task.

- Instantiating a `RecordReader` object that can work on each `InputSplit` class and producing records to the Map task as key-value pairs.

The `FileInputFormat` subclass and associated classes are commonly used for jobs that take inputs from HFDS. The `DBInputFormat` subclass is a specialized class that can be used to read data from a SQL database. `CombineFileInputFormat` is the direct abstract subclass of the `FileInputFormat` class, which can combine multiple files into a single split.

The InputSplit class

The abstract InputSplit class and its associated concrete classes represent a byte view of the input data. An InputSplit class is characterized by the following main attributes:

- The input filename
- The byte offset in the file where the split starts
- The length of the split in bytes
- The node locations where the split resides

In HDFS, an InputSplit class is created per file if the file size is less than the HDFS block size. For example, if the HDFS block size is 128 MB, any file with a size less than 128 MB resides in its own InputSplit class. For files that are broken up into blocks (size of the file is greater than the HDFS block size), a more complex formula is used to calculate InputSplit. The InputSplit class has an upper bound of the HDFS block size, unless the minimum size of a split is greater than the block size. Such cases are rare and could lead to locality problems.

Based on the locations of the splits and the availability of resources, the scheduler makes a decision on which node should execute the Map task for that split. The split is then communicated to the node that executes the task.

```
InputSplitSize = Maximum(minSplitSize,
Minimum(blocksize, maxSplitSize))

minSplitSize :
mapreduce.input.fileinputformat.split.minsize

blocksize: dfs.blocksize

maxSplitSize -
mapreduce.input.fileinputformat.split.maxsize
```

In previous releases of Hadoop, the minimum split size property was mapred.min.split.size and the maximum split size was given by the value of the property mapred.max.split.size. These are deprecated now.

The RecordReader class

Unlike InputSplit, the RecordReader class presents a record view of the data to the Map task. RecordReader works within each InputSplit class and generates records from the data in the form of key-value pairs. The InputSplit boundary is a guideline for RecordReader and is not enforced. On one extreme, a custom RecordReader class can be written to read an entire file (though this is not encouraged). Most often, a RecordReader class will have to read from a subsequent InputSplit class to present the complete record to the Map task. This happens when records overlap InputSplit classes.

The reading of bytes from a subsequent InputSplit class happens via the FSDataInputStream objects. Though this reading does not respect locality in itself, generally, it gathers only a few bytes from the next split and there is not a significant performance overhead. But in some cases where record sizes are huge, this can have a bearing on the performance due to significant byte transfers across nodes.

In the following diagram, a file with two HDFS blocks has the record **R5** spanning both blocks. It is assumed that the minimum split size is less than the block size. In this case, RecordReader is going to gather the complete record by reading bytes off the next block of data.

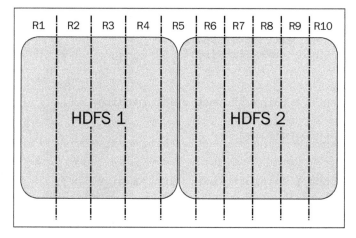

File with two blocks and record R5 spanning blocks

Hadoop's "small files" problem

Hadoop's problem with small files — files that are significantly smaller than the HDFS block size — is well known. When dealing with small files as input, a Map task is created for each of these files introducing bookkeeping overheads. The same Map task is able to finish processing in a matter of a few seconds, a processing time much smaller than the time taken to spawn and cleanup the task. Each object in the NameNode occupies about 150 bytes of memory. Many small files will proliferate in the presence of these objects and adversely affect NameNode's performance and scalability. Reading a set of smaller files is also very inefficient because of the large number of disk seeks and hops across DataNodes to fetch them.

Unfortunately, small files are a reality, but there are the following strategies to handle small files:

- Combining smaller files into a bigger file as a preprocessing step before storing it in HDFS and running the job. `SequenceFile` and `TFile` formats are popular ways of combining smaller files into a bigger file. Using **Hadoop archive files** (**HAR**) is another way of alleviating NameNode memory pressures. HAR is a meta-filesystem that resides on top of HFDS.

- Using `CombineFileInputFormat` to combine multiple smaller files into `InputSplit`. This also takes into consideration node and rack locality for better performance. It may not relieve the memory requirements of the NameNode though, as the number of files that need to be tracked still remains the same.

To illustrate the working of `CombineFileInputFormat`, we have a public NSF grant proposal abstracts dataset from the years 1990 to 2003 at `https://archive.ics.uci.edu/ml/datasets/NSF+Research+Award+Abstracts+1990-2003`. Though the dataset has 130,000 grant proposals, we will consider a subset of 441 grants. The standard output for a MapReduce Hadoop job that reads each line from the proposals spawns 441 input splits, as shown in following snippet. In this sample job, the number of reduce tasks has been set to zero:

```
14/04/10 07:50:03 INFO input.FileInputFormat: Total input paths to
process : 441
14/04/10 07:50:03 INFO mapreduce.JobSubmitter: number of splits:441
```

As we saw previously, inputs to a Hadoop MapReduce job are specified using the `InputFormat`, `InputSplit`, and `RecordReader` classes. In this program, we will combine all 441 proposals into a single split.

`CombineFileInputFormat` is an abstract class that facilitates input specifications to combine files. The only override that it expects the developer to fill is the `createRecordReader()` method. This is a method that instantiates a custom `RecordReader` class to read records. The `CombineFileInputFormat` class returns the `CombineFileSplit` object in the `getSplits()` method. Each split might be a combination of blocks from different files. If the `setMaxSplitSize()` method is used to set a maximum split size, local node files are combined in a split. Residue blocks are combined with other blocks from the same rack. However, if this value is not set, combining is not attempted at the node level; it is only attempted at the rack level. If the `setMaxSplitSize()` method is used to set the maximum split size to the block size in HDFS, default behavior is seen, that is, each block is a split.

The following code shows the concrete class based on this abstract class:

```
package MasteringHadoop;
import org.apache.hadoop.conf.Configuration;
import org.apache.hadoop.fs.FSDataInputStream;
import org.apache.hadoop.fs.FileSystem;
import org.apache.hadoop.fs.Path;
import org.apache.hadoop.io.LongWritable;
import org.apache.hadoop.io.Text;
import org.apache.hadoop.mapreduce.InputSplit;
import org.apache.hadoop.mapreduce.RecordReader;
import org.apache.hadoop.mapreduce.TaskAttemptContext;
import org.apache.hadoop.mapreduce.lib.input.*;
import org.apache.hadoop.util.LineReader;
import java.io.IOException;
public class MasteringHadoopCombineFileInputFormat extends
    CombineFileInputFormat<LongWritable, Text>{
    @Override
    public RecordReader<LongWritable, Text>
        createRecordReader(InputSplit inputSplit, TaskAttemptContext
            taskAttemptContext) throws IOException {
        return new CombineFileRecordReader<LongWritable,
          Text>((CombineFileSplit) inputSplit, taskAttemptContext,
          MasteringHadoopCombineFileRecordReader.class);
    }
}
```

Downloading the example code

You can download the example code files for all Packt books you have purchased from your account at `http://www.packtpub.com`. If you purchased this book elsewhere, you can visit `http://www.packtpub.com/support` and register to have the files e-mailed directly to you.

The `CombineFileFormat` class has an `isSplitable()` method. The default setting is true, but it can be made false to ensure that a file is processed by a single Map task in its entirety.

The following code shows the custom `RecordReader` class that is created to return records from `CombineFileSplit`. The difference between `CombineFileSplit` and `FileSplit` is the presence of multiple paths implying multiple offsets and lengths. The custom `RecordReader` class will be called for every file in the split. Therefore, it is mandatory for the constructor of the custom `RecordReader` class to have an `Integer` index that specifies the file that is being considered for record generation.

The second important method is `nextKeyValue()`, which generates the next key-value pair. The `getCurrentKey()` and `getCurrentValue()` methods return this generated key-value pair. In the following example, keys are byte offsets in the file and values are lines of text. A `LineReader` object is used to read each line:

```
public static class MasteringHadoopCombineFileRecordReader extends
    RecordReader<LongWritable, Text>{
        private LongWritable key;
        private Text value;
        private Path path;
        private FileSystem fileSystem;
        private LineReader lineReader;
        private FSDataInputStream fsDataInputStream;
        private Configuration configuration;
        private int fileIndex;
        private CombineFileSplit combineFileSplit;
        private long start;
        private long end;

        public MasteringHadoopCombineFileRecordReader
            (CombineFileSplit inputSplit, TaskAttemptContext
                context, Integer index) throws IOException{
            this.fileIndex = index;
            this.combineFileSplit = inputSplit;
            this.configuration = context.getConfiguration();
```

```
                    this.path = inputSplit.getPath(index);
                    this.fileSystem =
                        this.path.getFileSystem(configuration);
                    this.fsDataInputStream = fileSystem.open(this.path);
                    this.lineReader = new
                        LineReader(this.fsDataInputStream,
                            this.configuration);
                    this.start = inputSplit.getOffset(index);
                    this.end = this.start + inputSplit.getLength(index);
                    this.key = new LongWritable(0);
                    this.value = new Text("");


            }
        @Override
        public void initialize(InputSplit inputSplit,
            TaskAttemptContext taskAttemptContext) throws
                IOException, InterruptedException {
            //Overloaded in the constructor.
    }

        @Override
        public boolean nextKeyValue() throws IOException,
            InterruptedException {
            int offset = 0;
            boolean isKeyValueAvailable = true;
            if(this.start < this.end){
                offset = this.lineReader.readLine(this.value);
                this.key.set(this.start);
                this.start += offset;
            }

            if(offset == 0){
                this.key.set(0);
                this.value.set("");
                isKeyValueAvailable = false;
            }

            return isKeyValueAvailable;

        }

        @Override
        public LongWritable getCurrentKey() throws IOException,
            InterruptedException {
```

```
            return key;
        }


        @Override
        public Text getCurrentValue() throws IOException,
            InterruptedException {
            return value;
        }


        @Override
        public float getProgress() throws IOException,
            InterruptedException {
long splitStart = this.combineFileSplit.getOffset(fileIndex);
f(this.start < this.end){
                return Math.min(1.0f, (this.start -  splitStart)/
                    (float) (this.end - splitStart));
        }

        return 0;
        }


        @Override
        public void close() throws IOException {
            if(lineReader != null){
                lineReader.close();
            }
        }
    }
```

The Mapper class and the driver program are given in the following snippet. The most important line in the driver is that which sets InputFormat as job.setInputFormatClass(MasteringHadoop.MasteringHadoopCombineFileInputFormat.class). When the program is executed, the standard output obtained is also given after the snippet. The number of splits comes up as one. The size of the corpus in this case is 5 MB while the HDFS block size is 128 MB.

```
package MasteringHadoop;
import org.apache.hadoop.conf.Configuration;
import org.apache.hadoop.fs.Path;
import org.apache.hadoop.mapreduce.*;
import org.apache.hadoop.io.*;
import org.apache.hadoop.mapreduce.lib.input.FileInputFormat;
import org.apache.hadoop.mapreduce.lib.output.TextOutputFormat;
import org.apache.hadoop.util.GenericOptionsParser;
```

```java
import java.io.IOException;

public class CombineFilesMasteringHadoop {
    public static class CombineFilesMapper extends
        Mapper<LongWritable, Text, LongWritable, Text>{

        @Override
        protected void map(LongWritable key, Text value, Context
            context) throws IOException, InterruptedException {
            context.write(key, value);
        }
    }
    public static void main(String args[]) throws IOException,
        InterruptedException, ClassNotFoundException{
            GenericOptionsParser parser = new
                GenericOptionsParser(args);
            Configuration config = parser.getConfiguration();
            String[] remainingArgs = parser.getRemainingArgs();

            Job job = Job.getInstance(config, "MasteringHadoop-
                CombineDemo");
            job.setOutputKeyClass(LongWritable.class);
            job.setOutputValueClass(Text.class);
            job.setMapperClass(CombineFilesMapper.class);
            job.setNumReduceTasks(0);
job.setInputFormatClass(MasteringHadoop.MasteringHadoopCombineFile
    InputFormat.class);
            job.setOutputFormatClass(TextOutputFormat.class);
            FileInputFormat.addInputPath(job, new
                Path(remainingArgs[0]));
            TextOutputFormat.setOutputPath(job, new
                Path(remainingArgs[1]));
            job.waitForCompletion(true);
    }
}
```

The output is as shown as follows:

```
14/04/10 16:32:05 INFO input.FileInputFormat: Total input paths to
   process : 441
14/04/10 16:32:06 INFO mapreduce.JobSubmitter: number of splits:1
```

Filtering inputs

Filtering inputs to a job based on certain attributes is often required. Data-level filtering can be done within the Maps, but it is more efficient to filter at the file level before the Map task is spawned. Filtering enables only interesting files to be processed by Map tasks and can have a positive effect on the runtime of the Map by eliminating unnecessary file fetch. For example, files generated only within a certain time period might be required for analysis.

Let's use the 441-grant proposal file corpus subset to illustrate filtering. Let's process those files whose names match a particular regular expression and have a minimum file size. Both of these are specified as job parameters— filter.name and filter. min.size, respectively. Implementation entails extending the Configured class and implementing the PathFilter interface as shown in the following snippet. The Configured class is the base class for things that can be configured using Configuration. The PathFilter interface is the interface that contains an accept() method. The accept() method implementation takes in a Path parameter and returns true or false depending on whether the file has to be included in the input or not. The outline of the class is shown in the following snippet:

```
import org.apache.hadoop.conf.Configuration;
import org.apache.hadoop.conf.Configured;
import org.apache.hadoop.fs.FileSystem;
import org.apache.hadoop.fs.Path;
import org.apache.hadoop.fs.PathFilter;
import org.apache.hadoop.io.IntWritable;
import org.apache.hadoop.io.LongWritable;
import org.apache.hadoop.io.Text;
import org.apache.hadoop.mapreduce.Job;
import org.apache.hadoop.mapreduce.Mapper;
import org.apache.hadoop.mapreduce.lib.input.FileInputFormat;
import org.apache.hadoop.mapreduce.lib.input.TextInputFormat;
import org.apache.hadoop.mapreduce.lib.output.TextOutputFormat;
import org.apache.hadoop.util.GenericOptionsParser;
import java.io.IOException;
import java.util.regex.Matcher;
import java.util.regex.Pattern;

public static class MasteringHadoopPathAndSizeFilter extends
    Configured implements PathFilter {
        private Configuration configuration;
        private Pattern filePattern;
        private long filterSize;
```

```
private FileSystem fileSystem;

@Override
public boolean accept(Path path){
        //Your accept override implementation goes here
}

@Override
public void setConf(Configuration conf){
        //Your setConf override implementation goes here
}
}
```

An important change is to override the setConf() method. This method is used to set the private Configuration variable and read off any properties from it. In the driver class, the job has to be informed about the presence of a filter using the following line:

```
FileInputFormat.setInputPathFilter(job,
  MasteringHadoopPathAndSizeFilter.class);
```

The implementation of the setConf() method is as follows:

```
@Override
  public void setConf(Configuration conf){
      this.configuration = conf;

      if(this.configuration != null){
          String filterRegex =
              this.configuration.get("filter.name");

          if(filterRegex != null){
              this.filePattern =
              Pattern.compile(filterRegex);
          }

          String filterSizeString =
              this.configuration.get("filter.min.size");

          if(filterSizeString != null){
              this.filterSize =
                  Long.parseLong(filterSizeString);
          }

          try{
```

```
            this.fileSystem =
                FileSystem.get(this.configuration);
        }
        catch(IOException ioException){
            //Error handling
        }


    }
}
```

In the following code, the accept() method returns true for all directories.
The path of the current directory is one of the paths that will be provided to the
accept() method. It uses the Java regular expression classes such as Pattern
and Matches to determine whether any of the file paths match the expression and
sets a Boolean variable appropriately. A second check is done to determine the
file size and compare it with the file size filter. The FileSystem object exposes a
getFileStatus() method that returns a FileStatus object, which can be examined
for its file attributes via getters.

```
        @Override
        public boolean accept(Path path){
          boolean isFileAcceptable = true;
          try{
                if(fileSystem.isDirectory(path)){
                    return true;
                }

                if(filePattern != null){
                    Matcher m =
                        filePattern.matcher(path.toString());
                    isFileAcceptable = m.matches();
                }

                if(filterSize > 0){
                    long actualFileSize =
                        fileSystem.getFileStatus(path).getLen();
                    if(actualFileSize > this.filterSize){
                        isFileAcceptable &= true;
                    }
                    else{
                        isFileAcceptable = false;
                    }
                }

            }
```

```
      catch(IOException ioException){
         //Error handling goes here.

      }

      return isFileAcceptable;
   }
```

The following command line accepts files that have a999645 in their names and have sizes greater than 2,500 bytes. If either parameter is omitted, no filter is applied for that attribute.

```
hadoop jar MasteringHadoop-1.0-SNAPSHOT-jar-with-dependencies.jar
-D filter.name=.*a999645.* -D filter.min.size=2500 grant-subset
grant-subset-filter
```

Three files pass the test and the output is shown as follows. The filtering happens before the splits are decided.

```
14/04/10 21:34:38 INFO input.FileInputFormat: Total input paths to
  process : 3
14/04/10 21:34:39 INFO mapreduce.JobSubmitter: number of splits:3
```

The Map task

The efficiency of the Map phase is decided by the specifications of the job inputs. We saw that having too many small files leads to proliferation of Map tasks because of a large number of splits. Another important statistic to note is the average runtime of a Map task. Too many or too few Map tasks are both detrimental for job performance. Striking a balance between the two is important, much of which depends on the nature of the application and data.

 A rule of thumb is to have the runtime of a single Map task to be around a minute to three minutes, based on empirical evidence.

The dfs.blocksize attribute

The default block size of files in a cluster is overridden in the cluster configuration file, hdfs-site.xml, generally present in the etc/hadoop folder of the Hadoop installation. In some cases, a Map task might take only a few seconds to process a block. Giving a bigger block to the Map tasks in such cases is better. This can be done in the following ways:

- Increasing the fileinputformat.split.minsize parameter to be greater than the block size
- Increasing the block size of the input file stored in HDFS

The former leads to locality problems as InputSplit might have to import data from blocks residing in other nodes. The latter method preserves locality, but might require you to reload the file in HDFS. It can be done using the following command. A file tiny.dat.txt is being uploaded into HDFS with a block size of 512 MB. The default block size was 128 MB (in previous versions, it is 64 MB).

```
hadoop fs -D dfs.blocksize=536870912 -put tiny.dat.txt
tiny.dat.newblock.txt
```

> The number of Map tasks should not exceed 60,000 or 70,000 for any application.

There could be situations where Map tasks are CPU bound, that is, I/O is an insignificant part of the Map task runtime. In such cases, it is better to utilize all available computing resources within the cluster. Decreasing the fileinputformat.split.maxsize property to be less than the HDFS block size can help increase cluster resource utilization.

> Fewer Map tasks that exploit data locality are good for job performance. But in the face of failures, they might increase the job latency. A single Map task processes a significant chunk of the data and failure might hold up the entire job.

Sort and spill of intermediate outputs

The process of sending intermediate outputs from the Map tasks to the Reduce tasks involves complexity on both the Map side (as shown in the following diagram) and the Reduce side. Not only does the output of the Map tasks have to be partitioned based on the key to send it to the right Reduce task, but the keys within each partition have to be sorted as well. The partitioned data is then distributed to the appropriate reducers.

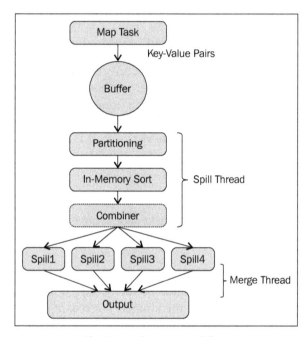

The Map task output workflow

The intermediate output records emitted by the Map task are not directly written on the disk. They are buffered in the local memory using a circular buffer before spilling them onto the disk. The size of this circular buffer is configured by the `mapreduce.task.io.sort.mb` property. The default value of this parameter is 100, that is, the circular buffer has a capacity of 100 MB. This property is overridden in the `mapred-default.xml` or `mapred-site.xml` file that is placed in the `etc/hadoop` directory of the Hadoop installation. All the properties discussed in this section go in the same config file. The buffered key-value records are serialized but not sorted.

Each key-value record is augmented with some accounting information. This accounting information has a constant value of 16 bytes per record regardless of the size of the actual key or value payload.

The soft threshold for the percentage of buffer that is allocated for the actual output record is given by the `mapreduce.task.io.sort.spill.percent` property. The default for this parameter is 0.8, that is, the output records from the buffer will be flushed to disk when the buffer becomes 80 percent full.

Before MAPREDUCE-64, the `io.record.sort.percent` property was a soft threshold for the percentage of the buffer that is allocated for accounting information. It had a default value of 0.05. Spills used to be triggered if the accounting information reached this threshold. This used to cause more spills and underutilization of the buffer, particularly for smaller records.

After this patch, the `io.record.sort.percent` property gets auto-tuned based on the record size instead of being set manually.

The spilling happens on a background thread after reaching the soft threshold for buffer occupancy. The Map task is not blocked to write onto the circular buffer when the spilling is going on. However, if the circular buffer reaches a hard limit, the Map task is blocked until the spill is complete. The spilling thread does a partition of the records based on the key, sorts the keys in memory within each partition, and writes them to a file. For every spill, there is a separate file that is written.

The method `map.sort.class` determines the sorting algorithm used for sorting keys. The default is QuickSort, implemented in `org.apache.hadoop.util.QuickSort`.

The partitioner class is determined by the `mapreduce.partitioner.class` property. The spill thread uses an instance of this class to determine which Reduce task partition the record has to be assigned to.

Once the Map task is complete, the spill files are merged, with keys sorted in each partition and written to a single output file. The `mapreduce.cluster.local.dir` parameter contains the directories where the output files are placed. The number of streams to merge simultaneously while writing the output is determined by the value of the `mapreduce.task.io.sort.factor` parameter. The default number is 10, that is, 10 open file handles will be present at a time during this step.

Each time a spill happens onto disk, the I/O required is three times a normal I/O operation. Once the spill file is written and the Map task has ended, it is read, merged to form a single output file, and rewritten to disk. It is best to spill only once at the very end of the Map task.

[If the merge step at the end of a Map is taking very less time, don't bother optimizing the sort and spill step.]

The sort and spill step can be made more efficient in the following ways:

- Increasing the size of the circular buffer by setting the `mapreduce.task.io.mb` property is one way to avoid or reduce the number of spills. When tweaking this parameter, it is good practice to monitor the Map task JVM heap size as well and increase it if necessary.

- Increasing the `mapreduce.task.io.sort.factor` property by a factor of 100 or so. This will make the merge process faster and reduce disk access.

- Writing efficient custom serializers for both keys and value types. The less the space taken up by serialized data, the more efficient the buffer usage.

- Writing **Combiners** to efficiently aggregate Map task outputs. This not only reduces the data transferred over the network to the Reduce task, but also helps in writing faster to the disk and lesser storage of the Map task spills and output files. The subsequent subsection gives more details about Combiners.

- Writing efficient key comparators and value grouping comparators can make a difference to the runtime of the sorting process.

[
MapReduce-4039

Sorting of keys within a single partition might not be necessary in many kinds of MapReduce applications. Termed as **Sort Avoidance**, it may lead to significant performance gains. Reducers need not wait for the all Map tasks to complete before starting off.

This enhancement is currently marked as open and could be coming in future releases.
]

Node-local Reducers or Combiners

Combiners are node-local reducers used to aggregate intermediate map output locally on individual mapper outputs. Combiners can help to reduce the amount of data that needs to be transferred across to reducers. The base class used to derive and implement a combiner is the same as that in the case of a reducer. However, depending on the application, the developer may choose to have different logic in the combiner and the reducer. The combiner is specified for a job using the call `setCombinerClass()`.

The JVM heap size for the Map task can be set using the `mapreduce.map.java.opts` parameter. The default value is `-Xmx1024m`.

If specified, the Combiner can be possibly called in two places:

- When the spills are being flushed onto disk by the spill thread
- When the spill files are being merged into a single output file to be consumed by the Reduce tasks

The former is called whenever a Combiner class is set for the job. The latter happens only if the number of spills exceeds the configuration value `mapreduce.map.combine.minspills`. The default value of this limit is three, that is, the Combiner is called during a merge only if there are three or more spills.

 The intermediate files from a Map task matching a regular expression pattern can be preserved even after the job exits. This is done by specifying the pattern in the `mapreduce.task.files.preserve.filepattern` property.

Fetching intermediate outputs – Map-side

The Reducer needs to fetch Map task output files over the network to execute the Reduce task. The network being a bottleneck in a distributed system, the following Map-side optimizations can alleviate this:

- The intermediate outputs of the Map tasks can be compressed using a suitable Compression codec. The configuration property `mapreduce.map.output.compress` can be set to `true` to enable compression. The type of compression codec to be used can be specified by the property `mapreduce.map.output.compress.codec`. There are many choices available for compression, which are detailed in later chapters.

- The Reduce tasks fetch the output partitions from the Map task using the HTTP protocol. The `mapreduce.tasktracker.http.threads` property is used to configure the number threads that can service Reduce task fetch HTTP requests. Each fetch would need a single thread to service the request. Setting this property to a very low value would increase latency in servicing requests due of request queuing. The default value of this property is 40, indicating 40 threads.

The Reduce task

The Reduce task is an aggregation step. If the number of Reduce tasks is not specified, the default number is one. The risk of running one Reduce task would mean overloading that particular node. Having too many Reduce tasks would mean shuffle complexity and proliferation of output files that puts pressure on the NameNode. It is important to understand the data distribution and the partitioning function to decide the optimal number of Reduce tasks.

 The ideal setting for each Reduce task to process is a range of 1 GB to 5 GB.

The number of Reduce tasks can be set using the `mapreduce.job.reduces` parameter. It can be programmatically set by calling the `setNumReduceTasks()` method on the `Job` object. There is a cap on the number of Reduce tasks that can be executed by a single node. It is given by the `mapreduce.tasktracker.reduce.maximum` property.

 The heuristic to determine the right number of reducers is as follows:

0.95 * (nodes * `mapreduce.tasktracker.reduce.maximum`)

Alternatively, you can use the following:

1.75 * (nodes * `mapreduce.tasktracker.reduce.maximum`)

At 0.95, each of the reducers can launch immediately after the Map tasks are completed, and at 1.75, the faster nodes will finish their first Reduce task and move onto the second one. This is a better setting for load balancing.

Fetching intermediate outputs – Reduce-side

The Reduce task fetches relevant partitions from a Map task as and when they finish. This is called the **Copy phase**. The number of Map tasks from whom a Reduce task can fetch data in parallel is determined by the value of the `mapreduce.shuffle.reduce.parallelcopies` parameter. The lower this value, the more the queuing on the Reduce side. The Reduce task might have to wait for an available slot to fetch data from a Map task.

In situations where a Reduce task cannot reach the output data of the Map task due to network connectivity issues, it retries the fetch in an exponential backoff fashion. The retries continue until the time value specified by the `mapred.reduce.copy.backoff` property is reached. After that, the Reduce task is marked as failed.

Merge and spill of intermediate outputs

Similar to the Map task's sort and spill, the Reduce task also needs to merge and invoke the Reduce on files on multiple Map task outputs. The next diagram illustrates this process. Depending on the size of the Map task output, they are either copied to a memory buffer or to the disk. The `mapreduce.reduce.shuffle.input.buffer.percent` property configures the size of this buffer as a percentage of the heap size allocated to the task.

The value of the `mapreduce.reduce.shuffle.merge.percent` property determines the threshold beyond which this buffer has to be spilt to disk. The default value of this setting is 0.66. The `mapreduce.reduce.merge.inmem.threshold` property sets the threshold for the number of map outputs that can reside in memory before a disk spill happens. The default value of this property is 1000. When either threshold is reached, the map outputs are written onto the disk.

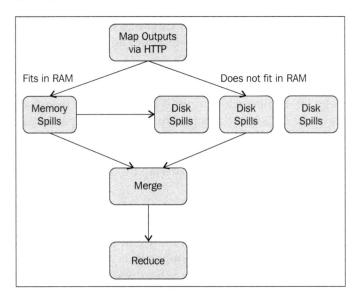

A background thread continuously merges the disk files. After all the outputs are received, the Reduce task moves into the **Merge** or **Sort** phase. Again, like the Map task merge, the number of file streams that are merged simultaneously is determined by the value of the `mapreduce.task.io.sort.factor` attribute. The tuning of these parameters can be done in a fashion similar to the Map-side spill and merge parameters. The key is to process as much as possible in the memory.

In later versions of Hadoop, two parameters, `mapreduce.reduce.merge.memtomem.enabled` and `mapreduce.reduce.merge.memtomem.threshold`, enable merging within the memory.

Any compression used for Map task outputs gets reversed in the memory during merging.

MapReduce output

The output is dependent on the number of Reduce tasks present in the job. Some guidelines to optimize outputs are as follows:

- Compress outputs to save on storage. Compression also helps in increasing HDFS write throughput.

- Avoid writing out-of-band side files as outputs in the Reduce task. If statistical data needs to be collected, the use of Counters is better. Collecting statistics in side files would require an additional step of aggregation.

- Depending on the consumer of the output files of a job, a splittable compression technique could be appropriate.

- Writing large HDFS files with larger block sizes can help subsequent consumers of the data reduce their Map tasks. This is particularly useful when we cascade MapReduce jobs. In such situations, the outputs of a job become the inputs to the next job. Writing large files with large block sizes eliminates the need for specialized processing of Map inputs in subsequent jobs.

Speculative execution of tasks

Stagglers are slow-running tasks that eventually complete successfully. A staggler Map task might not allow a Reduce task to start, thus delaying the completion of the job. Stagglers could be present because of hardware performance degradation or possible software misconfiguration.

Hadoop cannot automatically correct a staggler task but has the capability of identifying tasks that are running slower than normal. As a backup, it can spawn another equivalent task and use the results from the task that finishes first. The backup tasks can then be asked to terminate. This is termed **speculative execution**.

By default, Hadoop enables speculative execution. It can be turned off for Map tasks by setting `mapreduce.map.speculative` to `false` and for Reduce tasks by setting `mapreduce.reduce.speculative` to `false`.

The `mapreduce.job.speculative.speculativecap` is a property with values
between 0 and 1, indicating the percentage of running tasks that can be speculatively
executed. The default value of this property is 0.1. The `mapreduce.job.speculative.`
`slowtaskthreshold` and `mapreduce.job.speculative.slownodethreshold` are
two other configurable parameters whose values default to 1. They indicate how much
slower the tasks should be executing than the average. They are measured in terms of
standard deviation with respect to the average task progress rates.

MapReduce job counters

Counters are entities that can collect statistics at a job level. They can help in quality
control, performance monitoring, and problem identification in Hadoop MapReduce
jobs. Since they are global in nature, unlike logs, they need not be aggregated to be
analyzed. Counters are grouped into logical groups using the `CounterGroup` class.
There are sets of built-in counters for each MapReduce job.

The following example illustrates the creation of simple custom counters to
categorize lines into lines having zero words, lines with less than or equal to five
words, and lines with more than five words. The program when run on the grant
proposal subset files gives the following output:

```
14/04/13 23:27:00 INFO mapreduce.Job: Counters: 23
    File System Counters
        FILE: Number of bytes read=446021466
        FILE: Number of bytes written=114627807
        FILE: Number of read operations=0
        FILE: Number of large read operations=0
        FILE: Number of write operations=0
        HDFS: Number of bytes read=535015319
        HDFS: Number of bytes written=52267476
        HDFS: Number of read operations=391608
        HDFS: Number of large read operations=0
        HDFS: Number of write operations=195363
    Map-Reduce Framework
        Map input records=27862
        Map output records=27862
        Input split bytes=56007
        Spilled Records=0
        Failed Shuffles=0
        Merged Map outputs=0
        GC time elapsed (ms)=66
        Total committed heap usage (bytes)=62037426176
    MasteringHadoop.MasteringHadoopCounters$WORDS_IN_LINE_COUNTER
        LESS_THAN_FIVE_WORDS=8449
```

```
        MORE_THAN_FIVE_WORDS=19413
        ZERO_WORDS=6766
    File Input Format Counters
        Bytes Read=1817707
    File Output Format Counters
        Bytes Written=189102
```

The first step in creating a counter is to define a Java enum with the names of the counters. The enum type name is the counter group as shown in the following snippet:

```
public static enum WORDS_IN_LINE_COUNTER{
        ZERO_WORDS,
        LESS_THAN_FIVE_WORDS,
        MORE_THAN_FIVE_WORDS
    };
```

When a condition is encountered to increment the counter, it can be retrieved by passing the name of the counter to the getCounter() call in the context object of the task. Counters support an increment() method call to globally increment the value of the counter.

 An application should not use more than 15 to 20 custom counters.

The getCounter() method in the context has a couple of other overloads. It can be used to create a **dynamic counter** by specifying a group and counter name at runtime.

The Mapper class, as given in the following code snippet, illustrates incrementing the WORDS_IN_LINE_COUNTER group counters based on the number of words in each sentence of a grant proposal:

```
public static class MasteringHadoopCountersMap extends
    Mapper<LongWritable, Text, LongWritable, IntWritable> {
private IntWritable countOfWords = new IntWritable(0);
        @Override
        protected void map(LongWritable key, Text value,
            Context context) throws IOException,
                InterruptedException {

            StringTokenizer tokenizer = new
                StringTokenizer(value.toString());
            int words = tokenizer.countTokens();
if(words == 0)
    context.getCounter(WORDS_IN_LINE_COUNTER.ZERO_WORDS).increment(1);
            if(words > 0 && words <= 5)
```

```
context.getCounter(WORDS_IN_LINE_COUNTER.LESS_THAN_FIVE_WORDS)
    .increment(1);
              else
context.getCounter(WORDS_IN_LINE_COUNTER.MORE_THAN_FIVE_WORDS)
    .increment(1);
countOfWords.set(words);
              context.write(key, countOfWords);
          }
      }
```

Counters are global variables in a distributed setting and have to be used prudently. The higher the number of counters, the more are the overheads on the framework that keeps track of them. Counters should not be used to aggregate very fine-grained statistics of an application.

Handling data joins

Joins are commonplace in Big Data processing. They occur on the value of a join key and on a data type in the datasets that participate in a join. In this book, we will refrain from explaining the different join semantics such as inner joins, outer joins, and cross joins, and focus on inner join processing using MapReduce and the optimizations involved in it.

In MapReduce, joins can be done in either the Map task or the Reduce task. The former is called a **Map-side join** and the latter is called a **Reduce-side join**.

Reduce-side joins

Reduce-side joins are meant for more general purposes and do not impose too many conditions on the datasets that participate in the join. However, the shuffle step is very heavy on resources.

The basic idea involves tagging each record with a data source tag and extracting the join key in the Map tasks. The Reduce task receives all the records with the same join key and does the actual join. If one of the datasets participating in the join is very small, it can be distributed via a side channel such as the DistributedCache to every Reduce task.

For the Reduce-side joins to work, there are the following requirements:

- There needs to be a way of specifying the `InputFormat` and `Mapper` classes for the different datasets participating in the join. The `MultipleInputs` class is designed for this purpose. For a smaller file, the DistributedCache API can be used. A Map-side join, which will be explained later, shows how to use this side-file distribution channel.

- Secondary sorting capability needs to be there for optimal Reduce-side joins. The sorting of the join keys will happen, but it is important that the source is also sorted for each matching join key. By secondary sorting, one source occurs after the other, eliminating the need to hold all records for a particular key in the memory.

The following example illustrates Reduce-side joins. The dataset contains world cities and some information about the cities, the country code being one of them. It is available at `http://dev.maxmind.com/geoip/legacy/geolite/` in a CSV format. Countries have a two-letter ISO code. The `countrycodes.txt` file was taken from `http://www.spoonfork.org/isocodes.html`.

In this example and in subsequent examples of joins, the ISO code for the country is the join key. This key is used to get the country name and the total population of that country calculated by summing up the population of its individual cities. The join can be done by the following steps:

1. A custom `Writable` data type needs to be implemented to have the dataset tag information within the key. The following code shows the implementation of such a composite key:

```
package MasteringHadoop;

import org.apache.hadoop.io.IntWritable;
import org.apache.hadoop.io.Text;
import org.apache.hadoop.io.WritableComparable;

import java.io.DataInput;
import java.io.DataOutput;
import java.io.IOException;

public class CompositeJoinKeyWritable implements WritableComparabl
e<CompositeJoinKeyWritable> {

  private Text key = new Text();
```

```
private IntWritable source = new IntWritable();

public CompositeJoinKeyWritable(){

}

public CompositeJoinKeyWritable(String key, int source){

  this.key.set(key);
  this.source.set(source);

}

public IntWritable getSource(){
  return this.source;
}

public Text getKey(){
  return this.key;
}

public void setSource(int source){
  this.source.set(source);
}

public void setKey(String key){
  this.key.set(key);

}

@Override
public void write(DataOutput dataOutput) throws IOException {

  this.key.write(dataOutput);
  this.source.write(dataOutput);
}

@Override
public void readFields(DataInput dataInput) throws IOException {

  this.key.readFields(dataInput);
```

```java
      this.source.readFields(dataInput);

    }


    @Override
    public int compareTo(CompositeJoinKeyWritable o) {

      int result = this.key.compareTo(o.key);

      if(result == 0){
        return this.source.compareTo(o.source);
      }


      return result;
    }

    @Override
    public boolean equals(Object obj){

      if(obj instanceof CompositeJoinKeyWritable){

        CompositeJoinKeyWritable joinKeyWritable =
(CompositeJoinKeyWritable)obj;

        return (key.equals(joinKeyWritable.key) && source.
equals(joinKeyWritable.source));
      }

      return false;

    }
}
```

2. A custom `Partitioner` class needs to be implemented. `Partitioner` must partition the data based on the natural join key only; in this case, it is the ISO country code. This ensures that all the cities with the same country code are processed by the same Reduce task. The following code gives an implementation of a custom `Partitioner` class:

```
public static class CompositeJoinKeyPartitioner extends
    Partitioner<CompositeJoinKeyWritable, Text>{


        @Override

        public int getPartition(CompositeJoinKeyWritable
            key, Text value, int i) {

            return (key.getKey().hashCode() % i);

        }
    }
```

3. A custom grouping comparator needs to be written. Again, like the partitioner, the grouping has to be done on the natural key alone. The following code shows the grouping comparator for the composite key:

```
public static class CompositeJoinKeyComparator extends
    WritableComparator{

        protected CompositeJoinKeyComparator(){
            super(CompositeJoinKeyWritable.class, true);

        }

        @Override
        public int compare(Object a, Object b) {

            CompositeJoinKeyWritable compositeKey1 =
                (CompositeJoinKeyWritable) a;
            CompositeJoinKeyWritable compositeKey2 =
                (CompositeJoinKeyWritable) b;

            return compositeKey1.getKey()
                .compareTo(compositeKey2.getKey());

        }
    }
```

4. The `Mapper` classes have to be written for each kind of input datasets. In the following example, two `Mapper` classes are present: one for the city dataset and the other for the country dataset. The country dataset has a number less than the city dataset. This is done for efficiency. When a secondary sort is done on the dataset keys, the country dataset record appears before the city records at the Reducer:

```
public static class MasteringHadoopReduceSideJoinCountryMap
    extends Mapper<LongWritable, Text,
        CompositeJoinKeyWritable, Text>{

        private static short COUNTRY_CODE_INDEX = 0;
        private static short COUNTRY_NAME_INDEX = 1;

        private static CompositeJoinKeyWritable
            joinKeyWritable = new
                CompositeJoinKeyWritable("", 1);
        private static Text recordValue = new Text("");

        @Override
        protected void map(LongWritable key, Text value,
            Context context) throws IOException,
                InterruptedException {

            String[] tokens = value.toString().split(",", -
                1);

            if(tokens != null){
                joinKeyWritable.setKey(tokens[COUNTRY_CODE_
INDEX]);
                recordValue.set(tokens[COUNTRY_NAME_INDEX]);
                context.write(joinKeyWritable,
                    recordValue);
            }


        }
    }

    public static class
    MasteringHadoopReduceSideJoinCityMap extends
        Mapper<LongWritable, Text,
            CompositeJoinKeyWritable, Text>{

        private static short COUNTRY_CODE_INDEX = 0;


        private static CompositeJoinKeyWritable
```

```
            joinKeyWritable = new
                CompositeJoinKeyWritable("", 2);
        private static Text record = new Text("");

        @Override
        protected void map(LongWritable key, Text value,
            Context context) throws IOException,
                InterruptedException {

            String[] tokens = value.toString().split(",", -
                1);

            if(tokens != null){

joinKeyWritable.setKey(tokens[COUNTRY_CODE_INDEX]);
                record.set(value.toString());
                context.write(joinKeyWritable, record);
            }


        }
    }
```

5. The `Reducer` class takes advantage of secondary sorting to emit the joined records. The first value of the iterator is the country record. The name of the country is stored away and the population is calculated based on other records.

```
public static class MasteringHadoopReduceSideJoinReduce
    extends
            Reducer<CompositeJoinKeyWritable, Text, Text,
                LongWritable>{

        private static LongWritable populationValue = new
            LongWritable(0);
        private static Text countryValue = new Text("");
        private static short POPULATION_INDEX = 4;

        @Override
        protected void reduce(CompositeJoinKeyWritable key,
            Iterable<Text> values, Context context) throws
                IOException, InterruptedException {

            long populationTotal = 0;
            boolean firstRecord = true;
            String country = null;
```

```
for(Text record : values){

    String[] tokens =
        record.toString().split(",", -1);
    if(firstRecord){
        firstRecord = false;
        if(tokens.length > 1)
            break;
        else
          country = tokens[0];
    }
    else{
        String populationString =
            tokens[POPULATION_INDEX];

        if(populationString != null &&
            populationString.isEmpty() ==
                false){
            populationTotal +=
                Long.parseLong(populationString);
        }

    }
}

if(country != null){
    populationValue.set(populationTotal);
    countryValue.set(country);
    context.write(countryValue,
        populationValue);

}


    }
}
```

6. The driver program specifies all the custom data types that are required to do the Reduce-side join:

```
public static void main(String args[]) throws
IOException, InterruptedException, ClassNotFoundException{

        GenericOptionsParser parser = new
            GenericOptionsParser(args);
        Configuration config = parser.getConfiguration();
        String[] remainingArgs = parser.getRemainingArgs();

        Job job = Job.getInstance(config, "MasteringHadoop-
            ReduceSideJoin");

        job.setMapOutputKeyClass(CompositeJoinKeyWritable.class);
        job.setMapOutputValueClass(Text.class);
        job.setOutputKeyClass(Text.class);
        job.setOutputValueClass(LongWritable.class);

        job.setReducerClass(MasteringHadoopReduceSideJoinReduce
            .class);
        job.setPartitionerClass(CompositeJoinKeyPartitioner.
class);
        job.setGroupingComparatorClass(CompositeJoinKeyComparator
            .class);
        job.setNumReduceTasks(3);



        MultipleInputs.addInputPath(job, new
            Path(remainingArgs[0]), TextInputFormat.class,
                MasteringHadoopReduceSideJoinCountryMap.class);
        MultipleInputs.addInputPath(job, new
            Path(remainingArgs[1]), TextInputFormat.class,
                MasteringHadoopReduceSideJoinCityMap.class);

        job.setOutputFormatClass(TextOutputFormat.class);
        TextOutputFormat.setOutputPath(job, new
            Path(remainingArgs[2]));

        job.waitForCompletion(true);

    }
```

Map-side joins

Map-side joins, on the contrary, require either of two conditions satisfied in the datasets they join. These conditions are as follows:

- In addition to the presence of join keys, all inputs must be sorted using the join keys. The input datasets must have the same number of partitions. All records with the same key must reside in the same partition. Map-side joins are particularly attractive when operated on outputs of other MapReduce jobs. Such conditions are automatically satisfied in these cases. The `CompositeInputFormat` class can be used to run Map-side joins on such datasets. The configurations for inputs and join types can be specified using properties.

- If one of the datasets is small enough, side file distribution channels such as the DistributedCache can be used to do a Map-side join.

In the following example, the countries file is distributed across all nodes. During Map task setup, it is loaded into the memory onto a `TreeMap` data structure. The `setup()` method of the `Mapper` class is overridden to load the smaller data set in memory:

```
package MasteringHadoop;

import org.apache.hadoop.conf.Configuration;
import org.apache.hadoop.fs.FSDataInputStream;
import org.apache.hadoop.fs.FileSystem;
import org.apache.hadoop.fs.Path;
import org.apache.hadoop.io.LongWritable;
import org.apache.hadoop.io.Text;
import org.apache.hadoop.mapreduce.*;
import org.apache.hadoop.mapreduce.lib.input.TextInputFormat;
import org.apache.hadoop.mapreduce.lib.output.TextOutputFormat;
import org.apache.hadoop.util.GenericOptionsParser;
import org.apache.hadoop.util.LineReader;

import java.io.IOException;
import java.net.URI;
import java.net.URISyntaxException;
import java.util.TreeMap;

public class MasteringHadoopMapSideJoin {

    public static class MasteringHadoopMapSideJoinMap extends
        Mapper<LongWritable, Text, Text, LongWritable> {

        private static short COUNTRY_CODE_INDEX = 0;
```

```
private static short COUNTRY_NAME_INDEX = 1;
private static short POPULATION_INDEX = 4;


private TreeMap<String, String> countryCodesTreeMap = new
    TreeMap<String, String>();
private Text countryKey = new Text("");
private LongWritable populationValue = new
    LongWritable(0);


@Override
protected void setup(Context context) throws IOException,
    InterruptedException {

    URI[] localFiles = context.getCacheFiles();

    String path = null;
    for(URI uri : localFiles){
        path = uri.getPath();
        if(path.trim().equals("countrycodes.txt")){
            break;
        }

    }

    if(path != null){
        getCountryCodes(path, context);
    }


}
```

The getCountryCodes() private method, given as follows, is used to read the side file from the DistributedCache. Each line is processed and stored in the TreeMap instance. This method is a part of the Mapper class as well:

```
private void getCountryCodes(String path, Context context)
    throws IOException{

    Configuration configuration =
        context.getConfiguration();
    FileSystem fileSystem = FileSystem.get(configuration);
    FSDataInputStream in = fileSystem.open(new
        Path(path));
    Text line = new Text("");
```

```
LineReader lineReader = new LineReader(in,
    configuration);

int offset = 0;
do{
    offset = lineReader.readLine(line);

    if(offset > 0){
        String[] tokens = line.toString().split(",", -
            1);
        countryCodesTreeMap.put(tokens[COUNTRY_CODE_
            INDEX],

            tokens[COUNTRY_NAME_INDEX]);
    }

}while(offset != 0);


}
```

The map override method of the Mapper is where the join takes place. Each key is checked against the `TreeMap` data structure for a match. If a match exists, a joined record is emitted:

```
@Override
protected void map(LongWritable key, Text value, Context
    context) throws IOException, InterruptedException {

    String cityRecord = value.toString();
    String[] tokens = cityRecord.split(",", -1);

    String country = tokens[COUNTRY_CODE_INDEX];
    String populationString = tokens[POPULATION_INDEX];

    if(country != null && country.isEmpty() == false){

        if(populationString != null &&
            populationString.isEmpty() == false){

            long population =
                Long.parseLong(populationString);
```

```
                String countryName =
                    countryCodesTreeMap.get(country);

                if(countryName == null) countryName = country;

                countryKey.set(countryName);
                populationValue.set(population);
                context.write(countryKey, populationValue);

            }

        }
    }
}
```

The Reduce task is a simple task that reduces on the join key and calculates the total population in a country. The code is given as follows:

```
public static class MasteringHadoopMapSideJoinReduce extends
    Reducer<Text, LongWritable, Text, LongWritable>{

    private static LongWritable populationValue = new
        LongWritable(0);
    @Override
    protected void reduce(Text key, Iterable<LongWritable>
        values, Context context) throws IOException,
            InterruptedException {

        long populationTotal = 0;

        for(LongWritable population : values){
            populationTotal += population.get();
        }
        populationValue.set(populationTotal);
        context.write(key, populationValue);
    }
}
```

Summary

In this chapter, you saw optimizations at different stages of the Hadoop MapReduce pipeline. With the join example, we saw a few other advanced features available for MapReduce jobs. Some key takeaways from this chapter are as follows:

- Too many Map tasks that are I/O bound should be avoided. Inputs dictate the number of Map tasks.

- Map tasks are primary contributors for job speedup due to parallelism.

- Combiners increase efficiency not only in data transfers between Map tasks and Reduce tasks, but also reduce disk I/O on the Map side.

- The default setting is a single Reduce task.

- Custom partitioners can be used for load balancing among Reducers.

- DistributedCache is useful for side file distribution of small files. Too many and too large files in the cache should be avoided.

- Custom counters should be used to track global job level statistics. But too many counters are bad.

- Compression should be used more often. Different compression techniques have different tradeoffs and the right technique is application-dependent.

- Hadoop has many tunable configuration knobs to optimize job execution.

- Premature optimizations should be avoided. Built-in counters are your friends.

- Higher-level abstractions such as Pig or Hive are recommended instead of bare metal Hadoop jobs.

In the next chapter, we will look at Pig, a framework to script MapReduce jobs on Hadoop. Pig provides higher-level relational operators that a user can employ to do data transformations, eliminating the need to write low-level MapReduce Java code.

3
Advanced Pig

Running Java MapReduce jobs on Hadoop provides the most flexibility with the least abstraction. However, abstractions are necessary to infer patterns, accomplish common data manipulation tasks, reduce complexity, and flatten the learning curve. Pig is a platform that provides a framework and high-level abstractions to build MapReduce programs for Hadoop. It has a scripting language called **Pig Latin**. Pig Latin can be compared to SQL in terms of operator capabilities.

Developed at Yahoo! around the year 2006, Pig was used as a framework to specify ad hoc MapReduce workflows. In the following year, it was moved to Apache Software Foundation. The latest release of Pig is 0.12.1.

The official release of Pig is currently incompatible with Hadoop 2.2.0. It expects libraries from Hadoop 1.2.1. Running any Pig script fails, with the following exception:

```
Unexpected System Error Occured: java.lang.
IncompatibleClassChangeError: Found interface org.
apache.hadoop.mapreduce.JobContext, but class was
expected.
```

Fixing this requires a recompile of the Pig binaries. Run the following command and replace the newly generated `pig.jar` and `pig-withouthadoop.jar` files:

```
ant clean jar-all -Dhadoopversion=23
```

In this chapter, we will look at the advanced features of Pig by:

- Looking at how Pig is different when compared to SQL

- Analyzing how Pig Latin scripts are translated to MapReduce programs

- Delving into the advanced relational operators that Pig supports; we will delve deep into these relational operators and look at their applications with examples

- Studying ways to extend Pig beyond its off-the-shelf capabilities using User-defined Functions or UDFs that can implement a variety of interfaces; we will examine some of these interfaces

Pig versus SQL

SQL is a very popular query and data processing language. Any high-level language for data processing deserves comparison with SQL. In this section, we will compare Pig Latin with SQL. The comparison is as follows:

- Pig Latin is primarily a procedural language. SQL, on the other hand, is declarative in nature. The data pipeline in SQL is not expressed as the data transformations happen. However, in Pig Latin, each step of the data transformation in the pipeline is specified in order. It is possible to mimic this behavior in SQL with the use of intermediate temporary tables, but creating, managing, and cleaning up these intermediate tables can be cumbersome and error-prone. Though Pig Latin scripts are specified procedurally, the statements are executed lazily, that is, they are not executed until the value is absolutely required.

- Developers writing data flows in a declarative language such as SQL overly depend on the query optimizer to choose the right implementation for the data transformation step. SQL engines do provide hints, but the flexibility of choosing or plugging in an implementation of choice is not present. Pig Latin naturally comes with this flexibility.

- SQL is ideal for linear data flows—transformations that yield a single result set. However, data flows are often **Directed Acyclic Graphs (DAGs)**, where splitting data into streams, applying different transformation functions on each stream, and joining these streams are common operations. Implementing such DAGs in SQL require either repeating operations or materializing intermediate results. Pig handles data flow DAGs efficiently by reducing the number of disk reads and writes due to intermediate result materialization.

- SQL is not an **Extract-Transform-Load** (ETL) tool. It acts on data that is already present in a database. Pig facilitates UDFs, where users can specify Java code in the data flow. It allows for streaming, that is, insertion of an arbitrary executable in the data flow. Streaming can aid in the reuse of existing tools and code within the data-flow pipeline. These features of Pig make it a multiutility platform without the need for separate tools for ETL and processing.

- The procedural nature of Pig allows it to store data at any point during the data pipeline process. This can aid in introducing checkpoints manually and prevent the re-execution of the entire query from scratch on failures. This is particularly important when processing huge volumes of data, where data load and processing times are significantly large. SQL does not have this facility under the developers control, and it potentially requires the re-execution of significant portions of the query.

Different modes of execution

Pig has the following three modes of execution:

- **Interactive mode**: In this mode, a grunt shell is provided to the user. Users can type in Pig commands in an interactive session with Pig and the Hadoop cluster.

- **Batch mode**: In this mode, the user can write a series of Pig statements into a script file. The file can then be submitted for execution.

- **Embedded mode**: In this mode, any Java program can invoke Pig commands by importing the Pig libraries.

Apart from these modes of execution, Pig can either be executed locally, in the **local mode** using the local execution environment, or on a Hadoop cluster execution environment in the **mapreduce mode**. In the former mode, all commands are executed on a single system using the local filesystem. If the –x switch is not specified, Pig defaults to running in the **mapreduce** mode. Specifying the –x switch gives the user an option to run in the local or **mapreduce** mode and use the appropriate execution environment. The HADOOP_CONF_DIR environment variable is used to determine the Hadoop cluster for Pig to run MapReduce jobs.

The following code shows how to run Pig scripts in the local or mapreduce modes:

```
pig -x local …
pig  -x mapreduce …    OR pig …
```

Complex data types in Pig

Pig has primitive data types such as int, long, float, double, chararray, and bytearray. In addition, Pig also supports complex data types. Inputs and outputs to Pig's relational operators are specified using these complex data types. In some cases, the behavior of the operators depends on the complex data type used. These complex data types are as follows:

- Map: This data type should not be confused with the map function of MapReduce. The Map data type is an associative array data type that stores a chararray key and its associated value. There is no restriction on the data type of the value in a map. It can be a complex type too. If the type of the value cannot be determined, Pig defaults to the bytearray data type. The key and value association is syntactically done via the # symbol. The key values within a map have to be unique:

  ```
  [key#value, key1#value1…]
  ```

- Tuple: A Tuple data type is a collection of data values. They are of fixed length and are ordered. They can be compared to a record in a SQL table, without restrictions on the column types. Each data value is called a **field**. The ordering of values offers the capability to randomly access a value within a tuple:

  ```
  (value1, value2, value3…)
  ```

- Bag: A Bag data type is a container for tuples and other bags. They are unordered, that is, a tuple or a bag within a bag cannot be accessed randomly. There are no constraints on the structure of the tuples contained in a bag. Duplicate tuples or bags are allowed within a bag:

  ```
  {(tuple1), (tuple2)…}
  ```

 The Bag data type in Pig can be spilt into disks, making it possible to hold a large number of tuples that collectively might not fit in memory. This is not the case with Map or Tuple data types.

Compiling Pig scripts

The Pig architecture is layered to facilitate pluggable execution engines. Hadoop's MapReduce is an execution platform that is plugged into Pig. There are three main phases when compiling and executing a Pig script: preparing the logical plan, transforming it into a physical plan, and finally, compiling the physical plan into a MapReduce plan that can be executed in the appropriate execution environment.

The logical plan

The Pig statements are first parsed for syntax errors. Validation of the input files and input data structures happens during parsing. Type checking in the presence of a schema is done during this phase. A logical plan, a DAG of operators as nodes, and data flow as edges are then prepared. The logical plan cannot be executed and is agnostic of the execution layer. Optimizations based on in-built rules happen at this stage. Some of these rules are discussed later in the chapter. The logical plan has a one-to-one correspondence with the operators available. In the following script, two text files are loaded as data inputs and stored in Pig variables, also called relations. The inputs then go through transformations such as filtering out null values and a join operation of the two data inputs. Finally, the transformed data is grouped on a join key and aggregated over each group:

```
cc = load 'countrycodes.txt' using PigStorage(',') as
    (ccode:chararray, cname:chararray);
ccity = load 'worldcitiespop.txt' using PigStorage(',') as
    (ccode:chararray, cityName:chararray, cityFullName:chararray,
        region:int, population:long, lat:double, long:double);
filteredCcity = filter ccity by population is not null;
joinCountry = join cc by ccode, ccity by ccode;
generateRecords = foreach joinCountry generate cc::cname,
    ccity::cityName, ccity::population;
groupByCountry = group generateRecords by cname;
populationByCountry = foreach groupByCountry generate group,
    SUM(generateRecords.population);
```

A logical plan block diagram for the script is as shown in the following figure:

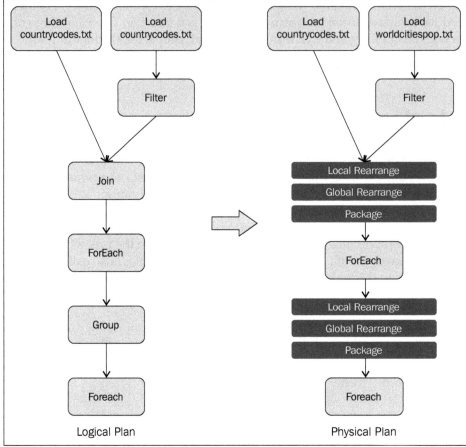

Logical and physical plans for Pig scripts

The physical plan

The physical plan is where the Pig compilation becomes aware of the execution platform. A translation of each operator into the physical form of execution happens during this stage. For the MapReduce framework, most operators have a one-to-one correspondence with the physical plan, except for a few of them. In addition to the logical operators, there are a few physical operators, which are the **Local Rearrange (LR)**, **Global Rearrange (GR)**, and **Package (P)** operators.

Logical operators such as GROUP, COGROUP, or JOIN are translated into a sequence of LR, GR, and P operators, as shown in the physical plan in the previous image. The LR operator corresponds to the shuffle preparation stage, where partitioning takes place based on the key. The GR operator corresponds to the actual shuffle between the Map and Reduce tasks. The P operator is the partitioning operator on the Reduce side.

The MapReduce plan

The final stage of Pig compilation is to compile the physical plan to actual MapReduce jobs. A Reduce task is required wherever an LR, a GR, and a P sequence is present in the physical plan. The compiler also looks for opportunities to put in Combiners wherever possible. The MapReduce plan for the physical plan in the previous image has two MapReduce jobs, one corresponding to the JOIN operator and the other to the GROUP operator in the logical plan. The following image shows the MapReduce plan for the query. The MapReduce task corresponding to the GROUP operator has a Combiner as well. It must be noted that the GROUP operation occurs in the Map task. This is possible because the output of **Reduce1** in the following image is sorted on the key:

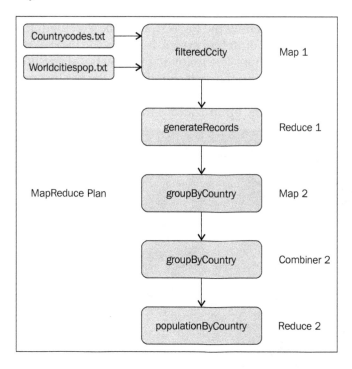

Development and debugging aids

There are three important commands that can help develop, debug, and optimize Pig scripts.

The DESCRIBE command

The DESCRIBE command gives the schema of a relation. This command is useful when you are a Pig Latin beginner and want to understand how operators transform the data. The output corresponding to the groupByCountry relation in the previous script code to find the population of the country is given as follows:

```
groupByCountry: {group: chararray,generateRecords: {(cc::cname:
    chararray,ccity::cityName: chararray,ccity::population: long)}}
```

The DESCRIBE output has the Pig syntax. In the preceding example, groupByCountry is a Bag data type that contains a group element and another bag, generateRecords.

The EXPLAIN command

EXPLAIN, on a relation, shows how the Pig script will be executed. It is useful when trying to optimize Pig scripts or debug errors. It shows the logical, physical, and MapReduce plans of the relation. The following screenshot shows the MapReduce plan for the second MapReduce job (corresponding to the GROUP operator) when the EXPLAIN command was executed on populationByCountry. You can use the EXPLAIN command to study the optimizations that went into the plans.

The ILLUSTRATE command

ILLUSTRATE is perhaps the most important development aid. ILLUSTRATE, on a relation, samples the data and applies the query on it. This can save a lot of time when debugging. The sample is significantly smaller than the data. This makes the code-test-debug cycle very fast. In many situations, the JOIN or FILTER operators might not yield any output on a sample of data. In such cases, ILLUSTRATE manufactures records that pass through these operators and inserts them into the sample dataset. The partial result of executing ILLUSTRATE on the populationByCountry relation is given in the following screenshot:

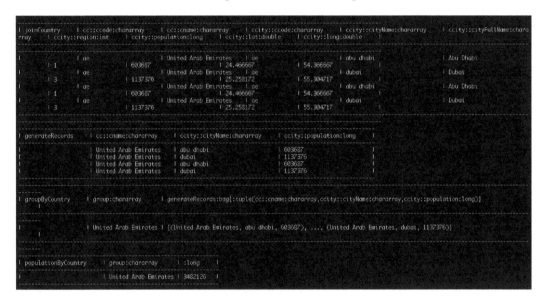

The advanced Pig operators

In this section, we will examine some of the advanced features and hints available in Pig operators.

The advanced FOREACH operator

The FOREACH operator is primarily used to transform every record of the input relation into a transformed record. A list of expressions is used to make this transformation. There are situations where the FOREACH operator can increase the number of output records. They are discussed in the following sections.

The FLATTEN operator

The FLATTEN keyword is an operator, though it looks like a UDF in syntax. It is used to *un-nest* nested tuples and bags. However, the semantics of the elimination of nesting is different when it is used on tuples when compared to bags.

FLATTEN on a nested tuple yields a single tuple, as shown in the following snippet. All the nested tuples are elevated to the topmost level.

Consider data of the following nature:

```
(1, (2, 3, 4))
X = FOREACH A GENERATE $0, FLATTEN($1);
```

This will yield (1,2,3,4) as the resulting tuple.

For bags, the situation becomes more complicated. When we un-nest a bag, we create new tuples. If we have a relation that is made up of tuples of the ({ (b,c), (d,e)}) form, and we apply GENERATE FLATTEN($0), we end up with the two tuples (b,c) and (d,e). In other words, FLATTEN does a cross-product, producing a row for every element in the bag.

Let's consider worldcitiespop.txt as an example:

```
cCity = load 'worldcitiespop.txt' using PigStorage(',') as
     (ccode:chararray, cityName:chararray, cityFullName:chararray,
        region:int, population:long, lat:double, long:double);
groupCcityByCcode = group cCity by ccode;
```

The groupCcityByCcode variable yields tuples with a nested bag, as shown in the following snippet. The number of such tuples is equal to the number of groups, in this case, the number of countries:

```
(ae, { (ae,ae,sharjah,Sharjah,6,543942,25.35731,55.403304),
(ae,ae,dubai,Dubai,3,1137376,25.258172,55.304717)})
```

The FLATTEN operator can be used on these tuples to ungroup them, yielding a record per city for this particular country, using the following code:

```
unGroupCcityByCcode = foreach groupCcityByCcode generate group,
     FLATTEN(cCity);
```

The result is a cross-product of the country code with each element of the nested bag, as follows:

```
(ae,ae,sharjah,Sharjah,6,543942,25.35731,55.403304)
(ae,ae,dubai,Dubai,3,1137376,25.258172,55.304717)
```

FLATTEN called on nested empty bags and empty tuples will yield no output records. This is because, mathematically, a cross-product between a nonempty and an empty set is an empty set. If this is not desired, it is good practice to replace empty bags and tuples with a constant bag.

The nested FOREACH operator

Relational operators can be applied within each record of a FOREACH operator. This is called a nested FOREACH or an inner FOREACH operator. Let's examine it with an example on the `worldcitiespop.txt` file. We want to find the details of the most populous city in each country. There can be many ways of solving this, but we will use the nested FOREACH operator in this case. The code is as follows:

```
ccity = load 'worldcitiespop.txt' using PigStorage(',') as
    (ccode:chararray, cityName:chararray, cityFullName:chararray,
        region:int, population:long, lat:double, long:double);
groupCcityByCcode = group cCity by ccode;
cityWithHighestPopulation = foreach groupCcityByCcode {
    citiesWithPopulation = filter cCity by (population is
        not null AND population > 0);
    orderCitiesWithPopulation = order citiesWithPopulation by
        population desc;
    topPopulousCity = limit orderCitiesWithPopulation 1;
    generate flatten(topPopulousCity); };
```

The steps performed are as follows:

1. The first step is to load `worldcitiespop.txt` based on a schema.

2. Then, group the data by country code. The nested FOREACH operator is the next statement. Flower braces ({) syntactically signify a nested FOREACH operator.

3. In the nested section, a variety of relational operators are applied to the group bag:

    1. A FILTER operator is applied on all the cities of the country to eliminate missing population values. A more efficient way will be to do the filtering before the FOREACH operator (refer to the *Best Practices* section). In this example, we will do the filtering in the nested FOREACH operator for illustration.

    2. The filtered city bag is sorted in descending order on the population of the city using the ORDER operators. Now, the first record is the most populous city.

3.   We use the `LIMIT` operator to select the first record.

4.   The last statement of a nested `FOREACH` operator is always the `GENERATE` method. Here, we generate the record for the most populous city. The `FLATTEN` operator is used to remove the bag nesting.

The tail of the final output is shown as follows:

```
(uz,tashkent,Tashkent,13,1978078,41.3166667,69.25)
(vc,kingstown,Kingstown,4,17995,13.1333333,-61.2166667)
(ve,maracaibo,Maracaibo,23,1948269,10.6316667,-71.6405556)
(vg,road town,Road Town,0,8449,18.4166667,-64.6166667)
(vn,ho chi minh city,Ho Chi Minh City,20,3467426,10.75,106.666667)
(vu,vila,Vila,8,35903,-17.7333333,168.3166667)
(wf,alele,Alele,0,901,-13.2333333,-176.15)
(ws,apia,Apia,0,40407,-13.8333333,-171.7333333)
(ye,aden,Aden,2,550744,12.7794444,45.0366667)
(yt,mamoudzou,Mamoudzou,0,54837,-12.7794444,45.2272222)
(za,cape town,Cape Town,11,3433504,-33.925839,18.423218)
(zm,lusaka,Lusaka,9,1267458,-15.4166667,28.2833333)
(zw,harare,Harare,4,2213701,-17.8177778,31.0447222)
```

 Currently, LIMIT, ORDER, DISTINCT, CROSS, FOREACH, and FILTER are the relational operators supported within a nested FOREACH operator in Pig.

The COGROUP operator

This operator is similar to a `GROUP` operation. Instead of collecting records of one input based on a key, it collects records of *n* inputs based on the key. The `GROUP` operator works on a single input relation, but a `COGROUP` operator can work on many input relations. `COGROUP` can be thought of as the first phase of a join — a `COGROUP` operator followed by a `FOREACH` operator that flattens the bags is an inner join. The following code shows a join between the `worldcitiespop.txt` and `countrycodes.txt` files using `COGROUP`:

```
cc = load 'countrycodes.txt' using PigStorage(',') as
    (ccode:chararray, cname:chararray);
ccity = load 'worldcitiespop.txt' using PigStorage(',') as
    (ccode:chararray, cityName:chararray, cityFullName:chararray,
        region:int, population:long, lat:double, long:double);
groupedCity = cogroup cc by ccode, ccity by ccode;
flattendGroupedCity = foreach groupedCity generate flatten(cc),
    flatten (ccity);
filteredGroup = filter flattendGroupedCity by cc::ccode ==
    ccity::ccode;
```

The maximum number of relations a COGROUP operator can group together is 127.

Operations such as semi-joins can be performed using the COGROUP operator.

 Semi-joins between two relations are the records in the first relation that have one or more matches on the join key in the second relation.

The UNION operator

The UNION operator is used to concatenate two or more datasets. Unlike SQL, the UNION operator in Pig does not impose any restrictions on the schema of the two datasets. If they are the same, the result will have the same schema. If one schema can be forced into the other schema by means of casts, the result will have this schema. Otherwise, the result will have no schema.

The UNION operator does not preserve the ordering of the tuples, and it does not eliminate any duplicate tuples. The UNION operator has an ONSCHEMA qualifier that is used to give a schema to the result. This schema is a set union of all the named fields between the datasets. The ONSCHEMA qualifier requires all the input relations to have a schema.

In our countrycodes.txt and worldcitiespop.txt files, the schemas do not match, and the result is without any schema. However, when we use the ONSCHEMA keyword along with the UNION operator, we see a schema. This schema is the union of the schemas of both relations. The following code illustrates this:

```
cc = load 'countrycodes.txt' using PigStorage(',') as
    (ccode:chararray, cname:chararray);
ccity = load 'worldcitiespop.txt' using PigStorage(',') as
    (ccode:chararray, cityName:chararray, cityFullName:chararray,
        region:int, population:long, lat:double, long:double);

unionCountryCity = union cc, ccity;
unionOnSchemaCountryCity = union onschema cc, ccity;
describe unionCountryCity;
describe unionOnSchemaCountryCity;
```

The schema comparison includes the names of the fields. The result of applying a UNION operator on datasets whose fields have different names will not have a schema. The workaround in such cases will be to introduce a FOREACH operator that renames fields to common names before the UNION statements.

The result of the Describe statements is as follows:

```
Schema for unionCountryCity unknown.
unionOnSchemaCountryCity: {ccode: chararray,cname:
    chararray,cityName: chararray,cityFullName: chararray,region:
        int,population: long,lat: double,long: double}
```

The CROSS operator

The CROSS operator performs the cross-set operations on two relations. The CROSS operator in Pig is implemented in parallel by constructing an artificial join key and then replicating records. This makes the CROSS operator very expensive, particularly in the shuffle and sort phases, as the records are replicated in each of the relations participating in the join for each artificial join key that was created.

However, there are situations where a CROSS operator is necessary. One such situation is a theta-join. Inner joins are based on equality of keys, that is, the equals-to operation is used to join the records across relations. However, there can be a need for inequality to determine record joins. This can be done by a CROSS operator followed by a FILTER operation on the join keys. The following hypothetical example illustrates using the CROSS operator for a theta-join. The join happens only if the value of a1 is less than the value of b1:

```
A = LOAD 'inputA.txt' AS (a0:chararray, a1:int);
B = LOAD 'inputB.txt' AS (b0:chararray, b1:int);
ACrossB = CROSS A, B;
thetaJoin = FILTER ACrossB BY a1 < b1;
```

Fuzzy joins are another variant of the join operation that can be done using the CROSS operator. An example is to self-join worldcitiespop.txt on cities within the same region code.

Specialized joins in Pig

Pig supports join optimizations that can be used out of the box depending on the dataset and nature of the join. These join optimizations increase the performance of Pig scripts and are highly recommended.

The Replicated join

In *Chapter 2*, *Advanced MapReduce*, we implemented Map-side joins and
Reduce-side joins as MapReduce jobs. When an input dataset for a join can be
made to fit in-memory, the join can take place Map-side by replicating the smallest
dataset across all the Map tasks. This is called a **Fragment-Replicate** join in Pig. It is
Pig's implementation of the Map-side join. Some of the key points to remember in a
Fragment-Replicate join are as follows:

- If the smaller file cannot be fit into memory, Pig throws an error and fails to
  execute. Pig also throws an error if the smaller file is greater than the value *l*
  for the `pig.join.replicated.max.bytes` property.

- The Fragment-Replicate join can be used to join more than two datasets.
  However, all datasets, except the first, will be loaded into memory.

- This replication of the input files across the different Map tasks happens via
  the DistributedCache, very similar to the implementation we discussed in
  Chapter 2, *Advanced MapReduce*.

- The Fragment-Replicate join can only be used to do an inner join and a
  left-outer join. Right-outer and full-outer joins are not possible. This is
  because the left relation is fragmented and the right relation is replicated
  entirely. When the join processor gets a record from the right relation, it
  has only a local view of the left relation and does not know if a matching
  key exists in some other split of the left relation.

Using the `replicated` keyword specifies a Fragment-Replicate join. In the following
example, `countrycodes.txt` and `worldcitiespop.txt` are joined using this join. It
must be noted that `countrycodes.txt` is the smaller relation and comes later in the
join specification:

```
cc = load 'countrycodes.txt' using PigStorage(',') as
    (ccode:chararray, cname:chararray);
ccity = load 'worldcitiespop.txt' using PigStorage(',') as
    (ccode:chararray, cityName:chararray, cityFullName:chararray,
        region:int, population:long, lat:double, long:double);
joinCountryCity = join ccity by ccode, cc by ccode using
    'replicated';
```

Skewed joins

The presence of skews in data can hurt join performances by overloading a single Reduce task. Skews are statistical quirks, where a single or small number of keys have a significantly large number of records. Pig helps alleviate such a situation by providing **Skewed joins**. The idea here is to sample one of the input relations to a join and plot a histogram of the records for each key.

The histogram is then analyzed, and keys that have a large number of records are split. Each split is sent to a different Reduce task. In this way, load balancing of the records on the Reduce end is achieved. However, this also requires replicating the other input relation so that each of these load-balanced Reduce tasks has all the relevant records for a successful join.

Some of the key points to remember when executing a Skewed join are as follows:

*   Skewed joins work only with two datasets. If there are more than two datasets that need to be joined, the responsibility is on the developer to break it down into multiple two-way joins.

*   Sampling and constructing a histogram adds a performance overhead when using this join type. The average overhead observed is around 5 percent.

*   The second relation of the join is the dataset that will be sampled.

*   Pig is influenced by the value of the `pig.skewedjoin.reduce.memusage` Java parameter to decide how many additional Reduce tasks need to spawned to process a skewed key. The default value of this attribute is 0.5, that is, 50 percent of the JVM heap is available for the Reduce task to perform the join.

The `skewed` keyword is used to indicate a Skewed join. The following example shows its usage:

```
cc = load 'countrycodes.txt' using PigStorage(',') as
    (ccode:chararray, cname:chararray);
ccity = load 'worldcitiespop.txt' using PigStorage(',') as
    (ccode:chararray, cityName:chararray, cityFullName:chararray,
        region:int, population:long, lat:double, long:double);
joinCountryCity = join cc by ccode, ccity by ccode using 'skewed';
```

The Merge join

Again, as we saw in *Chapter 2*, *Advanced MapReduce*, it is possible to do a Map-side join if both the inputs are sorted on the join key. Pig has an implementation of this kind of join, which is known as a **Sort join** or **Merge join**.

The join algorithm works by making the second relation a side file and the first relation the input to Map tasks. The side file is sampled for the keys, and an index is built using a MapReduce job. The index is a mapping between the key and offset, where the key records the start in the file. Once this index is built, another MapReduce job is started with the first relation as the input file. Each record is read and looked up in the index for the corresponding offset in the second file. The records are read from the second relation, and the join is done.

The following example shows a Merge join using `countrycodes.txt` and `worldcitiespop.txt`. Again, note that `countrycodes.txt` is the file for which the index will be built. The `merge` keyword is used to indicate a Merge join:

```
cc = load 'countrycodes.txt' using PigStorage(',') as
    (ccode:chararray, cname:chararray);
ccity = load 'worldcitiespop.txt' using PigStorage(',') as
    (ccode:chararray, cityName:chararray, cityFullName:chararray,
        region:int, population:long, lat:double, long:double);
joinCountryCity = join cc by ccode, ccity by ccode using 'merge';
```

A variant of a Merge join is a **Merge-sparse join**. This is used when one of the relations is very sparse, that is, only a small number of records are matched during a join. This join type is still under experimentation. Currently, only inner joins are supported using the Merge-sparse join algorithm.

User-defined functions

User-defined functions or **UDFs**, are functions that can be implemented by the developer to extend the functionality of Pig and add custom processing. These functions can be called in almost all Pig operators. UDFs are written in Java. From Pig 0.8 onwards, Python UDFs are supported. In the latest version of Pig, in addition to Python and Java, UDFs can be written in Jython, JavaScript, Ruby, and Groovy.

Other than Java, the rest of the language bindings do not support all interfaces of Pig. For example, the load and store interfaces are not supported by the other language bindings. In this book, we will use Java to build and illustrate the power of UDFs.

There is a repository of Java UDFs called **piggy bank**. This is a public repository where you can take advantage of UDFs written by others and contribute your own UDFs to the community.

Before using a UDF in Pig, it is necessary to register the JAR file in the Pig script. The registration is done using the REGISTER command. In addition to an instance of the UDF class per Map or Reduce task, Pig creates an instance where the logical and physical plans for the script are created. This is done mainly for validation.

 Each Map and Reduce task gets its own copy of UDF. States cannot be shared across Map and Reduce tasks; however, it can be shared within the same Map or Reduce task.

Pig UDFs can be broadly classified into the following types:

- Evaluation functions
- Load functions
- Store functions

Let's examine each one of them in detail.

The evaluation functions

As the name suggests, these are functions used for evaluation. The following example shows a custom upper UDF and its usage within a Pig script. All evaluation functions are extended from the org.apache.pig.EvalFunc base class. The most important method to override is the exec method. The EvalFunc class takes a generic type that signifies the return type of UDFs. The input to the exec method is a Tuple type. This Tuple has to be unwrapped using the get() method, and the resulting data item has to be processed by the exec method. The simplest of UDFs only has to override the exec method:

```
package MasteringHadoop;
import org.apache.pig.EvalFunc;
import org.apache.pig.data.Tuple;
import java.io.IOException;

public class UPPER extends EvalFunc<String>{


    @Override
    public String exec(Tuple objects) throws IOException {

        if(objects == null || objects.size() == 0){
            return null;
        }
        try{
```

```
        String inputString = (String) objects.get(0);
        return inputString.toUpperCase();
    }
    catch(Exception ex){

        throw new IOException("Error processing input ", ex);
    }


  }
}
register MasteringHadoop-1.0-SNAPSHOT-jar-with-dependencies.jar;
cc = load 'countrycodes.txt' using PigStorage(',') as
    (ccode:chararray, cname:chararray);
ccCapitalized = foreach cc generate
    MasteringHadoop.UPPER(cc.cname);
```

The aggregate functions

These UDFs are evaluation functions that are applied on groups. The in-built functions such as SUM and COUNT are functions of this kind. Aggregate UDFs take in a bag of values and return a scalar.

> The entire record can be passed into UDFs by using *. When the entire record is passed, it is wrapped within another tuple. For example, to get the second element of a record, input.get(0).get(1) has to be executed. The first get() call unwraps the record from the tuple.

The Algebraic interface

Aggregate functions that implement the Algebraic interface can be used for local aggregation via Combiners. In *Chapter 2*, *Advanced MapReduce*, we studied how Combiners can help reduce data flow from Map tasks to Reduce tasks and also speed up the query by reducing the amount of IO.

An **algebraic** function is any function that can be divided into three functions: the initial function, the intermediate function, and the final function. If these three functions are applied in a cascading fashion, it is marked as an algebraic function. In other words, the data is divided into fragments, and the initial function is applied on it, followed by the intermediate function on its results, and finally, the final function on the results of the intermediate function. The COUNT function is an example of an algebraic function, where the initial function is count; the intermediate and final functions are both sums of the results.

A **distributive** function is a special case of an algebraic function where all three subfunctions do the same computation. SUM is an example of a distributive function.

Pig provides the org.apache.pig.Algebraic interface, which can be implemented to make the UDF algebraic. The following example shows a COUNT aggregate UDF implementing an algebraic interface.

Using an algebraic function translates to using Combiners on the Map task to execute the Initial and Intermediate static class exec functions. The Reduce task will execute the Final class' exec function:

```
package MasteringHadoop;

import org.apache.pig.Algebraic;
import org.apache.pig.EvalFunc;
import org.apache.pig.backend.executionengine.ExecException;
import org.apache.pig.data.DataBag;
import org.apache.pig.data.Tuple;

import java.io.IOException;
import java.util.Iterator;

public class COUNT extends EvalFunc<Long> implements Algebraic {

    protected static Long count(Tuple input) throws
        ExecException{
        DataBag dataBag = (DataBag) input.get(0);
        return dataBag.size();
    }

    protected static Long sum(Tuple input) throws ExecException{

        long returnSum = 0;
        DataBag dataBag = (DataBag) input.get(0);
        for(Iterator<Tuple> it = dataBag.iterator();
            it.hasNext();){
            Tuple tuple = it.next();
            returnSum += (long)tuple.get(0);
        }
        return returnSum;

    }

    static class Initial extends EvalFunc<Long>{

        @Override
```

```java
        public Long exec(Tuple objects) throws IOException {
            return count(objects);
        }
    }

    static class Intermediate extends EvalFunc<Long>{

        @Override
        public Long exec(Tuple objects) throws IOException {
            return sum(objects);
        }
    }

    static class Final extends EvalFunc<Long>{

        @Override
        public Long exec(Tuple objects) throws IOException {
            return sum(objects);
        }
    }


    @Override
    public Long exec(Tuple objects) throws IOException {
        return count(objects);
    }


    @Override
    public String getInitial() {
        return Initial.class.getName();
    }

    @Override
    public String getIntermed() {
        return Intermediate.class.getName();
    }

    @Override
    public String getFinal() {
        return Final.class.getName();
    }
}
```

The Accumulator interface

In many cases, when a GROUP or COGROUP operator is used, all the bags of tuples for a particular key might not fit in memory. Also, the UDF might not need to see all the tuples at one go. Pig allows UDFs to implement the Accumulator interface to handle these situations. Instead of passing the entire record set at once, Pig incrementally passes subsets of the records for a given key through this interface.

Though the Algebraic interface alleviates the memory problem by aggregating early, there are many functions that are not algebraic. These functions might still be able to aggregate by accumulation and might not need to see the entire dataset.

Let's implement the UDF LongMax, which finds the biggest value in a bag using the Accumulator interface. As shown in the following snippet, the three methods that need to be implemented are accumulate, getValue, and cleanup. The accumulate method is called whenever an intermediate set of records is passed to UDFs. The cleanup method is called after each key is processed:

```java
package MasteringHadoop;

import org.apache.pig.Accumulator;
import org.apache.pig.EvalFunc;
import org.apache.pig.backend.executionengine.ExecException;
import org.apache.pig.data.DataBag;
import org.apache.pig.data.Tuple;

import java.io.IOException;
import java.util.Iterator;

public class LONGMAX extends EvalFunc<Long> implements
    Accumulator<Long> {

    private Long intermediateMax = null;

    @Override
    public Long exec(Tuple objects) throws IOException {
        return max(objects);
    }

    @Override
    public void accumulate(Tuple objects) throws IOException {
        Long newIntermediateMax = max(objects);

        if(newIntermediateMax == null){
            return;
```

```
        }

    if(intermediateMax == null){
        intermediateMax = Long.MIN_VALUE;
    }

    intermediateMax = Math.max(intermediateMax,
        newIntermediateMax);

  }

@Override
public Long getValue() {
    return intermediateMax;
}

@Override
public void cleanup() {
    intermediateMax = null;
}

protected static Long max(Tuple input) throws ExecException{
    long returnMax = Long.MIN_VALUE;
    DataBag dataBag = (DataBag) input.get(0);
    for(Iterator<Tuple> it = dataBag.iterator();
        it.hasNext();){
        Tuple tuple = it.next();
        Long currentValue = (Long)tuple.get(0);
        if(currentValue > returnMax){
            returnMax = currentValue;
        }
    }
    return returnMax;

  }

}
```

The filter functions

Filter functions are also evaluation functions, but return a `Boolean` value. They can be used anywhere a `Boolean` expression is being evaluated. They are most commonly used as part of the `FILTER` operator. They implement the `FilterFunc` interface.

The load functions

These are functions that do input handling in Pig scripts. They implement the `LoadFunc` abstract class and are used along with the `LOAD` statement. The following example is a simple CSV file loader UDF. The methods that need to be overridden are `setLocation`, `getInputFormat`, `prepareToRead`, and `getNext`.

The `setLocation` function is used to inform the load location. The loader should in turn communicate this to `InputFormat`. The `setLocation` method might be called many times by Pig.

The `prepareToRead` method gets the `RecordReader` object of the `InputFormat` class. This `RecordReader` can then be used to read and parse records in the `getNext` function. The `getNext` method does the actual record parsing into Pig complex types. In the following example, it takes each line and parses record tuples.

The `getInputFormat` method gives Pig the `InputFormat` class used by the loader. Pig calls `InputFormat` in the same manner as a MapReduce Hadoop job. The following code snippet illustrates the CSV file loader UDF:

 If files have to be read recursively from directories in HDFS, `PigFileInputFormat` and `PigTextInputFormat` can be used. These Pig-specific `InputFormat` classes are found in the `org.apache.pig.backend.hadoop.executionengine.mapReduceLayer` package. `TextInputFormat` and `FileInputFormat`, present natively in Hadoop, can only read files one level deep in the directory structure.

```
package MasteringHadoop;

import org.apache.hadoop.io.Text;
import org.apache.hadoop.mapreduce.InputFormat;
import org.apache.hadoop.mapreduce.Job;
import org.apache.hadoop.mapreduce.RecordReader;
import org.apache.hadoop.mapreduce.lib.input.FileInputFormat;
import org.apache.hadoop.mapreduce.lib.input.TextInputFormat;
import org.apache.pig.LoadFunc;
import org.apache.pig.backend.hadoop.executionengine
    .mapReduceLayer.PigSplit;
import org.apache.pig.data.DataByteArray;
import org.apache.pig.data.Tuple;
import org.apache.pig.data.TupleFactory;

import java.io.IOException;
```

```
import java.util.ArrayList;


public class CsvLoader extends LoadFunc {
    private RecordReader recordReader = null;
    private TupleFactory tupleFactory =
        TupleFactory.getInstance();
    private static byte DELIMITER = (byte)',';
    private ArrayList<Object> tupleArrayList = null;


    @Override
    public void setLocation(String s, Job job) throws IOException {
        FileInputFormat.setInputPaths(job, s);
    }

    @Override
    public InputFormat getInputFormat() throws IOException {
        return new TextInputFormat();
    }


    @Override
    public void prepareToRead(RecordReader recordReader, PigSplit
        pigSplit) throws IOException {
        this.recordReader = recordReader;
    }

    @Override
    public Tuple getNext() throws IOException {
        try{

            if(recordReader.nextKeyValue()){

                Text value  = (Text)
                    recordReader.getCurrentValue();
                byte[] buffer = value.getBytes();

                tupleArrayList = new ArrayList<Object>();

                int start = 0;
                int i = 0;
```

```
                        int len = value.getLength();

                        while(i < len){

                            if(buffer[i] == DELIMITER){

                                readFields(buffer, start, i);
                                start = i + 1;

                            }
                            i++;
                        }

                        readFields(buffer, start, len);

                        Tuple returnTuple =
                            tupleFactory.newTupleNoCopy(tupleArrayList);
                        tupleArrayList = null;

                        return returnTuple;


                    }

                }
                catch(InterruptedException ex){
                    //Error handling

                }
                return null;


            }


            private void readFields(byte[] buffer, int start, int i){
                if(start == i){
                    //Null field
                    tupleArrayList.add(null);
                }
                else{
                    //Read from start to i
```

```
        tupleArrayList.add(new DataByteArray(buffer, start,
            i));
    }

  }


}
```

The store functions

Store UDFs are similar to load UDFs. They extend the abstract class, `StoreFunc`, and deal with Hadoop's `OutputFormat` family of classes and `RecordWriter`. The methods to override in the `StoreFunc` abstract class are `putNext`, `getOutputFormat`, `setStoreLocation`, and `prepareToWrite`.

Pig performance optimizations

In this section, we will look at different performance parameters and how to tune them for optimized Pig script execution.

The optimization rules

Pig applies optimization rules on the generated logical plan for a Pig script. By default, all rules are enabled. The `pig.optimizer.rules.disabled` property can be used to disable rules. The `-optimizer_off` command-line option can also be used when executing a Pig script to disable rules. Some rules are mandatory and cannot be disabled. The `all` option disables all the non-mandatory rules:

```
set pig.optimizer.rules.disabled <comma-separated rules list>
```

Alternatively, you can use the following command:

```
pig -t|-optimizer_off [rule name | all]
```

> FilterLogicExpressionSimplifier is turned off by default. Setting the property pig.exec.filterLogicExpressionSimplifier to true can turn it on.

Most of the optimization rules discussed in the following section are simple and borrowed from database query optimizations:

- `PartitionFilterOptimizer`: This rule pushes all filtering upstream to the +er. Many loaders are partition-aware and will be instructed to load a partition with the filter predicate.

- `FilterLogicExpressionSimplifier`: Filter statement expressions are simplified by turning on this rule. Some of the simplifications done are as follows:

  - **Constant Pre-calculations**: Any expression that evaluates to a constant is precalculated:

    `X = FILTER A BY $0 > 2*5;` is simplified to `X = FILTER A BY $0 > 10;`

  - **Eliminations of negations**: Any negations in filter expressions are removed without a change in logic:

    `X = FILTER A BY NOT(NOT ($0 > 10) OR $0 > 20);` is simplified to `X = FILTER A BY $0 > 10 AND $0 <= 20;`

  - **Elimination of implied expressions in AND**: Any redundant logical conditions in an AND expression is eliminated:

    `X = FILTER A BY $0 > 5 AND $0 > 10;` is simplified to `X = FILTER A BY $0 > 10;`

  - **Elimination of implied expression in OR**: Any redundant logical conditions in an OR expression is eliminated:

    `X = FILTER A BY $0 > 5 OR $0 > 15;` is simplified to `X = FILTER A BY $0 > 5;`

  - **Elimination of equivalence**: Any equivalence in an expression is simplified:

    `X = FILTER A BY $0 != 5 AND $0 > 5;` is simplified to `X = FILTER A BY $0 > 5;`

  - **Elimination of filtering in presence of complementary expressions in OR**: Filtering is not done when there are complementary expressions in OR:

    No filtering is done in the case of `X = FILTER A BY $0 <= 5 OR $0 > 5;`

- ° **Elimination of 'always' true expressions**: Any filtering expression that always results in a true logical evaluation is eliminated:

  ```
  X = FILTER A BY 1 == 1;
  ```

- `SplitFilter`: This optimizer rule tries to split filter statements. The `SplitFilter` optimization, when combined with other filter optimizations, can be very effective in terms of performance. In the following example, the `SplitFilter` optimization will split the `joinCountryFilter` relation into two filters:

```
joinCountryFilter1 = filter joinCountry by
    INDEXOF(cc::ccode, 'a', 0) == 0;
joinCountryFilter = filter joinCountryFilter1 by population > 0;

cc = load 'countrycodes.txt' using PigStorage(',') as
    (ccode:chararray, cname:chararray);

ccity = load 'worldcitiespop.txt' using PigStorage(',') as
    (ccode:chararray, cityName:chararray,
        cityFullName:chararray, region:int,
            population:long, lat:double, long:double);
joinCountry = join cc by ccode, ccity by ccode;
store joinCountry into 'country-code-join-pig' using
    PigStorage(',');
joinCountryFilter = filter joinCountry by
    INDEXOF(cc::ccode, 'a', 0) == 0 and population > 0;
```

- `PushUpFilter`: The idea behind this optimization is to push filter statements upstream in the data pipeline. The effect of such a move is the reduction of records that are to be processed. In the `SplitFilter` example, once the filters are split, `PushUpFilter` moves `joinCountryFilter1` and `joinCountryFilter` before the `JOIN` statement and directly after the `LOAD` statements.

- `MergeFilter` : The `MergeFilter` rule is the exact complement of `SplitFilter`. The `SplitFilter` rule is applied before `PushUpFilter`, but `MergeFilter` is applied after the application of `PushUpFilter`. Multiple filters on the same dataset are combined as a single filter:

```
X = FILTER A BY $0 > 10;
```
and
```
Y = FILTER X BY $1 > 10;
```
will be combined as
```
Y = FILTER A BY ($0 > 10 AND $1 > 10);
```

- PushDownForEachFlatten: The FLATTEN operation within a FOREACH statement generally produces more tuples than the input. Adhering to the principle of processing the least number of records in the data pipeline, the PushDownForEachFlatten optimization pushes these FOREACH statements downstream. In the following example, the FOREACH statement will be moved after the JOIN statement:

```
X = FOREACH A GENERATE FLATTEN($0), $1;
Y = JOIN X BY $1, B BY $1;
```

- LimitOptimizer: Similar to PushUpFilter, the idea here is to move the LIMIT operator statements upstream. This reduces the number of records processed downstream.

- ColumnMapKeyPrune: The idea behind this optimization is to get the loader to load only the required columns of data. If the loader is unable to do this, a FOREACH statement is inserted just after the load call. This optimization works on map keys as well.

- AddForEach: The AddForEach optimization is used to prune columns as soon as the script does not require it. In the following example, column1 is no longer used after the ORDER statement:

```
A = LOAD 'input.txt' AS (column1, column2);
X = ORDER A by column1;
Y = FILTER X by column2 > 0;
```

  A FOREACH operator is added in between the ORDER and FILTER statements:

```
X1 = FOREACH X GENERATE column2;
Y = FILTER X1 by column2 > 0;
```

- MergeForEach: This optimization merges multiple FOREACH statements into one FOREACH statement. This saves iterating over the dataset multiple times. This optimization is only possible if the following three preconditions are satisfied:
    - The FOREACH has no FLATTEN operator within it.
    - The FOREACH statements are consecutive.
    - The subsequent FOREACH statement is not nested. This is not applicable for the first FOREACH in the sequence.

- GroupByConstParallelSetter: In a statement executing GROUP ALL, even if PARALLEL is used to set the number of Reduce tasks, only one Reduce task is used. The rest of the Reduce tasks return empty results. This optimization automatically sets the number of Reduce tasks to one.

Measurement of Pig script performance

UDFs are developer-written functions that might require performance profiling to identify hotspots. Pig gives a couple of statistics on UDFs using Hadoop counters. A setting called `pig.udf.profile` can be set to `true`. With this setting enabled, Pig tracks the time taken to execute a particular UDF, and also the frequency of UDF invocation. The `approx._microsecs` function measures the approximate time spent in UDFs, and `approx._invocations` gives the developer the number of times UDFs were called during execution.

> By setting `pig.udf.profile`, counters are enabled during Hadoop job executions. As we saw in the previous chapter, counters are global, and they add overhead on the tracking of Hadoop jobs. This setting should be judiciously used, preferably in test settings only.

Combiners in Pig

In the previous chapter, we saw how Combiners reduce disk I/O and save on the amount of data sent over the network from the Map to the Reduce tasks. In Pig, Combiners are invoked based on the structure of the script. The following are a few conditions under which Combiners are invoked:

- A non-nested `FOREACH` statement is used
- All the projections in a `FOREACH` statement are expressions on the grouped columns, or any UDFs used are algebraic functions, that is, they implement the `Algebraic` interface

> Combiners are used in nested `FOREACH` statements as long as `DISTINCT` is the only operator used within the nesting.

A Combiner is not used under the following conditions:

- If the script fails the rules explained previously
- If there is any statement present between a `GROUP` and `FOREACH` statement; post Pig 0.9, the `LIMIT` operator is an exception to this rule

> The logical optimizer might push any `FILTER` operators that come after `FOREACH` using the `PushupFilter` optimizer. This might prevent the use of Combiners.

Memory for the Bag data type

Bags are the only complex data types that are spilt into disks if they don't fit in memory. The `pig.cachedbag.memusage` setting determines the percentage of memory allocated to bags. The default setting is 0.2, that is, 20 percent of the memory is shared between all bags in the application.

Number of reducers in Pig

Unlike bare metal MapReduce, Pig determines the number of Reduce tasks automatically based on the size of the inputs. The input data size is divided by the value in the `pig.exec.reducers.bytes.per.reducer` parameter to figure out the number of Reduce tasks. The default value for the parameter is 1000000000 (1GB). However, the maximum number of Reduce tasks is capped by the value in setting `pig.exec.reducers.max`. Its default value is 999.

The class that implements the algorithm used to calculate the number of Reduce tasks is in value of setting `pig.exec.reducer.estimator`. A custom algorithm can override this as long as the class implements the `org.apache.pig.backend.hadoop.executionengine.mapReduceLayer.PigReducerEstimator` interface and the full class name is assigned to the setting. Arguments can be passed to this custom algorithm by providing a value to the `pig.exec.reducer.estimator.arg` setting. This value will be passed to the constructor as a string parameter.

The multiquery mode in Pig

By default, Pig executes in the multiquery mode. All the statements in a Pig script are executed as one Pig job. One such query is as follows:

```
#Multi-query execution can be turned off explicitly by the -M or -
no_multiquery switch.
```

```
pig -M <script> or pig -no_multiquery <script>
```

DUMP should be avoided as it disables multiquery execution, resulting in the revaluation of relations and making the Pig script inefficient. Instead, a good practice is to use STORE. The interactive command DUMP forces the Pig compiler to avoid multiquery executions.

When a multiquery execution takes place, it is important for the user to distinguish between successful and failed executions of jobs. The STORE command outputs will have different paths, and the result of execution can be discerned by looking at the files. Also, at the end of execution, Pig gives out a result code indicating the status of the script execution. The following table gives the different result codes and their meaning:

Return code	Meaning
0	Success
1	Retrievable errors
2	Failure (all)
3	Failure (partial)

Best practices

The optimization rules in the previous section change the logical plan of a Pig script to enhance performance. We know that these rules will help develop efficient scripts. There are a few other practices that can speed up Pig scripts. These best practices cannot be made into rules as they are application and data specific. Also, the optimization rules tend to be conservative and might not guarantee the application of the rule.

The explicit usage of types

Pig supports many types, both primitive and complex. Type usages can speed up your scripts, sometimes up to 2X. For example, in Pig, all numerical computations without type specifications are considered as double computations. The double type in Pig takes up 8 bytes of storage, while an int type takes up 4 bytes. The computation using int is faster than the computation involving the double type.

Early and frequent projection

As we saw with the AddForEach and ColumnMapKeyPrune optimizers, it is a good practice to project only fields that are absolutely necessary downstream. This helps in reducing the overall data that needs to be transferred and processed downstream. It is also good practice to check your scripts for unused fields. Projecting only the necessary fields after each operation using a FOREACH statement can eliminate unused fields. Projecting early and often is a Pig best practice.

Early and frequent filtering

Similar to early projection, it is efficient to filter early and often. Again, filtering reduces the amount of data being transferred and processed downstream. Filtering reduces data by reducing the number of records, while projection reduces data by reducing the number of fields in the dataset.

 If filtering removes an insignificant number of records, and the operation of filtering is expensive, it might not be efficient to filter early and often. Understanding your data is important when implementing this practice.

The usage of the LIMIT operator

Very often, we are interested in sampling or perusing the top few records of our results. The LIMIT operator can be used to do this. As we saw in the LimitOptimizer rule, LIMIT operations will be pushed upstream, reducing the overall processing time.

The usage of the DISTINCT operator

There are two ways of finding the number of distinct elements in a field: one is to use the GROUP operator and generate the group key, and the other is to use the DISTINCT operator available in Pig. The latter is more efficient than the former.

The reduction of operations

MergeForEach and MergeFilter merge consecutive FOREACH and FILTER statements to a single FOREACH or FILTER statement. Look out for such opportunities where combining multiple operations is possible. Reducing the number of operators in the data pipeline increases the performance of a Pig script.

The usage of Algebraic UDFs

When UDFs are developed and the nature of the processing is algebraic, it is good practice to write UDFs that implement the Algebraic interface. Combiners are called when algebraic UDFs work on grouped data. The usage of Combiners enhance the job performance in MapReduce.

The usage of Accumulator UDFs

Accumulator UDFs can be used to reduce the amount of memory required by UDFs by taking the input in chunks.

Eliminating nulls in the data

A JOIN or GROUP operation on relations send all NULL keys to a single Reduce task. If FLATTEN is used to unwrap the grouping, all NULL records will be eliminated. However, this elimination happens after the Reduce task is executed. Actively filtering for nulls before a JOIN or GROUP/COGROUP operator can improve the script performance significantly by getting rid of Reduce tasks on the NULL keys.

The usage of specialized joins

The second input of a regular join is streamed instead of bringing it to memory. This is a regular join optimization that exists in Pig. When joining datasets of different sizes, it is more efficient to get the dataset with a larger number of records as the last input to the join:

```
C = JOIN small_file BY s, large_file by F;
```

As we saw in the *Specialized joins in Pig* section, a number of other join optimizations can be leveraged in Pig.

Compressing intermediate results

A Pig script might get compiled into a number of MapReduce jobs. Each job might produce intermediate output. The output can be compressed using the LZO compression codec. This will not only help save on HDFS storage but will also help in faster job execution by reducing load times.

The pig.tmpfilecompression property determines whether intermediate file compression is switched on or off. By default, the value is false. The pig.tmpfilecompression.codec property value is the codec used for compression. Currently, Pig accepts gz and lzo as possible values for this parameter. Though the GZIP compression codec provides better compression, it is not preferred because of it slowing down during execution times.

Combining smaller files

In *Chapter 2, Advanced MapReduce*, we saw the problems associated with small files and the usage of CombineFileInputFormat. Pig now has in-built support for combining smaller files. This reduces the number of splits, and in turn, the number of Map tasks.

The pig.splitCombination property can be set to true to combine smaller files. The size of each split is given by pig.maxCombinedSplitSize. This property value takes the suggested size in bytes of the input to each Map task. Smaller files are combined until this limit is reached.

 Combining small files works well for the in-built PigStorage loader. If you are writing a custom loader, the loader must be stateless across invocations to the prepareToRead method. Also, the loader must not implement the IndexableLoadFunc, OrderedLoadFunc, and CollectableLoadFunc interfaces.

Summary

In this chapter, we went through the advanced features of Pig. We looked into the optimizations that Pig has to offer. The following are a few key takeaways from this chapter:

- As a rule, try to use Pig in as many situations as you can. Pig's abstractions, development aids, and flexibility can save you both time and money. Stretch Pig's capabilities before reverting to MapReduce jobs.

- The logical plan optimizations might change the order of statement execution. Use EXPLAIN and ILLUSTRATE extensively to study Pig scripts.

- Help Pig to execute your script faster by following some of the guidelines mentioned in this chapter. Try to make your UDFs implement the Algebraic or Accumulator interface, ideally both.

- Understand the data you are trying to process. Specialized support is available for some kinds of data quirks, such as Skewed joins for joins on skewed data.

In the next chapter, we will look at advanced features of a higher-level SQL abstraction on Hadoop MapReduce called Hive.

4
Advanced Hive

SQL is a popular data-processing language that has been around for four decades. There are scores of people who are already familiar with Relational Data Stores and SQL. A natural step in onboarding more users onto Hadoop is to flatten the learning curve by bringing in concepts they are well versed with. Hive introduces relational and SQL concepts into Hadoop MapReduce. In the chapter on Pig, you saw the advanced usage of Pig scripts to author MapReduce workflows. In this chapter, we will delve into the advanced usage of Hive.

Apache Hive is often described as a data warehouse infrastructure. Traditionally, business intelligence is gathered from a data warehouse, a database that stores data from many sources within an enterprise. This database stores both historical and current data in an enterprise. This data store is primarily queried for reporting and analytics. Traditionally, infrastructure that made data warehouses consisted of **Relational Databases (RDBMS)**, and the query language used to perform analysis and generate reports was SQL. Data warehouse infrastructure used to be made of Relational Data Stores and queried using SQL. Special star or snowflake schemas were used to model these data stores. Apache Hive continues this tradition of SQL, but it changes the underlying data store to HDFS. The queries are translated into MapReduce jobs. The variant of SQL used in Hive queries is called **HiveQL**.

In this chapter, we will discuss the following topics:

- The architecture of Hive on a Hadoop cluster
- The data types supported by Hive, underlying file formats, and data model
- The different query plan optimizers available with Hive and their significance
- The extensibility options provided by Hive, such as UDFs, UDAFs, and UDTFs

The Hive architecture

The following diagram shows the Hive architecture. We will look at each component in detail:

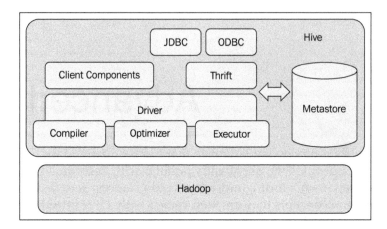

The Hive metastore

The metastore is a database for system-related metadata. It stores details about the tables, partitions, schemas, column types, and table locations. It can be accessed via the Thrift interface, making it possible to read this data using clients written in many different programming languages. The data is stored in a relational database system and uses an **Object-relational mapping** (**ORM**) layer to read and write data into the store. The choice of using an RDBMS for the metastore was made to reduce the latency when serving this information to the Hive query compiler.

The ORM layer of the metastore allows a pluggable model where any RDBMS can be plugged into Hive. The default RDBMS used is Apache Derby, an open source relational data store. In practice, organizations use MySQL and other popular RDBMS suites to host the metastore. The data in the metastore imposes structures on otherwise raw HDFS files. This makes it critical to protect the metastore from crashes by regular backups or replication. The metastore is only accessed during compilation and never when MapReduce jobs are run.

The Hive compiler

The compiler takes a HiveQL query and translates it into MapReduce jobs. A parser parses the query and builds an **abstract syntax tree (AST)**. The AST is checked for types and semantic consistencies. Metadata from the metastore is used to achieve this step. The output of the checks is an operator DAG. A series of optimization transformations are then applied on the DAG. The transformations are chained, and the output is an optimized operator tree. Users are allowed to add their transformations by implementing the `Transform` interface. We will discuss some of the optimizations later in this chapter.

The optimized DAG is then translated into a physical plan. The physical plan is a set of MapReduce and HDFS jobs. A HDFS job is used to read and write data from HDFS.

The Hive execution engine

The execution engine takes the plan generated by the compiler and executes the job strictly in order of their dependencies. The plan is communicated to each task in the Hadoop cluster via a `plan.xml` file. This file is distributed across the cluster using a side channel such as DistributedCache. The job outputs are stored in temporary locations. On the completion of the entire query, if a store location is specified, these files are moved to appropriate locations as specified by the **Data Manipulation Language (DML)**. In the case of a query without a store location, the results are served directly from the temporary location.

The supporting components of Hive

The Hive infrastructure has a number of supporting components, which are as follows:

- A **Driver** is the component that handles query submissions. It is responsible for orchestrating the life cycle of a query by invoking the components in the correct order to fulfill it. The Driver also spawns sessions and keeps track of session statistics.

- There are many client components that are used to submit queries to Hive. The notable ones are **Command Line Interface (CLI)**, a web interface, and JDBC/ODBC connectors. Thrift serialization is used extensively as the serialization library in Hive.

- Extensibility components, such as the **SerDe** and **ObjectInspector** interfaces, are present to help users integrate with different data types and legacy data. **User-defined Functions (UDFs)** and **User-defined Aggregate Functions (UDAFs)** are custom functions that can be written by the user to extend Hive's capabilities.

Data types

Hive supports all the primitive numeric data types such as TINYINT, SMALLINT, INT, BIGINT, FLOAT, DOUBLE, and DECIMAL. In addition to these primitive data types, Hive also supports string types such as CHAR, VARCHAR, and STRING data types. Like SQL, the time indicator data types such as TIMESTAMP and DATE are present. BOOLEAN and BINARY miscellaneous types are available too.

A number of complex types are also available. Complex types can be composed from other primitive or complex types. The complex types available are as follows:

- STRUCTS: These are groupings of data elements similar to a C-struct. The dot notation is used to dereference elements within a struct. A field within column C defined as STRUCT {x INT, y STRING} can be accessed as A.x or A.y.

  The syntax for this is STRUCT<field_name : data_type>

- MAPS: These are key-value data types; providing the key within square braces can access a value. A value of a map column *M* that maps from key *x* to value *y* can be accessed by *M[x]*.There is no restriction on the type stored by the value, though the key needs to be of a primitive type.

  The syntax for this is MAP<primitive_type, data_type>

- ARRAYS: These are lists that can be randomly accessed through their position. The syntax to access an array element is the same as a map. However, what goes in the square braces is a zero-based index of the element.

  The syntax for this is ARRAY<data_type>

- UNIONS: This is a union-type available in Hive. It can hold an element of one of the data types specified in the union.

  Syntax: UNIONTYPE<data_type1, data_type2...>

Functions and data types in Hive are case insensitive.

Hive Version >= 0.7.0 – UNIONTYPE complex data type is available.

Hive Version >= 0.8.0 – TIMESTAMP and BINARY data types are available.

Hive Version >= 0.11.0 – DECIMAL data type is available.

Hive Version >= 0.12.0 – DATE and VARCHAR data types are available.

Hive Version >= 0.13.0 – CHAR data type is available.

File formats

Hive supports a number of file formats out of the box. In this section, we will inspect some of these file formats and their utilities.

Compressed files

For some use cases, storing files in a compressed format within HDFS is advantageous. This strategy not only uses less storage, it also can reduce query times. Hive provides importing files stored in GZIP and BZIP2 formats directly into tables. During query execution, these files are decompressed and given as inputs to Map tasks. However, files compressed with GZIP and BZIP2 compression schemes cannot be split and are processed within a single Map task.

In practice, files stored in these compressed file formats are loaded into a table whose underlying data format is a Sequence file. Sequence files can be split and distributed to different Map tasks.

The `io.seqfile.compression.type` property tells Hive how the compression of the Sequence file should happen. It can take two values, `RECORD`, where each record is compressed and, `BLOCK`, where 1MB of the file is buffered before compressing it.

Lempel–Ziv–Oberhumer (LZO) compression is a lossless compression codec that trades compression for speed. If a Hadoop cluster needs to use the LZO compression, it has to be installed on each node within the cluster. By setting `mapreduce.output.fileoutputformat.compress.codec` to the LZO codec and `mapreduce.output.fileoutputformat.compress` to `true` for the Hadoop cluster, we can enable LZO compression for the output files. Setting the Hive property `hive.exec.compress.output` to `true` makes Hive query outputs to be stored in the LZO compressed format.

ORC files

ORC stands for **Optimized Row Columnar** files. This is a file format particularly attractive for Hive. These files are similar to RCFiles (Row Columnar Files), but have additional optimizations.

The following diagram shows the structure of an ORC file. It contains groups of row data called stripes. These stripes are typically 250MB in size. At the end of the file is a file footer and postscript section. The file footer contains information such as the stripe metadata, the number of rows in each stripe, and statistics such as count, minimum, maximum, and sum of data in each stripe.

Each stripe also has a footer that contains local statistics for an individual stripe. The key characteristic of an ORC file is that it stores records in a columnar format. Each column is contiguously stored for all rows. This increases the I/O efficiency for aggregate queries. The following diagram is a schematic of an ORC file:

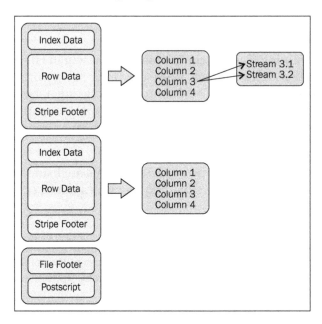

The Parquet files

Parquet is another wide columnar store for Hive. From Hive 0.10.0 to 0.12.0, Parquet was available as an external package that needed to be explicitly installed. However, in Hive 0.13.0, it is natively available in Hive. Parquet is interesting when there is a need to store nested information in records.

> **SerDe** stands for **Serialization and Deserialization**. They are used to read and write the rows in a Hive table. The SerDe module sits in between the file format and object representation of the row:
>
> HDFS File -> InputFileFormat -> <key,value> -> DeSerializer -> Row Object
>
> Row Object -> Serializer -> <key,value> -> OutputFileFormat -> HDFS file

The data model

Hive data is organized as databases. A **database** is a logical collection of Hive tables. A database within Hive assigns a namespace for its tables. If no namespace is assigned to Hive tables, it belongs to the `default` namespace. The creation of a database results in the creation of an HDFS directory for the files in the database. This directory serves as the namespace for the tables. The `CREATE DATABASE MasteringHadoop` command creates a MasteringHadoop database. When we list the HDFS directory structure, we see a directory created for this database, as shown:

```
drwxr-xr-x   - sandeepkaranth supergroup          0 2014-05-15 08:55
/user/hive/warehouse/masteringhadoop.db
```

A **table** is the basic unit of data storage similar to traditional RDBMS. It logically groups records of the same type. Records are rows corresponding to typed columns. A table maps to a single directory within HDFS. Hive also allows imposing structures on existing data locations via **external tables**. Metadata stored within Hive for each table includes the column types and list of columns. It also includes other information such as the owner of the table, serialization and deserialization information (SerDe) for the columns, data storage formats, and bucketing-related metadata. Databases and tables are stored in the HDFS location specified by the `hive.metastore.warehouse.dir` property. These properties are defined in the `hive-default.xml` or `hive-site.xml` file in the Hive installation configuration (`conf`) directory.

 When specifying the `LOCATION` for an `EXTERNAL` table in HDFS, Hive expects the data files to be in a directory.

Partitions are divisions of the table based on distinct column values. When partition columns are specified, all the records corresponding to distinct values or value combinations of the columns are stored in a subdirectory within the `table` directory. Partitions are used as prefilters to prune unnecessary records from getting processed, helping decrease the query latency and I/O. It must be noted that partitions also increase the number of files in HDFS, correspondingly the number of Map tasks and intermediate outputs. The right number of partitions has to be worked out for best performance.

 A `DROP` table on an `EXTERNAL` table does not delete the data in HDFS.

Buckets or **clusters** are files in the leaf-level directories that correspond to records that have the same column-value hash. A Hive user can specify the number of buckets per partition, or per table if partitions are not present. Each record is placed in this bucket, generally by taking the hash of the bucketed column modulo to the number of buckets specified. Buckets are useful to sample data.

Let's take the `worldcitiespop.txt` file and create a table out of it. The following **Data Definition Language** (DDL) query shows how a schema can be imposed on an external table:

```
CREATE EXTERNAL TABLE MasteringHadoop.worldcities_external(code
VARCHAR(5), name STRING, fullName STRING, region INT, population
BIGINT, lat FLOAT, long FLOAT)
COMMENT 'This is the world cities population table'
ROW FORMAT DELIMITED FIELDS TERMINATED BY ','
STORED AS TEXTFILE
LOCATION '/user/sandeepkaranth/worldcitiespop';
```

The keyword, EXTERNAL, is used to indicate an existing table. There are keywords associated with every bit of metadata that is stored in the Metastore. ROW FORMAT is used to specify the serialization and deserialization semantics of a table. If ROW FORMAT is not specified, or ROW FORMAT DELIMITED is specified, a Hive native SerDe is used to produce the table rows. The STORED AS clause specifies the underlying file format used by the table, and LOCATION indicates the place where the table data is stored within HDFS. When the EXTERNAL keyword is used, no additional HDFS directories are created.

> In Hive, it is mandatory that each table maps to an HDFS directory, including an EXTERNAL table. In the example, `worldcitiespop` is an HDFS directory that contains the `worldcitiespop.txt` file. Hive disallows the imposing of the table structure directly on a file.

Now, let's create a table that is not external using the following DDL query:

```
CREATE TABLE MasteringHadoop.worldcities(code VARCHAR(5), name
STRING, fullName STRING, region INT, population BIGINT, lat FLOAT,
long FLOAT)
COMMENT 'This is the world cities population table'
PARTITIONED BY (region_p INT)
CLUSTERED BY (code) SORTED BY (code) INTO 2 BUCKETS
ROW FORMAT DELIMITED FIELDS TERMINATED BY ','
STORED AS SEQUENCEFILE;
```

This table definition specifies a partition column within the table. It also indicates the number of buckets, that is, two, within each partition. The underlying file format of the table is the SEQUENCEFILE format. A partition column cannot have the same name as any other column. When loading data into the table, the partition column must be treated as a separate column.

Bucketing information is specified by the CLUSTERED keyword. In the preceding example, we cluster the data based on the country code and specify a sort column within each bucket. The number of buckets is specified as two. When bucketing, it is very important to set the number of Reduce tasks to be equal to the number of buckets to populate the right number of buckets. This can be done in a couple of ways. One of the ways is to set the number of Reduce tasks explicitly for every job. The other way is to let Hive automatically bucket the data by setting the hive. enforce.bucketing property to true.

Using the following DML query, we will populate the previous table using the external table we created:

```
set hive.enforce.bucketing = true;
set hive.enforce.sorting = true;
set hive.exec.dynamic.partition = true;
set hive.exec.dynamic.partition.mode=nonstrict;
set hive.exec.max.dynamic.partitions.pernode=1000;
FROM MasteringHadoop.worldcities_external
INSERT OVERWRITE TABLE MasteringHadoop.worldcities
PARTITION(region_p)
SELECT code, name, fullName, region, population, lat, long, region
WHERE region IS NOT NULL;
```

 A table definition that has a column with the same name as the partition column throws the error FAILED: SemanticException [Error 10035]: Column repeated in partitioning columns.

The end result is a table with partitions based on the distinct value of the region code. Each partition has two buckets that are sorted on the country code. The underlying HDFS directory structure for the partitions is given below. Each partition is a separate directory. The distinct value of the column that is stored in the partitioned column is part of the directory name.

```
drwxr-xr-x   - sandeepkaranth supergroup          0 2014-05-15 11:55 /user/hive/warehouse/masteringhadoop.db/worldcities/region_p=91
drwxr-xr-x   - sandeepkaranth supergroup          0 2014-05-15 11:55 /user/hive/warehouse/masteringhadoop.db/worldcities/region_p=92
drwxr-xr-x   - sandeepkaranth supergroup          0 2014-05-15 11:55 /user/hive/warehouse/masteringhadoop.db/worldcities/region_p=93
drwxr-xr-x   - sandeepkaranth supergroup          0 2014-05-15 11:55 /user/hive/warehouse/masteringhadoop.db/worldcities/region_p=94
drwxr-xr-x   - sandeepkaranth supergroup          0 2014-05-15 11:55 /user/hive/warehouse/masteringhadoop.db/worldcities/region_p=95
drwxr-xr-x   - sandeepkaranth supergroup          0 2014-05-15 11:55 /user/hive/warehouse/masteringhadoop.db/worldcities/region_p=96
drwxr-xr-x   - sandeepkaranth supergroup          0 2014-05-15 11:55 /user/hive/warehouse/masteringhadoop.db/worldcities/region_p=97
drwxr-xr-x   - sandeepkaranth supergroup          0 2014-05-15 11:55 /user/hive/warehouse/masteringhadoop.db/worldcities/region_p=98
drwxr-xr-x   - sandeepkaranth supergroup          0 2014-05-15 11:55 /user/hive/warehouse/masteringhadoop.db/worldcities/region_p=99
```

On inspecting a partition directory, we see the buckets as files. Each of the partitions has two files, indicating two buckets.

```
-rw-r--r--   3 sandeepkaranth supergroup       3627 2014-05-15 11:55 /user/hive/warehouse/masteringhadoop.db/worldcities/region_p=99/000000_0
-rw-r--r--   3 sandeepkaranth supergroup     183750 2014-05-15 11:55 /user/hive/warehouse/masteringhadoop.db/worldcities/region_p=99/000001_0
```

Dynamic partitions

Partitioning can be of three types: static, dynamic, and hybrid. If the partition information for a column is available during compile time, it is termed a statically partitioned column. The user, when defining the tables, specifies the values taken up by the column. In contrast, for dynamically partitioned columns, the partitions are defined and determined during a query execution.

> Partitions are HDFS directories and can be directly added to HDFS using the hdfs put command. However, the metastore has the master information for all the tables. It will not be aware of any partition that is directly added to HDFS. Hive provides a command to automatically update the metastore and recover the partition. The command is MSCK REPAIR TABLE tableName;. On Amazon EMR, the command is ALTER TABLE tableName RECOVER PARTITIONS;.

The DML query to populate the `MasteringHadoop.worldcities` table is dynamically partitioned. The values for the `region_p` column are determined when this table is populated from the `MasteringHadoop.worldcities_external` table. In the `INSERT..SELECT` DML query as the previous one, all dynamically partitioned columns should come at the end of the `SELECT` statement and appear in the same order as they appear in the `PARTITION` directive. The `region_p` partition column value comes from the region column of the `EXTERNAL` table and is specified last in the `SELECT` statement.

Semantics for dynamic partitioning

Some key semantics when using the dynamic partitioning feature in Hive are as follows:

- By default, dynamic partitioning is turned off in Hive. It can be enabled by setting the value of `hive.exec.dynamic.partition` to `true` in the `hive-default.xml` or `hive-site.xml` configuration file.

- If partitions with the same values as the dynamically loaded data already exist, the existing partitions will be overwritten.

- A `NULL` or empty partition column will be sent to a partition determined by the value of the `hive.exec.default.partition.name` property. The default value of this property is `__HIVE_DEFAULT_PARTITION__`.

- Dynamic partitions are governed and limited by the following three important properties:

    ○ The `hive.exec.max.dynamic.partitions` property imposes a limit on the total number of partitions that can be created by a DML query. The default value is 1,000. If the number of partitions exceeds 1,000, an exception is raised by the MapReduce job.

    ○ The `hive.exec.max.dynamic.partitions.pernode` property imposes a limit on the total number of partitions that can be created by a single Map or Reduce task. The default value is 100. A fatal error is raised if a task exceeds this limit.

- ° The `hive.exec.max.created.files` property imposes a limit on the number of files created by all Map and Reduce tasks globally when a DML query is executed. The default value is 100,000.

> The following fatal error is displayed when a Reduce task exceeds the number of dynamic operations:
>
> ```
> 2014-05-15 08:46:27,647 FATAL [Thread-17]: ExecReducer
> (ExecReducer.java:reduce(282)) -
> org.apache.hadoop.hive.ql.metadata.HiveFatalException:
> [Error 20004]: Fatal error occurred when node tried to
> create too many dynamic partitions. The maximum number
> of dynamic partitions is controlled by
> hive.exec.max.dynamic.partitions and
> hive.exec.max.dynamic.partitions.pernode. Maximum was
> set to: 100
> ```

- By default, a query with all dynamically partitioned columns is not allowed. This is because the value of the `hive.exec.dynamic.partition.mode` property is set to `strict`. In the preceding example, we have no statically partitioned columns. In order for the query to work, the dynamic partition mode property has to be set to `nonstrict`.

Indexes on Hive tables

In an RDBMS, indexing is used for a faster lookup of data, which in turn relates to faster queries. Indexes are data structures that enable random and efficient access of database records based on keys. An index itself might not store the entire record, but only a pointer to the record. Hive indexes are similar to nonclustered indexes from traditional databases. They keep track of mapping between the data and relevant HDFS blocks they reside in. This enables a MapReduce job to figure out only the relevant blocks to process queries.

In the following example, an index is created using two different handlers, **compact** and **bitmap**. A Hive index is nothing but a table in HDFS. The `DEFERRED REBUILD` directive is used to instruct Hive to populate the index at a later stage. An `ALTER INDEX` command can be issued to build the index at a later point of time:

```
USE MasteringHadoop;
CREATE INDEX worldcities_idx_compact ON TABLE worldcities (name)
AS 'COMPACT' WITH DEFERRED REBUILD;
CREATE INDEX worldcities_idx_bitmap ON TABLE worldcities (name) AS
'BITMAP' WITH DEFERRED REBUILD;
DESCRIBE masteringhadoop__worldcities_worldcities_idx_compact__;
```

The output of the DESCRIBE operation on the compact index tables is shown as follows. For each partition and bucket, the index table holds an array of offsets. These offsets can be used to directly get the block of data:

```
hive> DESCRIBE
masteringhadoop__worldcities_worldcities_idx_compact__;
OK
name                    string
_bucketname             string
_offsets                array<bigint>
region_p                int

# Partition Information
# col_name               data_type                comment

region_p                 int
Time taken: 0.078 seconds, Fetched: 9 row(s)
```

Bitmap indexes are used when the number of possible values taken by the indexed column is less. The index table structure for a Bitmap index is also similar, but the information encoded is different. The _bitmaps field stores a bit for each record in the table. If the value is present in the record, this particular bit is turned on, otherwise it is turned off. The index table structure of a bitmap index is shown as follows:

```
hive> DESCRIBE masteringhadoop__worldcities_worldcities_idx_bitmap__;
OK
name                    string
_bucketname             string
_offset                 bigint
_bitmaps                array<bigint>
region_p                int

# Partition Information
# col_name               data_type                comment

region_p                 int
Time taken: 0.083 seconds, Fetched: 10 row(s)
```

Hive query optimizers

After type checking and semantic analysis of the query, a number of rule-based transformations are applied to optimize the query. We will discuss some of these optimizations here. Custom optimizations can be written by implementing the `org.apache.hadoop.hive.ql.optimizer.Transform` interface. This interface has one method that takes in a `ParseContext` object and returns another after the transformation. The `ParseContext` object has the current operator tree, among other information.

The following are the few optimizations that are already available with Hive 0.13.0:

- `ColumnPruner`: This operator tree is walked to determine the minimal number of columns in the base table that are required to fulfill the query. Any additional columns in the base table are pruned away by inserting a `SELECT` statement when reading the base tables. This reduces the amount of data read, processed, and written.

- `GlobalLimitOptimizer`: When a `LIMIT` operator is used in a query, this particular optimizer sets `GlobalLimitCtx`. This assists other optimizer rules that appear downstream to take smarter and efficient decisions.

- `GroupByOptimizer`: When the `GROUP BY` key is a superset of the bucketing and sorting keys, the grouping can be done on the Map side. This optimizer takes care of modifying the plan accordingly. The ordering of the keys must be the same too.

- `JoinReorder`: Based on user-specified hints, tables that are to be streamed are processed last in a join operation.

- `PredicatePushdown`: This is a term carried forward from the RDBMS world. It is a misnomer and is actually Predicate Pushup. The idea here is to move predicates that filter out data upstream close to the data source. This will enable less record processing downstream, saving both I/O and network bandwidth costs. A significant query speed can be achieved with this. By default, `PredicatePushdown` is switched off. Setting the `hive.optimize.ppd` property to `true` enables `PredicatePushdown`.

- `PredicateTransitivePropagate`: This optimization rule propagates a predicate to other relations in a join. When two tables are joined and the join key of one table is filtered, the filtering predicate can be used on the other table as well.

- BucketingSortingReduceSinkOptimizer: If the source and destination tables are bucketed and sorted on the same keys in the same order, no Reduce task is required to conduct join or insert operations on these tables. For example, in the INSERT OVERWRITE A SELECT * FROM B; query, if the A and B keys are bucketed and sorted on the same table, Map tasks are sufficient to fulfill the query completely. Eliminating Reduce means making the query faster as there is no need for the shuffle/sort step.

- LimitPushdownOptimizer: If no filter operators are present in a statement having the LIMIT operator, the Map tasks of the query can be optimized to retrieve a top K result. This top K result can then be passed to the LIMIT operator. This greatly reduces the number of records flowing through the shuffle/sort stage.

- NonBlockingOpDeDupProc: This optimization merges projections and filters them into single statements.

- PartitionPruner: To prevent the metastore from memory issues, partition names are fetched first, and then, each partition information is retrieved based on the need.

- ReduceSinkDeDuplication: If two Reduce tasks have the same partition columns and order, they can be merged into a single task.

- RewriteGBUsingIndex: A GROUP BY operation can be conducted by conducting a table scan on the index table rather than on the base table. This is possible if the key columns have an index over them. For example, SELECT COUNT(k) FROM A GROUP BY k can be written as SELECT SUM(_count_of_k) FROM index_table GROUP BY k;. This optimization might not be applicable for all GROUP BY queries.

- StatsOptimizer: There can be many queries that can be answered directly from the metastore statistics. Queries involving MIN, MAX, and COUNT are some examples of queries that can potentially be answered without spawning any MapReduce task. This optimizer detects this possibility and optimizes the query.

Advanced DML

The Data Manipulation Language provided by Hive is equivalent in features to any state-of-the-art SQL system. They provide standard operations such as the JOIN, GROUP BY, and UNION operations. The semantics might vary marginally depending on the operation. Different kinds of optimization hints are also present.

The GROUP BY operation

The GROUP BY operation is the same as in standard SQL, except for a few advanced features:

- **Multi-Group-By Inserts**: It is possible to have multiple GROUP BY clauses within a single query. The output can be written to multiple tables or HDFS files. For example, the following query is possible:

```
FROM src_table INSERT OVERWRITE TABLE id_count SELECT id,
COUNT(id) GROUP BY id INSERT OVERWRITE TABLE id_sum SELECT id,
SUM(id_value) GROUP BY id;
```

- **Map-side aggregation for GROUP BY**: By setting the hive.map.aggr property to true, it is possible to enforce one level of aggregation on the Map tasks. This will yield a better-performing query.

ORDER BY versus SORT BY clauses

Hive has both an ORDER BY and a SORT BY clause to sort the output of a query. The difference between the two is that ORDER BY imposes a total order on query results, but SORT BY imposes order only on the rows in a Reduce task. If there are multiple Reduce tasks, the output data will only have a partial order when SORT BY is used.

It is easy to see that the ORDER BY clause requires a single Reduce task to achieve total order on the query, a bottleneck to sort large datasets. Hive enforces the need for a LIMIT operator by default when an ORDER BY clause is used. This is governed by the hive.mapred.mode setting. The default value is strict. By setting it to nonstrict, the compiler does not impose the mandatory LIMIT restriction. However, this is not recommended.

The JOIN operator and its types

The JOIN operators are very important to process data on multiple datasets or tables. A number of JOIN operator variants are facilitated in Hive. Hive provides a number of join optimization options based on the nature of the data. The following are some important properties and optimizations in the JOIN operator:

- Hive supports inner joins, outer joins, and the left semi-join. All joins are based on the equality operator. Fuzzy and theta joins are not supported.
- A multitable join is allowed. The number of MapReduce jobs depends on the number of key columns participating in the join. If the same key columns are used to join multiple tables, a single MapReduce job will be used.

- By default, the last table participating in the join is streamed to the Reduce task. The rest of the tables are buffered. It is important to place the biggest table at the end when conducting a join for better performance. The user can explicitly specify a `STREAMTABLE` hint to override the default. For example, consider the `SELECT /*+ STREAMTABLE(A)*/  A.x, B.x, C.x FROM A JOIN B ON (A.key = B.key) JOIN C ON (B.key = C.key);` query. The `STREAMTABLE` hint instructs the Hive compiler to stream table A. By default, it will have streamed table C.

- A `WHERE` clause appearing in a `JOIN` statement filters rows after the `JOIN` operator is executed. It is good practice to colocate the `WHERE` clause filters in the `JOIN` itself with the `ON` clauses, where the `JOIN` keys are specified.

Map-side joins

When one of the tables participating in a join is small, the join operation can be conducted directly on the Map task. This can be specified by the `MAPJOIN` hint in Hive. For example, `SELECT /*+ MAPJOIN(A) */ A.x, B.x FROM A JOIN B ON (A.key = B.key)` hints that A being a smaller table can be loaded into memory and a Map-side join can be performed.

If the tables participating in a join are bucketized on the join columns, and the number of buckets of one table is equal or a multiple of the number of buckets in the other table, a Map-side join can be done. Though this is not the default behavior, it can be enabled by setting the `hive.optimize.bucketmapjoin` property to `true`. This is also known as the **bucketized map-side join**.

If the tables participating in a join are bucketized on the join columns, have the same number of buckets, and the buckets are sorted on the join columns, a sort-merge operation can be done to join the two tables. However, this is again not the default behavior. In addition to setting the `hive.optimize.bucketmapjoin` property to `true`, the `hive.optimize.bucketmapjoin.sortedmerge` property has to be set to `true`, and `hive.input.format` has to be set to `org.apache.hadoop.hive.ql.io.BucketizedHiveInputFormat`. This is also known as the **bucketized sort-merge join**.

Setting the `hive.auto.convert.join` property to `true` automatically converts a join to a Map-side join. The `MAPJOIN` hint is no longer required. However, the hint is mandatory for the bucketized map-side and sort-merge joins.

Advanced aggregation support

The primary use case of Hive is analytics on data warehouses. This calls for advanced aggregation support to collect and report statistics from data on different dimensions.

Hive supports GROUPING SETS, where more than one GROUP BY operation can be done on a single table. It is equivalent to executing two different GROUP BY queries and then applying UNION on them. The following command shows the usage of GROUPING SET:

`SELECT x, y, SUM(z) FROM X GROUP BY x, y GROUPING SETS( (x,y), y);`

This query is equivalent to UNION of the SELECT x, y, SUM(z) FROM X GROUP BY x,y; and SELECT null, y, SUM(z) FROM X GROUP BY y; queries.

Cubes are multidimensional data structures used to drill down, roll up, and aggregate facts. Hive simulates cubes' queries by aggregating facts over all combinations of dimensions. For example, SELECT x, y, z, SUM(a) FROM X GROUP BY x, y, z WITH CUBE; is equivalent to the SELECT x,y,z, SUM(a) FROM X GROUP BY x,y,x GROUPING SETS ((x,y,z), (x,y), (y,z), (x,z), (x), (y), (z), ()); query.

Hive also supports the ROLLUP command to compute aggregates at each hierarchy level. A query of the SELECT x, y, z, SUM(a) FROM X GROUP BY x,y,z WITH ROLLUP; form is equivalent to SELECT x,y,z, SUM(a) FROM X GROUP BY x,y,z GROUPING SETS ((x,y,z) , (x,y), (x), ());.

There is an implicit assumption of the x hierarchy being drilled down to y, and y can in turn being drilled down to z. The ROLLUP directive creates a number of rows for every single input row. In the preceding example, for every input row, four output rows are generated with three group keys. The higher the cardinality of the group keys, the worse it gets at the Map and Reduce task boundaries. In these cases, it is better to spawn multiple MapReduce jobs. The cardinality threshold, beyond which an additional job is launched, is given by the hive.new.job.grouping.set. cardinality setting.

Other advanced clauses

There are many other clauses for the advanced usage of Hive queries:

- The EXPLODE user-defined table generation function can be used to produce multiple rows for a single input row. For example, EXPLODE on an array type column produces a row for each element of the array.

- A bucket can be sampled by the TABLESAMPLE keyword. The query syntax is SELECT cols FROM table_name TABLESAMPLE(i OUT OF n). Here, the i bucket is sampled in a total of n buckets. The TABLESAMPLE directive can also be used to sample at a block level. Giving a percentage value for sampling in the TABLESAMPLE directive does this. It must be noted that the granularity of sampling is a block in this case. TABLESAMPLE can be used to sample data based on the input split size and number of rows as well.

- Hive provides a few virtual columns that can be used in specialized queries. INPUT__FILE__NAME gives the Map tasks an input filename, and BLOCK__OFFSET__INSIDE__FILE gives the global position of the file.

- The EXPLAIN command for a query gives the AST, execution DAG with the dependencies, and description of each stage within the DAG.

UDF, UDAF, and UDTF

Like in Pig, UDFs are one of the most important extensibility features in Hive. Writing a UDF in Hive is simpler, but the interfaces do not define every override method that is needed to make the UDF complete. This is because UDFs can take any number of parameters, and it is difficult to provide a fixed interface. Hive uses Java reflection under the hood when executing the UDF to figure out the parameter list for the function.

These are the following three kinds of UDFs in Hive:

- **Regular UDFs**: These UDFs take in a single row and produce a single row after application of the custom logic.

- **UDAFs**: These are aggregators that take in multiple rows but output a single row. SUM and COUNT are examples of in-built UDAFs.

- **UDTFs**: These are generator functions that take in a single row and produce multiple rows as outputs. The EXPLODE function is a UDTF.

The following code example shows how a simple UDF is written. Every UDF is extended from the UDF class present in `org.apache.hadoop.hive.ql.exec` package. It has no override methods, but at least one `evaluate` method has to be part of the class. The following UDF takes in a `String` type and returns another by converting the input string to uppercase. Any number of evaluate methods can be written, and the correct one is chosen by Hive during runtime:

```
package MasteringHadoop;

import org.apache.hadoop.hive.ql.exec.UDF;

public class TOUPPER extends UDF{

    public String evaluate(String input){

        return input.toUpperCase();
    }

}
```

The following Hive statements show how to deploy and run this UDF. The JAR file containing the UDF must be registered, and the Hive metastore has to be instructed on the presence of this UDF. After this, the UDF can be used as any other built-in function within Hive:

```
add jar MasteringHadoop-1.0-SNAPSHOT-jar-with-dependencies.jar;
CREATE TEMPORARY FUNCTION MASTERINGHADOOPTOUPPER AS
'MasteringHadoop.TOUPPER';
SELECT MASTERINGHADOOPTOUPPER(name) FROM
MasteringHadoop.worldcities;
```

A UDAF is slightly more complicated to implement. As we saw in the previous two chapters, aggregations can happen either in the Map or Reduce tasks or both. The UDAF has to be ready to handle all these possibilities. The following code shows a UDAF that finds the maximum of a set of `BIGINT` numbers. As with the UDF, the UDAF extends the `UDAF` class. Instead of an evaluate method, the evaluator classes have to be declared in a UDAF. At runtime, Hive reflects on the UDAF extension and calls the methods on the evaluator classes.

Any number of evaluator classes can be present within a UDAF. They all have to extend the `UDAFEvaluator` base class. The only override the `UDAFEvaluator` base class provides is the `init()` method. In the following example, we create a `MaximumBigIntEvaluator` class to compare and select the maximum value of the `BIGINT` value.

The `init()` method is used to initialize the internal state of the evaluator. Other than the `init()` method, there is an `iterator()` method that will be called for each value that needs aggregation. The `iterator()` method has to update the state of the evaluator. Null values are ignored. The `terminatePartial()` method is called by the Hive runtime whenever it wants a partial result. This generally happens when Map-side aggregations are done. The evaluator has to return the aggregation state so far. The `merge()` function is called by Hive when two partial aggregations need to be aggregated. It generally happens on the Reduce side, where partial results from Maps are merged. Finally, the `terminate()` method is called to get the final aggregation result:

```
package MasteringHadoop;

import org.apache.hadoop.hive.ql.exec.UDAF;
import org.apache.hadoop.hive.ql.exec.UDAFEvaluator;
import org.apache.hadoop.io.LongWritable;


public class BIGINTMAX extends UDAF {

    public static class MaximumBigIntEvaluator
        implements UDAFEvaluator{

        private Long max;
        private boolean empty;


        public MaximumBigIntEvaluator(){
            super();
            init();
        }


        @Override
        public void init() {
            max = (long)0;
            empty = true;
        }


        public boolean iterate(LongWritable value){
            if(value != null){

                long current = value.get();
```

```
                        if(empty){
                            max = current;
                            empty = false;

                        }
                        else{

                            max = Math.max(current, max);
                        }


                    }
                    return true;


            }


            public LongWritable terminatePartial(){
                return empty ? null : new LongWritable(max);

            }

            public LongWritable terminate(){
                return empty ? null : new LongWritable(max);

            }

            public boolean merge(LongWritable value){
              iterate(value);
              return true;
            }

        }

    }
```

These methods are mandatory for a UDAF to work properly. The following diagram shows the application of the evaluator methods:

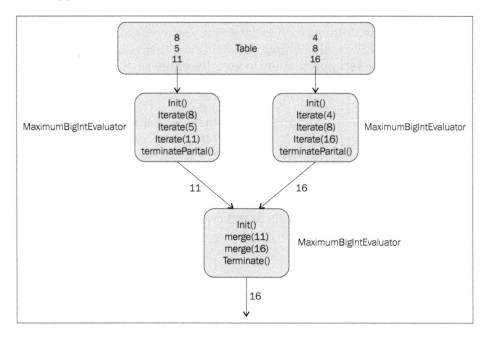

Summary

Hive, through its query language HiveQL, brings in SQL and Relational database concepts to Hadoop. The primary use case for Hive is data warehousing and analytical querying for applications such as Business Intelligence. The supporting components of Hive are built to assist this use case. For example, row-columnar file formats are very efficient when performing aggregations on columns.

The key takeaways from this chapter are as follows:

- In Hive, a close look has to be kept on the file format used by the underlying table. Text files can be inefficient. Sequence files are better off as they are compressed. Specialized files such as RC and ORC are more suited both in terms of I/O and query performance.

- Compression brings in efficiency. Both intermediate and final outputs can be compressed. It is better to avoid compression techniques such as GZIP that cannot be split. Snappy is an alternative compression technique that can be split.

- Partitioning large tables is good practice. This helps pre-filter relevant data when processing queries. However, too many partitions put pressure on HDFS.

- Use Map-side joins wherever possible. Order smaller tables to the left-hand side of your join. Settings such as `hive.auto.convert.join` help optimize joins automatically without hints. The `hive.mapjoin.smalltable.filesize` property can be set appropriately to keep the entire small table in memory. However, care has to be taken to see that the JVM has enough memory to fit the table.

- `ORDER` statements should be avoided as they use a single reducer. All the optimizations from *Chapter 2, Advanced MapReduce*, can be applied on the Hadoop cluster running Hive queries. This will have a positive influence on the performance of the query.

In the next chapter, we will look at Hadoop I/O in detail, particularly file compression and serialization/deserialization of data to and from Hadoop-based files.

5
Serialization and Hadoop I/O

Hadoop is about big data, and whenever data is handled, discussion and detailing of IO becomes an integral part of the setup. Data needs to be ingested via the network or loaded from an external persistent media. The ingested data needs to be staged during the extraction and transformation steps. Finally, the results need to be stored for consumption by downstream analysis processes for serving data, reporting, and visualization. Each of these stages involves understanding the underlying data storage structure, data formats, and data models. These aspects help in tuning the entire data-handling pipeline for efficiency of storage and speed.

In this chapter, we will look into the IO features and capabilities of Hadoop. Specifically, we will cover the following topics:

- Serialization and deserialization support and their necessity within Hadoop
- Avro—an external serialization framework
- Data compression codecs available within Hadoop and their tradeoffs
- Special file formats in Hadoop and their features

Data serialization in Hadoop

Though we see data in a structured form, the raw form of data is a sequence or stream of bits. This raw form of data is the one that travels over the network and is stored in RAM or any other persistent media. **Serialization** is the process of converting structured data into its raw form. **Deserialization** is the reverse process of reconstructing structured forms from the data's raw bit stream form.

In Hadoop, different components talk to each other via **Remote Procedure Calls (RPCs)**. A caller process serializes the desired function name and its arguments as a byte stream before sending it to the called process. The called process deserializes this byte stream, interprets the function type, and executes it using the arguments that were supplied. The results are serialized and sent back to the caller. This workflow naturally calls for fast serialization and deserialization. Network bandwidth is at a premium and requires the serialized representation of the function name and its arguments to have the smallest possible payload. Different processes might evolve differently, and the entire serialization-deserialization process might need to be backward compatible and extensible. Processes running on different machines might have different configurations and leverage different platform components, making interoperability a desired feature of the serialization-deserialization library. These properties of serialization and deserialization are not limited to network data, but extend to storage, both volatile and persistent.

Writable and WritableComparable

Serialization and deserialization in Hadoop is done via the `Writable` interface. This interface has two methods, `void write(DataOutput out)` and `void readFields(DataInput in)`. The `write` method serializes the object into a byte stream. The `readFields` method is the deserialization method that reads off of an input byte stream and converts it into an object.

Inherited from the `Writable` interface is the `WritableComparable` interface. This interface is a combination of the `Writable` and `Comparable` interfaces. Classes implementing this interface not only facilitate serializing and deserializing, but also comparison of values. Having a Hadoop data type implement this interface can come in very handy to sort and group data objects. An example was seen in *Chapter 2, Advanced MapReduce*, when the join operator was implemented using a custom `WritableComparable` type.

Out of the box, Hadoop supports a number of `WritableComparable` wrappers. Each `WritableComparable` wrapper wraps a Java primitive type. For example, an `IntWritable` wrapper class wraps an `int` data point, and a `BooleanWritable` wrapper wraps a `boolean` type.

Hadoop supports the `VIntWritable` and `VLongWritable` classes. These are the variable length equivalents of the fixed length `IntWritable` and `LongWritable` types. A value between -112 and 127 is encoded as a single byte using a variable-length number type. However, larger values are encoded in a way that the first byte indicates the sign and the number of bytes that follow. Variable-length `Writable` types save space, on average, when the distribution of the numeric value has a high variance. Lesser values need lesser storage.

In *Chapter 2, Advanced MapReduce*, we implemented a custom `WritableComparable` class for the Reduce-side join operation. The `CompositeJoinKeyWritable` class was a composite key of the country code of the data source. Other than the `write` and `readFields` overrides, the `compareTo` function was overridden to provide a comparison of these custom types.

As we saw in the `CompositeJoinKeyWritable` class, under the hood, `Writable` types serialize their payload in a specific way. Let's take the `IntWritable`, `LongWritable`, `VIntWritable`, and `VLongWritable` classes as examples and see the raw bytes that their values are serialized to.

The following method takes a `Writable` type and serializes it as a stream of bytes. It uses the `write` method to write the payload of the `Writable` type into a byte stream. The byte stream is converted into a hexadecimal string for display on the console. The `org.apache.hadoop.util.StringUtils` utility class has some static functions that help us convert a byte array to a hexadecimal string:

```
public static String serializeToByteString(Writable writable)
  throws IOException {

    ByteArrayOutputStream outputStream = new
        ByteArrayOutputStream();
    DataOutputStream dataOutputStream = new
        DataOutputStream(outputStream);
    writable.write(dataOutputStream);
    dataOutputStream.close();
    byte[] byteArray = outputStream.toByteArray();
    return StringUtils.byteToHexString(byteArray);
    }
```

The following code instantiates each of the four classes we consider in this example to study Hadoop serialization. We will take three numbers (100 representing a small integer, 1048576 a normal integer, and 4589938592L a long integer) as the payload for these objects:

```
public static void main(String[] args) throws IOException{

    IntWritable intWritable = new IntWritable();
    VIntWritable vIntWritable = new VIntWritable();
    LongWritable longWritable = new LongWritable();
    VLongWritable vLongWritable = new VLongWritable();

    int smallInt = 100;
    int mediumInt = 1048576;
    long bigInt = 4589938592L;

    System.out.println("smallInt serialized value using
        IntWritable");
    intWritable.set(smallInt);
    System.out.println(serializeToByteString(intWritable));

    System.out.println("smallInt serialized value using
        VIntWritable");
    vIntWritable.set(smallInt);
    System.out.println(serializeToByteString(vIntWritable));

    System.out.println("mediumInt serialized value using
        IntWritable");
    intWritable.set(mediumInt);
    System.out.println(serializeToByteString(intWritable));

    System.out.println("mediumInt serialized value using
        VIntWritable");
    vIntWritable.set(mediumInt);
    System.out.println(serializeToByteString(vIntWritable));

    System.out.println("bigInt serialized value using
        LongWritable");
    longWritable.set(bigInt);
    System.out.println(serializeToByteString(longWritable));

    System.out.println("bigInt serialized value using
        VLongWritable");
    vLongWritable.set(bigInt);
    System.out.println(serializeToByteString(vLongWritable));
}
```

The program uses `IntWritable` and `VIntWritable` as the wrapper classes for the small and medium integers. `LongWritable` and `VLongWritable` are used for the large integer. The output when these numbers are serialized into a byte array is shown as follows:

```
smallInt serialized value using IntWritable
00000064
smallInt serialized value using VIntWritable
64
mediumInt serialized value using IntWritable
00100000
mediumInt serialized value using VIntWritable
8d100000
bigInt serialized value using LongWritable
000000011194e7a0
bigInt serialized value using VLongWritable
8b011194e7a0
```

The `IntWritable` class uses a fixed length of four bytes to represent an integer regardless of the value stored within it. The `VIntWritable` class is smarter, and the number of bytes it uses depends on the value of the payload. For the number 100, `VIntWritable` uses only a single byte. There is a similar difference in the `LongWritable` and `VLongWritable` serialized values too.

 Text is a `Writable` version of the `String` type. It represents a collection of UTF-8 characters. Hadoop's `Text` class is mutable when compared to Java's `String` class.

Hadoop versus Java serialization

A question that pops up at this point is why Hadoop uses the `Writable` interface and does not rely on Java serialization. Let's try to serialize the values in the previous example using Java data types and serialization. For Java serialization, we will use the following static method:

```
public static String javaSerializeToByteString(Object o) throws
    IOException{
    ByteArrayOutputStream outputStream = new
        ByteArrayOutputStream();
    ObjectOutputStream objectOutputStream = new
        ObjectOutputStream(outputStream);
    objectOutputStream.writeObject(o);
```

```
objectOutputStream.close();

byte[] byteArray = outputStream.toByteArray();
return StringUtils.byteToHexString(byteArray);


}
```

Java provides the `ObjectOutputStream` class to serialize an object into a byte stream. The `ObjectOutputStream` class supports a `writeObject` method. The three numbers are serialized using the following code:

```
System.out.println("smallInt serialized value using Java
    serializer");
System.out.println(javaSerializeToByteString(new
    Integer(smallInt)));

System.out.println("mediumInt serialized value using Java
    serializer");
System.out.println(javaSerializeToByteString(new
    Integer(mediumInt)));

System.out.println("bigInt serialized value using Java
    serializer");
System.out.println(javaSerializeToByteString(new Long(bigInt)));
```

The output is as follows:

```
smallInt serialized value using Java serializer
aced0005737200116a6176612e6c616e672e496e746567657212e2a0a4f7818738
    02000149000576616c7565787200106a6176612e6c616e672e4e756d62657
        286ac951d0b94e08b020000787000000064
mediumInt serialized value using Java serializer
aced0005737200116a6176612e6c616e672e496e746567657212e2a0a4f7818738
    02000149000576616c7565787200106a6176612e6c616e672e4e756d6265
        7286ac951d0b94e08b020000787000100000
bigInt serialized value using Java serializer
aced00057372000e6a6176612e6c616e672e4c6f6e673b8be490cc8f23df020001
    4a000576616c7565787200106a6176612e6c616e672e4e756d62657286ac9
        51d0b94e08b0200007870000000011194e7a0
```

Very clearly, the serialized value is way bigger than the serialized values of a `Writable` class. Hadoop is all about serializing and deserializing either on disk or on the wire, and compactness is highly valued. Java serialization takes way more bytes to represent an object.

Java serialization's inefficiency stems from the fact that Java does not make any assumption about the class of the serialized value. This entails tagging every serialized value with class-related metadata. `Writable` classes, on the other hand, read the fields from the byte stream and assume that the byte stream is of its type. This leads to higher performance due to the compactness of the representation. The cost is a steeper learning curve for the Hadoop newbie. Another downside is that `Writable` classes are locked into the Java programming language.

Creating custom `Writable` classes is tedious as the developer has to take care of the class format on the wire. Briefly, **Record IO** was introduced within Hadoop. This feature came with a record definition language and a compiler that could translate record specifications to `Writable` classes. Eventually, this has been deprecated, and Avro has been suggested as the alternative.

> Before Hadoop 0.17, any MapReduce program had to use Writable classes for Map and Reduce task keys and values. However, post this release, any serialization framework can be integrated with MapReduce jobs in Hadoop. This has led to the usage of a number of alternate serialization frameworks. Each framework brought in performance gains either in terms of representation compactness or speed of serialization and deserialization, or both.

Avro serialization

Avro is a popular data serialization framework that is part of Apache Software Foundation. Its key features are as follows:

- It supports a number of data structures for serialization.
- It is neutral to particular programming languages and provides fast and compact binary serialization.
- Code generation is optional in Avro. Data can be read, written, or used in RPCs without having to generate classes or code.

Avro uses **schemas** during the reading and writing of data. Schemas make the compact representation of the serialized object conducive. The self-describing capability of schemas makes it possible to get rid of object-type metadata to be present along with the serialized byte stream, the method used in Java serialization. The schemas are described in the **Javascript Object Notation** (**JSON**) format that has evolved as a popular object description notation on the Web. Schema changes can be handled by having both the old and new schema available when processing data.

The following are two schema files used in Avro. The first file is the schema of the `worldcitiespop.txt` file, and the second file is the schema of the `countrycodes.txt` file:

```
{"namespace": "MasteringHadoop.avro",
 "type": "record",
 "name": "City",
 "fields": [
     {"name": "countryCode", "type": "string"},
     {"name": "cityName",  "type": "string"},
     {"name": "cityFullName", "type": "string"},
     {"name": "regionCode", "type": ["int","null"]},
     {"name": "population", "type": ["long", "null"]},
     {"name": "latitude", "type": ["float", "null"]},
     {"name": "longitude", "type": ["float", "null"]}
 ]
}

{"namespace": "MasteringHadoop.avro",
 "type": "record",
 "name": "Country",
 "fields": [
     {"name": "countryCode", "type": "string"},
     {"name": "countryName",  "type": "string"}
 ]
}
```

Schema files are self-explanatory and the JSON notation makes them readable. Avro supports all the standard primitive data types. In addition, Avro also supports complex data types such as unions. Null value fields are unions of the null and field types. Unions are syntactically represented as JSON arrays.

Let's take the `worldcitiespop.txt` file, a file in CSV text format, and convert it into an Avro file using the `City` schema specified previously. The following code gives the important steps to write Avro files. Most of the conversion happens in the static method, `CsvToAvro`. This method takes in `csvFilePath`, the output of `avroFilePath`, and the path to `schemaFile`. There is a special `Schema` class in Avro, and parsing the schema file initializes an object of this class. The schema is not code generated, so we use the `GenericRecord` class to initialize the schema and write the data points. If the schema is used to generate code, the result will be a `City` class that can be imported directly in the following code, like any other Java class.

The `DataFileWriter` class is used to write the actual records into the file. It has a `create` method that creates the output Avro file. Using a `BufferedReader` object, we read each city record from the CSV file one line at a time. The `getCity` helper method takes the line, splits it into tokens separated by a comma, and generates a `GenericRecord` object. The `GenericData.Record` class is used to instantiate an Avro record. This class constructor takes in a `Schema` object.

Writing to a `GenericRecord` object requires a `put` method that takes in the name of the record field and the corresponding value. The `isNumeric` method is used to validate the tokenized `String` to see whether it is a number or not. Bad records are skipped and not written into the Avro file. If `put` is not used on a field, this particular field is assumed to be `null`:

```
public static void CsvToAvro(String csvFilePath, String
    avroFilePath, String schemaFile) throws IOException{

        //Read the schema
        Schema schema  = (new Schema.Parser()).parse(new
            File(schemaFile));
        File avroFile = new File(avroFilePath);

DatumWriter<GenericRecord>datumWriter = new
    GenericDatumWriter<>(schema);
DataFileWriter<GenericRecord>dataFileWriter = new
    DataFileWriter<>(datumWriter);
dataFileWriter.create(schema,avroFile);


BufferedReader bufferedReader = new BufferedReader(new
    FileReader(csvFilePath));
        String commaSeparatedLine;
while((commaSeparatedLine = bufferedReader.readLine()) != null){

GenericRecord city = getCity(commaSeparatedLine, schema);

dataFileWriter.append(city);
        }

dataFileWriter.close();

    }


private static GenericRecord getCity(String commaSeparatedLine,
    Schema schema){

GenericRecord city = null;
```

```
String[] tokens = commaSeparatedLine.split(",");

        //Filter out the bad tokens
if(tokens.length == 7){
city = new GenericData.Record(schema);
city.put("countryCode", tokens[0]);
city.put("cityName", tokens[1]);
city.put("cityFullName", tokens[2]);

if(tokens[3] != null && tokens[3].length() > 0 &&isNumeric(tokens[3]))
{
city.put("regionCode", Integer.parseInt(tokens[3]));
            }


if(tokens[4] != null && tokens[4].length() > 0
    &&isNumeric(tokens[4])){
city.put("population", Long.parseLong(tokens[4]));
            }


if(tokens[5] != null && tokens[5].length() > 0
    &&isNumeric(tokens[5])){
city.put("latitude", Float.parseFloat(tokens[5]));
            }

if(tokens[6] != null && tokens[6].length() > 0
    &&isNumeric(tokens[6])){
city.put("longitude", Float.parseFloat(tokens[6]));
                }
            }

return city;


        }


public static boolean isNumeric(String str)
    {
try
        {
double d = Double.parseDouble(str);
        }
catch(NumberFormatException nfe)
        {
return false;
        }
return true;
    }
```

Avro and MapReduce

There is extensive support for Avro serialization and deserialization in a Hadoop MapReduce job. In Hadoop 1.X, there were the `AvroMapper` and `AvroReducer` specialized classes that needed to be used. However, in Hadoop 2.X, the built-in `Mapper` and `Reducer` classes can be reused. `AvroKey` can be used as the input or output types to both the `Mapper` and `Reducer` classes.

There is a special `InputFormat` class called `AvroKeyInputFormat`, which can be used to read `AvroKey` from the input files. The following code finds the population of each country using the `worldcitiespop.avro` file that was generated using the previous program. The `Mapper` code is given in the following code. We pass the schema as a string using a side channel. In the following code, it is passed through the `Configuration` object by setting a key on it. `DistributedCache` can also be used to pass the schema file around. The `setup` method is overridden to read the schema in the Map task.

The `map` method reads the `GenericRecord` datum object based on the schema passed to it:

```
package MasteringHadoop;

import org.apache.avro.Schema;
import org.apache.avro.generic.GenericRecord;
import org.apache.avro.mapred.AvroKey;
import org.apache.avro.mapreduce.AvroJob;
import org.apache.avro.mapreduce.AvroKeyInputFormat;
import org.apache.hadoop.conf.Configuration;
import org.apache.hadoop.fs.Path;
import org.apache.hadoop.io.*;
import org.apache.hadoop.mapreduce.*;
import org.apache.hadoop.mapreduce.lib.output.TextOutputFormat;
import org.apache.hadoop.util.GenericOptionsParser;

import java.io.File;
import java.io.IOException;
import java.net.URI;
import java.net.URISyntaxException;

public class MasteringHadoopAvroMapReduce {

private static String citySchema = "{\"namespace\":
    \"MasteringHadoop.avro\",\n" +
```

```
              " \"type\": \"record\",\n" +
              " \"name\": \"City\",\n" +
              " \"fields\": [\n" +
                      {\"name\": \"countryCode\", \"type\":
              \"string\"},\n" +
                      {\"name\": \"cityName\",  \"type\":
              \"string\"},\n" +
                      {\"name\": \"cityFullName\", \"type\":
              \"string\"},\n" +
                      {\"name\": \"regionCode\", \"type\":
               [\"int\",\"null\"]},\n" +
                      {\"name\": \"population\", \"type\": [\"long\",
              \"null\"]},\n" +
                      {\"name\": \"latitude\", \"type\": [\"float\",
              \"null\"]},\n" +
                      {\"name\": \"longitude\", \"type\": [\"float\",
              \"null\"]}\n" +
              " ]\n" +
                  "}";


      public static class MasteringHadoopAvroMapper extends
          Mapper<AvroKey<GenericRecord>, NullWritable, Text,
             LongWritable>{

      private Text ccode = new Text();
      private LongWritable population = new LongWritable();
      private String inputSchema;

            @Override
      protected void setup(Context context) throws IOException,
          InterruptedException {
      inputSchema = context.getConfiguration().get("citySchema");
              }

            @Override
      protected void map(AvroKey<GenericRecord> key, NullWritable value,
          Context context) throws IOException, InterruptedException {

      GenericRecord record = key.datum();
                String countryCode = (String)
                record.get("countryCode");
                Long cityPopulation = (Long) record.get("population");

      if(cityPopulation != null){
```

```
ccode.set(countryCode);
population.set(cityPopulation.longValue());
context.write(ccode, population);

        }

    }
}
```

The following `Reducer` code reduces on the country code and sums up the population. The `main` function sets up the `Job` configuration. There is a specialized `AvroJob` class that can be used to specify Avro-specific properties on the `Job` configuration:

```
public static class MasteringHadoopAvroReducer extends
    Reducer<Text, LongWritable, Text, LongWritable>{

private LongWritable total = new LongWritable();


        @Override
protected void reduce(Text key, Iterable<LongWritable> values,
    Context context) throws IOException, InterruptedException {
long totalPopulation = 0;

for(LongWritable pop : values){
totalPopulation += pop.get();
            }

total.set(totalPopulation);
context.write(key, total);
        }
    }




public static void main(String args[]) throws IOException,
    InterruptedException, ClassNotFoundException,
        URISyntaxException{

GenericOptionsParser parser = new GenericOptionsParser(args);
        Configuration config = parser.getConfiguration();
```

```
        String[] remainingArgs = parser.getRemainingArgs();

        config.set("citySchema", citySchema);

            Job job = Job.getInstance(config, "MasteringHadoop-
                AvroMapReduce");

        job.setMapOutputKeyClass(AvroKey.class);
        job.setMapOutputValueClass(Text.class);
        job.setOutputKeyClass(Text.class);
        job.setOutputValueClass(LongWritable.class);

        job.addCacheFile(new URI(remainingArgs[2]));

        job.setMapperClass(MasteringHadoopAvroMapper.class);
        job.setReducerClass(MasteringHadoopAvroReducer.class);
        job.setNumReduceTasks(1);

            Schema schema  = (new Schema.Parser()).parse(new
                File(remainingArgs[2]));
        AvroJob.setInputKeySchema(job, schema);

        job.setInputFormatClass(AvroKeyInputFormat.class);
        job.setOutputFormatClass(TextOutputFormat.class);

        AvroKeyInputFormat.addInputPath(job, new Path(remainingArgs[0]));
        TextOutputFormat.setOutputPath(job, new Path(remainingArgs[1]));

        job.waitForCompletion(true);

        }
    }
```

Avro and Pig

Pig has been extended to support Avro. AvroStorage implements both the LoadFunc
and StoreFunc interfaces to support loading from and writing to Avro files. However,
Pig's Avro integration has some limitations and assumptions, which are as follows:

* Nested record types are not supported in AvroStorage.

* Union support is only for nulls.

* It is assumed that all files in a directory and subdirectories have the
  same schema.

- When `AvroStorage` is used to store data in the Avro format, all fields will be null-valued unions. This is because there are no non-null-valued fields in Pig.

- `TUPLE` wrappers might be present in the Avro file when `STORE` is called on a Pig relation.

- JSON-encoded Avro files are not supported.

- `AvroStorage` does not implement map data types.

- The column-pruning optimization is not present when `AvroStorage` is used.

The following example shows the loading of the `countrycodes.avro` file into a Pig relation. It is important to register a number of JAR files for `AvroStorage` to work well in Pig:

```
REGISTER avro-1.4.0.jar
REGISTER json-simple-1.1.jar
REGISTER piggybank.jar
avroCountry = LOAD 'countrycodes.avro' USING
AvroStorage('{"namespace": "MasteringHadoop.avro",
  "type": "record",
  "name": "Country",
  "fields": [
      {"name": "countryCode", "type": "string"},
      {"name": "countryName",  "type": "string"}
  ]
}');
```

Avro and Hive

Hive has a SerDe module called `AvroSerde`, which can read and write Hive tables using Avro. It automatically infers the schema of the Hive table from the Avro input. For most Avro types, there are corresponding Hive table types. If some Avro types do not exist in Hive, they are automatically converted to a type that is available in Hive.

 Avro has the concept of enums, while Hive does not. All enum types in Avro are converted to a string type in Hive.

Let's build a Hive table on the external Avro file with the `country.avschema` schema. The Hive DDL statement is as follows:

```
CREATE EXTERNAL TABLE avrocountry
ROW FORMAT SERDE 'org.apache.hadoop.hive.serde2.avro.AvroSerDe'
STORED AS
```

```
INPUTFORMAT
'org.apache.hadoop.hive.ql.io.avro.AvroContainerInputFormat'
OUTPUTFORMAT
'org.apache.hadoop.hive.ql.io.avro.AvroContainerOutputFormat'
LOCATION '/user/sandeepkaranth/avrocountrydata'

TBLPROPERTIES ( 'avro.schema.literal'='
{"namespace": "MasteringHadoop.avro",
 "type": "record",
 "name": "Country",
 "fields": [
     {"name": "countryCode", "type": "string"},
     {"name": "countryName",  "type": "string"}
 ]
}')
;
```

The key pieces of the DDL statement are as follows:

- The usage of `AvroContainerInputFormat` as `InputFormat` of the table.

- The usage of `AvroContainerOutputFormat` as `OutputFormat` of the table.

- The specification of the schema in `TBLPROPERTIES`. The schema can be specified in a file either by a link to the schema file or literally, as shown in the DDL statement. If specified by a link or URL, the property name changes to `avro.schema.url` instead of `avro.schema.literal`.

The describe of the `avrocountry` table shows the interpreted Hive table schema from the Avro schema, as shown:

```
hive> describe avrocountry;
OK
countrycode        string                        from deserializer
countryname        string                        from deserializer
Time taken: 0.155 seconds, Fetched: 2 row(s)
```

 When writing tables, all null-valued columns should be specified as a union of the column type and null in the Avro-schema definition.

Comparison – Avro versus Protocol Buffers / Thrift

Avro has its share of competing serialization/deserialization libraries. The popular libraries among them are **Thrift** and **Protocol Buffers**. Avro differs from these frameworks in the following ways:

- Avro supports dynamic typing and can support static typing if performance is the need of the hour. Protocol Buffers and Thrift have **Interface Definition Languages (IDLs)** to specify schemas and their types. These IDLs are used to generate code for serialization and deserialization. Using IDLs brings down the flexibility in building generic data-processing pipelines.

- Avro is built into Hadoop, while the rest are not. The Hadoop ecosystem components also support Avro, as we saw in the case of Hive and Pig.

- Avro's schema definition is in JSON and not in any proprietary IDL. This makes it popular among developers as JSON has evolved as the object notation for the Web. It also makes Avro a language neutral.

File formats

There are a number of file formats that are data structures by themselves. In the chapter on Hive, we saw ORC files, an optimized form of record columnar file storage. There are a few other popular file container formats supported by Hadoop. We will look at them in this section.

The Sequence file format

A **Sequence** file is a container format for binary key-value pairs. Each record in a Sequence file contains a key and its associated value. Sequence files are used to combine smaller files into a single large file to alleviate the small file problem in Hadoop. In this situation, the filename forms the key and the file contents are the values associated with the key. Sequence files have a broader applicability as they can be split into configurable blocks. They can be combined with fast compression methods such as LZO or Snappy and can provide speed as well as storage and bandwidth.

The next image shows the format of a Sequence file. The start of the file has a magic number, a binary representation of the letters SEQ. A version byte and header follow it. The header stores the metadata of the file, such as the key and value class names, as a string. If the key or value is of the Text class, a `org.apache.hadoop.io.Text` string is embedded in the header. The class names are followed by Booleans that indicate whether compression is enabled, and block compression is enabled in this order. The compression codec class name to be used is then specified, followed by user-related metadata as key-value pairs. The header ends with a sync marker to denote the end of the header. These sync markers are allowed to get a record boundary in the file. They are randomly generated markers. The overhead due to the sync markers is kept below 1 percent of the total file size. This means the markers appear at the end of a group of records.

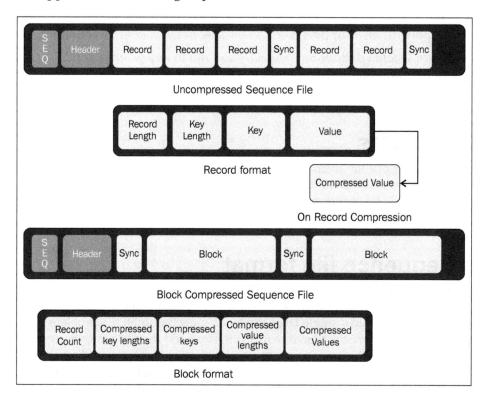

Each record contains record-related metadata, such as the record and key lengths. The actual key and value bytes follow the metadata. The lengths are 4-byte integer values serialized using the `IntWritable` class. When record compression is enabled, the value bytes are compressed using the codec specified in the header. There is no change to the record structure.

The keys are not compressed when compression is enabled.

During block compression, records are grouped into blocks. The minimum block size is determined by the property `io.seqfile.compress.blocksize` parameter. A sync marker is written at the beginning of each block. The sync marker is 16-bytes long, and is generated by taking a hash of the `(UID() + '@' + time or internet address)` expression. Block compression compresses the keys too. Blocks use a `VIntWritable` serialization to store the counts, key lengths, and keys.

Reading and writing Sequence files

The following code illustrates reading and writing using the `SequenceFile` format. The `writeSequenceFile` method takes a path to the file to be converted and the output file path. The `SequenceFile` class has a `createWriter` static method to create a writer handle. The `append` method on the writer takes in a key and value and appends it to the file. The following code takes in a CSV file and writes a line number as the key and line string as the value:

```
package MasteringHadoop

import org.apache.hadoop.conf.Configuration;
import org.apache.hadoop.fs.FileSystem;
import org.apache.hadoop.fs.Path;
import org.apache.hadoop.io.*;
import org.apache.hadoop.util.ReflectionUtils;

import java.io.BufferedReader;
import java.io.IOException;
import java.io.InputStreamReader;
import java.net.URI;


public class MasteringHadoopSequenceFile {

public static void writeSequenceFile(String textFile, String
    seqFile) throws IOException{

        Path readPath = new Path(textFile);
        Path writePath = new Path(seqFile);
        Configuration conf = new Configuration(false);
```

```
FileSystem fs = FileSystem.get(URI.create(textFile), conf);
BufferedReaderbufferedReader = null;
SequenceFile.WritersequenceFileWriter = null;

try{

    bufferedReader = new BufferedReader
                        (newInputStreamReader
                              (fs.open(readPath)));

    sequenceFileWriter = SequenceFile.createWriter(conf,
    SequenceFile.Writer.file(writePath),
    SequenceFile.Writer.keyClass(LongWritable.class),
    SequenceFile.Writer.valueClass(Text.class));
          String line = null;
    LongWritable key = new LongWritable();
          Text value = new Text();
    long lineCount = 0;

    while((line = bufferedReader.readLine()) != null){
        key.set(lineCount);
        lineCount++;
        value.set(line);
        sequenceFileWriter.append(key, value);


        }


    }
catch(IOException ioEx){
ioEx.printStackTrace();
    }
finally{
if(sequenceFileWriter != null)
sequenceFileWriter.close();

if(bufferedReader != null)
bufferedReader.close();
    }
  }
```

The following function reads the Sequence file using `SequenceFile.Reader`. From the Sequence file headers, we can infer the type of the key and value. `ReflectionUtils` has some utility methods to create objects based on these types. The `syncSeen` method gives an indication about the sync markers within the file as the file is being read:

```
public static void readSequenceFile(String seqFile) throws
    IOException{

        Path readPath = new Path(seqFile);
        Configuration conf = new Configuration(false);
FileSystem fs = FileSystem.get(URI.create(seqFile), conf);

SequenceFile.Reader reader = null;

try{
reader = new SequenceFile.Reader(conf,
    SequenceFile.Reader.file(readPath));
        Writable key =
      (Writable)ReflectionUtils.newInstance(reader.getKeyClass(),
        conf);
        Writable value =
      (Writable)ReflectionUtils.newInstance(reader.getValueClass(),
        conf);

while(reader.next(key,value)){
System.out.println("key: " + key.toString());
if(reader.syncSeen()){
System.out.println("sync: ");
            }

        }
    }
catch(IOException ioEx){
ioEx.printStackTrace();
    }
finally{
if(reader != null){
reader.close();
        }
    }

  }


public static void main(String[] args){

try{
```

```
writeSequenceFile(args[0], args[1]);
readSequenceFile(args[1]);
        }
catch(IOException ioEx){
ioEx.printStackTrace();
        }

    }

}
```

A Sequence file can also be read using the following Hadoop command:

```
hadoop fs -text /user/sandeepkaranth/countrycodes.seq
```

The MapFile format

MapFile is the same as SequenceFile in structure. Additionally, it provides an index for the keys in the file. MapFile keys have to be of the WritableComparable type and values have to be of the Writable type. In SequenceFile, any serialization framework can be used to serialize the keys and values.

When MapFile is created, it has two associated files, one for the data and another for the index. Both these files are of the SequenceFile type. The data SequenceFile contains all the data records sorted by the key. The index SequenceFile contains the key and the file offset where the key is present. The keys in the index file are sampled. Not every key occurs in the index file. The interval of the sample is given by the value in the io.map.index.interval property. The following example illustrates the data and index files in the countrycodes.map file:

```
hadoop fs -ls countrycodes.map/

Found 2 items

-rw-r--r--   3 sandeepkaranth supergroup        10033 2014-06-08 14:20
countrycodes.map/data

-rw-r--r--   3 sandeepkaranth supergroup          166 2014-06-08 14:35
countrycodes.map/index


hadoop fs -text countrycodes.map/index
127    5088


hadoop fs -text countrycodes.map/data
241   vi,Virgin Islands (USA)
242   vn,Vietnam
```

243   vu,Vanuatu

244   wf,Wallis and Futuna Islands

245   ws,Samoa

246   ye,Yemen

247   yt,Mayotte

248   yu,Yugoslavia

249   za,South Africa

250   zm,Zambia

251   zr,Zaire

252   zw,Zimbabwe

The MapFile format can be useful to process Map-side joins. The sorted nature of the data and index files can be used to force splits of the datasets participating in a join into a single Map task. The APIs to create files in the MapFile format are similar to the APIs for SequenceFile creation.

The following code shows how SequenceFile can be converted into MapFile. The MapFile.fix() static method shown in the following code is used to achieve this:

```
    public static void writeMapFile(String seqFile) throws
  IOException {

        Path readPath = new Path(seqFile);
        Path mapPath = new Path(readPath, MapFile.DATA_FILE_NAME);

        Configuration conf = new Configuration(false);
        FileSystem fs = FileSystem.get(URI.create(seqFile), conf);

        SequenceFile.Reader reader = null;

        try{
            reader = new SequenceFile.Reader(conf,
                SequenceFile.Reader.file(mapPath));
            Class keyClass = reader.getKeyClass();
            Class valueClass = reader.getValueClass();

            MapFile.fix(fs, readPath, keyClass, valueClass, false,
                conf);

        }
        catch(IOException ioEx){
            ioEx.printStackTrace();
        }
```

```
        catch(Exception ex){
            ex.printStackTrace();
        }
        finally{
            if(reader !=  null){
                reader.close();
            }
        }


    }
```

Other data structures

Hadoop also supports other persistent data structures that are variants of `MapFile`. Some of them are as follows:

- `SetFile`: This file format stores a set of keys and allows set operations on the keys. The key difference in the `SetFile` API when compared to the `MapFile` API is that the `append` method of `SetFileWriter` takes in only a key and no value. Under the hood, the value is `NullWritable`. The file structure remains the same, as in, it has both the index and the data `SequenceFile` methods.

- `ArrayFile`: This particular file format can be thought of as the complement of `SetFile`. It stores only values and no keys. Like an array, the key for a particular value is `LongWritable`, which contains a record number. The API method, `append`, takes in only a value.

- `BloomMapFile`: This file format is a variant of `MapFile`. In addition to the index and data files, it has a bloom file. This bloom file is a file that encodes a Dynamic Bloom filter. For large files in the key-value format with sparse keys, the lookup of the key on the index might not be fast enough. A Bloom filter is a probabilistic data structure that encodes the presence of keys in a few bits and can provide quick answers to the `MapFileget()` method.

Compression

A recurring theme that appears in this book is the need to save storage and network data transfer. When dealing with large volumes of data, anything that reduces these two properties gives an efficiency boost both in terms of speed and cost. Compression is one such strategy that can help make a Hadoop-based system efficient.

All compression techniques are a tradeoff between speed and space. The higher the space savings, the slower the compression technique, and vice versa. Each compression technique is also tunable for this tradeoff. For example, the gzip compression tool has options -1 to -9, where -1 optimizes for speed and -9 for space.

The following figure shows the different compression algorithms in the speed-space spectrum. The gzip tool does a good job of balancing out both storage and speed. Techniques such as LZO, LZ4, and Snappy are very fast, but their compression ratio is not very good. Bzip2 is a slower technique, but has the best compression.

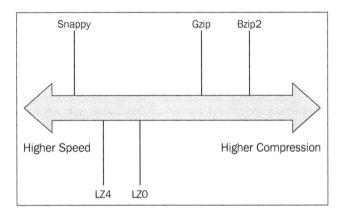

Codecs are concrete implementations of these compression techniques. All compression codecs in Hadoop have to implement the `CompressionCodec` interface in their implementing classes. Codecs are found in the `org.apache.hadoop.io.compress` package. There is a default codec in Hadoop, the compression of which is based on the `DEFLATE` algorithm.

 The `DEFLATE` compression is similar to gzip, but does not contain additional headers and footers.

Splits and compressions

Map tasks act on each split of data, generally a file block stored in HDFS. However, the majority of the compression algorithms do not allow you to read the file at arbitrary points. Though implementations such as gzip are block-based compression techniques, these blocks are no way related to or aware of HDFS blocks. In these situations, Hadoop does not try to split the file, and it provides the entire file to a single Map task. This can turn unwieldy in many situations.

For some compression formats such as LZO, there are indexing tools that can process the LZO file and build an index of the compressed blocks. This index can be used by an appropriate `InputFormat` method to determine the number of splits and their offsets. For example, `LzoTextInputFormat` has the capability to read a LZO-based file index and decide the Map task input splits.

However, compression techniques such as bzip2 support splitting natively. These split points are indicated by means of synchronization markers. Hadoop recognizes the different compression formats of files using the extension of the file.

There are a number of strategies that can be used when compression is enabled:

- The application can split the files as a preprocessing step and use well-known compression techniques such as gzip on each file split. These compressed file chunks can be stored in HDFS. For optimality, the post-compressed size of a file chunk has to be nearly equal to the HDFS block size. In this case, it does not matter whether the compression algorithm is splittable or not.

- Splittable compressions such as bzip2 can be applied on the file. However, this technique is the slowest of the supported compression codecs. An alternative is to use LZO, and then build an index on top of it.

- There are a number of file formats, such as `SequenceFile`, `MapFile`, and `RCFile`. These file formats support splitting natively. They can be compressed as well, as we saw in the File Formats section of this chapter.

- The preferred method in the industry is to store data in specialized file formats. They provide a balanced view between speed and compression.

Scope for compression

In *Chapter 2*, *Advanced MapReduce*, we saw a number of places in the MapReduce pipeline where compression increases job speed and reduces storage needs. We will summarize it in this subsection:

- All compressed inputs are decompressed and processed within the Map task. The codec to be used is determined by the file extension. In some cases, such as LZO compression with indexing, appropriate `InputFormat` classes should be used to supply the appropriate splits.

- The `mapreduce.map.output.compress` property can be set to `true` to enable compression of intermediate outputs. The codec to be used for compression can be set using the `mapreduce.map.output.compress.code` property. The default is `org.apache.hadoop.compress.DefaultCodec`.

- The compression of job outputs can be enabled by setting the `mapreduce. output.fileoutputformat.compress` property to `true`. The codec can be specified by setting `mapreduce.output.fileoutputformat.compress. codec`. For `SequenceFile` outputs, there is a special `mapreduce.output. fileoutputformat.compress.type` property, which determines the granularity at which the compression should happen. The default value for this is `RECORD`, indicating that each record will be compressed. Record groupings can also be compressed by setting this value to `BLOCK`.

Summary

Big data processing involves data representation either in storage or in transit over the network. Compact representation, fast transformations, extensibility, and backward compatibility of the data representation are desired properties. Some key takeaways from this chapter related to data representation are as follows:

- Hadoop provides inbuilt serialization/deserialization mechanisms using the `Writable` interface. The `Writable` classes are serialized more compactly than Java serialization.

- Avro is a flexible and extensible data serialization framework. It serializes data in binary and is supported by Hadoop, MapReduce, Pig, and Hive.

- Avro provides dynamic typing, eliminating the need for code generation. The schema can be stored with the data and read by any subsystem.

- Compression techniques trade speed and storage savings. Hadoop supports many compression codecs along this tradeoff spectrum. Compression is a very important optimization parameter for big data processing.

- Hadoop supports specialized container file formats such as `SequenceFile` and `MapFile`. These formats support splitting and compression. Hadoop also supports persistence of specialized data structures such as `ArrayFile`, `SetFile`, and `BloomMapFile`.

In the next chapter, we will look at YARN, the heart of resource management in Hadoop 2.X, and how it generalizes the Hadoop platform.

6
YARN – Bringing Other Paradigms to Hadoop

Yet Another Resource Negotiator (**YARN**) is a cluster resource management layer that was introduced in Hadoop 2.0. As we saw briefly in *Chapter 1*, *Hadoop 2.X*, YARN separates out the responsibilities of the JobTracker daemon. JobTracker was responsible for:

- Resource arbitration within a Hadoop cluster
- MapReduce job management

The problem with the JobTracker model was that it became the single point of failure in the compute layer of a Hadoop cluster. Any failure in JobTracker meant trashing the running jobs and starting all over again. JobTracker's singular nature also became a scaling bottleneck. All job communications, scheduling, and resource management were controlled by the JobTracker master daemon.

The tightly coupled functions of JobTracker made it rigid, allowing a single computing paradigm, MapReduce, to be onboarded onto the cluster. MapReduce is not suitable for a variety of emerging applications and force-fitting solutions to all problems using this paradigm is not prudent.

YARN takes care of cluster resource management and application scheduling. It is agnostic to the kind of application that is executing or any of its internals. Resource negotiation happens strictly through protocols. MapReduce becomes an application in YARN. Like MapReduce, other applications can be written to run on a cluster that can request for CPU, memory, and other resources from YARN via defined protocols and execute.

In this chapter, we will be:

- Delving into the architecture of YARN
- Building a simple YARN non-MapReduce application and looking at:
  - The modules that constitute a YARN application
  - The core steps to build out each module
  - The protocols used to communicate with YARN components
- Discussing YARN scheduling variants
- Glancing at YARN commands

The YARN architecture

The following figure illustrates the architecture of a YARN-based cluster. There are five major component types in a YARN cluster. They are as follows:

- **Resource Manager (RM)**: This is a per-cluster daemon that is solely responsible for allocating and managing resources available within the cluster.
- **Node Manager (NM)**: This is a per-node daemon that is responsible for local resource management. It is also the node-local representative of the RM.
- **Application Master (AM)**: This is a per-application daemon that encapsulates all application-specific logic and libraries. The AM is responsible for negotiating resources from the RM and working with the NM to execute them to completion.
- **Container**: This is an abstract representation of a resource set that is given to a particular application. The AM is a specialized container that is used to bootstrap and manage the entire application's life cycle.
- **Client**: This is the entity in the cluster that can submit applications to the RM and specify the type of AM that needs to be spawned to execute the application.

Resource Manager (RM)

The Resource Manager has the following two main components:

- **Scheduler**
- **ApplicationsManager**

The Scheduler is responsible for allocating resources to the various applications that are running in the cluster. It is a pure entity and does not have any insight into the status of the application. The Scheduler does not guarantee restarts on application or hardware failures. Scheduling is done based on the global model of the cluster the RM is aware of. It uses queues and capacity parameters during the allocation process.

The scheduling policy can be plugged into the Scheduler. The two popular scheduling policies in Hadoop 1.X were **CapacityScheduler** and **FairScheduler**. These policies continue to exist in Hadoop 2.X.

The ApplicationsManager is the component responsible for handling application submissions made by clients. In addition, it also bootstraps applications by negotiating the container on behalf of the application for the Application Master. The ApplicationsManager also provides the services of restarting the Application Master in case of failures. The following image illustrates the architecture of a YARN-based cluster:

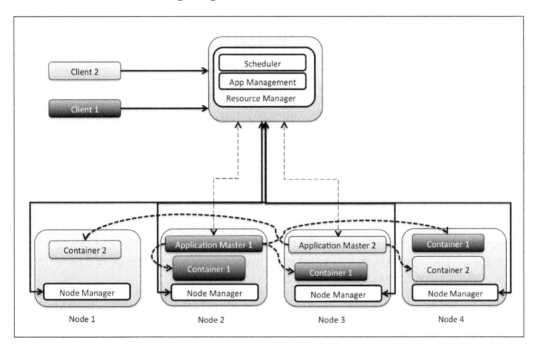

The RM is loosely coupled and interacts via a couple of public interfaces and one private interface. It has the following interfaces:

- A public interface for clients to submit jobs (**Application-Client Protocol**)
- A public interface for AMs to request for resources (**Application-Master Protocol**)
- An internal interface for NM interactions

Resource allocation is dynamic and is agnostic to the internals of the application or its optimizations. This makes efficient resource utilization within clusters possible. AMs send resource requests with the following parameters:

- Number of containers that will be required, for example, 100 containers
- The specifications of resources in each container, for example, 2 CPUs and 4GB RAM
- The locality preferences for the container at the node or rack level
- Priorities of requests within an application

The RM's Scheduler gets these requests, and based on the cluster state image it has built using heartbeats from NMs, it allocates containers to AMs. The container exits are relayed back to the AMs. In the case of scarcity of cluster resources, the RM might request AMs to give back a few containers. If no containers are released after a certain timeout, the RM might terminate the container. The RM's request for resource release can be treated as a warning to save any critical data and work state that the AM might be executing.

Application Master (AM)

On application submission, the ApplicationsManager negotiates a container with the Scheduler. The container is used to bootstrap the AM for this particular application. Once spawned, the AM will periodically send heartbeats to the RM. The heartbeats are used to perform the following actions:

- Report whether the AM is alive
- Request resources for the application

In response to these heartbeats, the RM allocates containers and the AM is free to use them. The onus to interpret and handle container terminations and other application-related faults is completely up to the AM.

The AM interacts with the RM using the Application-Master protocol. The AM gathers the status of its containers directly from the NM. It can also start and stop containers allocated to it by interacting with the NM. The NM-related interactions are done via the **ContainerManager** protocol.

In YARN, the resource model follows the concept of late binding. The container spawned might not be related to the AM's request. It is only bound to a lease sought out by the AM. The state at which the AM requests resources might change by the time the resource is allocated. The allocated resource can be used for purposes other than what it is originally intended for.

Let's illustrate late binding by means of a hypothetical example using the MapReduce Application Master. We know that HDFS replicates each block of a file among nodes in a cluster. A Map task preferably runs on the same node as the input block. When the MR AM requests for containers, it assigns a Map task to the container whose data is local or close to the allocated container node. The decision happens only after the AM receives the containers, and in a dynamic fashion.

 Hadoop 1.X had a web interface for the JobTracker. This web interface (generally listening on port 50030) is no longer available in Hadoop 2.X because the JobTracker is absent.

Node Manager (NM)

The NMs are per-node daemons that do local container management, ranging from authentication to resource monitoring. They report to the RM using heartbeats. A **Container Launch Context** (**CLC**) record is used to specify container metadata such as dependencies, data file paths, and environment variables. Based on the values in the CLC, an NM spawns a container.

Resources might be shared between containers by the same tenant. Download of resources and dependencies from external sources is also possible by providing their URLs. NMs are responsible for termination of containers, either on request by the AM or on decree from the RM. An NM has the authority to terminate a container if the container breaches its lease. Termination includes cleanup, such as deletion of any local data that the container might have.

Monitoring of local physical resources such as CPU, memory, and disk health falls in the NM's purview. It reports these parameters to the RM. The RM scheduler can take decisions on container scheduling based on the load or health of the node.

The NM provides services such as log aggregation to the application. Standard output and error logs spewed by an application are uploaded to HDFS upon application completion. NMs can also be configured to have pluggable **auxiliary services**. For example, an auxiliary service to persist local data until an application's termination, rather than container termination, can be useful in some scenarios. In the MapReduce use case, map outputs need to be transferred to the reducers. Auxiliary services can be used to achieve this. Any additional configuration required for these services can be specified by the CLC.

YARN clients

The YARN client is responsible for submitting an appropriate CLC for the AM. As we discussed earlier, the AM itself runs in a container whose resources are negotiated by the RM. Registering the AM is also the responsibility of the client. The client is free to provide other services to its consumers.

Developing YARN applications

YARN can bring in other computing paradigms to Hadoop. In Hadoop 2.X, MapReduce, Pig, and Hive are all Application Master libraries and their corresponding clients. Developers can write their own applications using the YARN API and leverage the existing infrastructure running Hadoop. Also, enterprises can have lots of data assets in HDFS already, and writing custom applications can leverage this without a need to provision new clusters or migrate the existing data.

Storm is a real-time stream-processing engine that has been ported onto YARN, bringing in the paradigm of moving data to compute nodes. **Spark** is another project that is on YARN and can leverage the existing Hadoop infrastructure to provide in-memory data transformations, including MapReduce. There are a number of projects in development that exhibit Hadoop's capability as a generic cluster-computing platform.

In this section, let's look at how to write a simple YARN application. The application takes in a shell command and executes it on a predefined number of nodes on the Hadoop cluster. We will need to write both the Application Master and Client programs.

Writing YARN clients

YARN clients submit applications to the RM via `ApplicationClientProtocol`. The result is the assignment of `ApplicationId` to the client. The client then needs to communicate the specifications of the container that deploys the Application Master. The Application Master is like a program that needs to be started and executed independently. These specifications include the location of the Application Master libraries, any environment variables required for the execution of the Application Master, and arguments to actually run the program.

The following code is a snippet from the shell command application. We write a run method that will be called from the `DistributedShellClient` main method. Arguments are passed to the `main` method from the command line. The arguments are the Application Master JAR path, shell command, and number of containers that execute this command. Let us see how to write a YARN client with the following steps:

1. The first step is to create a `YarnConfiguration` object. The `YarnConfiguration` class is the subclass of the `Configuration` class that is used in Hadoop MapReduce. The successful creation of the `YarnConfiguration` object means that the application is able to read the necessary config files, such as the `yarn-site.xml` file. The defaults of properties are present in the `yarn-default.xml` file. The `yarn-site.xml` file is generally found in the `etc/hadoop` folder relative to the Hadoop installation directory.

2. The application client now has to initialize a `YarnClient` object. This is done via a factory method called `createYarnClient`. The `YarnClient` object is initialized using the configuration that was created earlier. Based on the configuration passed, the `YarnClient` object resolves the RM end point. During initialization, `YarnClient` creates a proxy for the RM. All communication happens via the proxy. The proxy encapsulates the `ApplicationClientProtocol` object. A start call on the `YarnClient` object is called to get the client machinery up and running.

3. An alternative approach will be for developers to create the proxies by themselves and manage it. The `ApplicationClientProtocol` object is a proxy type that can be created and used. However, it is recommended to use the former method.

4. The `YarnClient` has a `createApplication` method that is used to get the `YarnClientApplication` object. Since `YarnClient` encapsulates a proxy for the RM, it also contains methods to retrieve properties about the RM and manage applications submitted to the RM.

   The code is as follows:

```
package MasteringYarn;
import org.apache.hadoop.conf.Configuration;
import org.apache.hadoop.fs.FileStatus;
import org.apache.hadoop.fs.FileSystem;
import org.apache.hadoop.fs.Path;
import org.apache.hadoop.yarn.api.ApplicationConstants;
import org.apache.hadoop.yarn.api.records.*;
import org.apache.hadoop.yarn.client.api.YarnClient;
import
org.apache.hadoop.yarn.client.api.YarnClientApplication;
import org.apache.hadoop.yarn.conf.YarnConfiguration;
```

```
import org.apache.hadoop.yarn.exceptions.YarnException;
import org.apache.hadoop.yarn.util.Apps;
import org.apache.hadoop.yarn.util.ConverterUtils;
import org.apache.hadoop.yarn.util.Records;
import java.io.File;
import java.io.IOException;
import java.util.Collections;
import java.util.HashMap;
import java.util.Map;

public class DistributedShellClient {
private Configuration conf = new YarnConfiguration();

    public void run(String[] args) throws YarnException,
        IOException, InterruptedException {

YarnConfiguration yarnConfiguration = new
    YarnConfiguration();
YarnClient yarnClient = YarnClient.createYarnClient();
        yarnClient.init(yarnConfiguration);
        yarnClient.start();

YarnClientApplication yarnClientApplication =
    yarnClient.createApplication();
```

5. Once `YarnClientApplication` is created, the next step is to request a container in order to bootstrap the Application Master. Container specifications are described in a `ContainerLaunchContext` class in YARN. In the `org.apache.hadoop.yarn.util` package, there is a special `Records.newRecord` static factory method that instantiates different classes.

6. Going through the documentation of the `ContainerLaunchContext` class will give a glimpse of the properties that can be specified when launching a container. ACLs, commands, environment variables, local resources, binary service data, and security token setters are present in any `ContainerLaunchContext` object. In the following code, the `ContainerLaunchContext` object is instantiated and the `setCommands` method is called to set the list of commands that need to be executed upon the container launch. In our case, we will specify the command to launch the Application Master present in the `DistributedShellApplicationMaster` class that we will define later.

7. Launching the Application Master requires the necessary classes or JAR files to be present locally. The next step is to specify the JAR file containing the logic of the Application Master using the setLocalResources method on the ContainerLaunchContext object. In this example, the HDFS path to the JAR file will be taken as the local resource. The path of this file is specified as a command-line argument. Other side channels can also be used to distribute resources locally to containers.

8. Similarly, if any environment variables need to be set up for the smooth functioning of the container, it can be set up using the setEnvironment method on the ContainerLaunchContext object.

9. The most important pieces of specification needed by the RM to launch any container are CPU and memory requirements of the container. In this example, the Application Master container needs around 100MB of memory and a single core to execute. This is specified using a Resource object. The Resource object is an abstract representation of the container's compute requirements. The Resource object can currently model CPU and memory. CPU is modeled in units called virtual cores. It is an integer value, and the configuration has to map a virtual core to the actual physical core. Usually, this mapping is 1:1. The memory is modeled in megabytes (MB). The setVirtualCores and setMemory methods on the Resource object are used to specify them:

```
    //container launch context for application master
ContainerLaunchContext applicationMasterContainer =
    Records.newRecord(ContainerLaunchContext.class);
        applicationMasterContainer.setCommands(
                Collections.singletonList("$JAVA_HOME/bin/java
    MasteringYarn.DistributedShellApplicationMaster " +
                                            args[2]   +
                                            " "       +
                                            args[3]   +
                                            " "       +
                                            "1>"      +
                                            ApplicationConstants.
    LOG_DIR_EXPANSION_VAR + "/stdout "   +
                                            "2>"      +

    ApplicationConstants.LOG_DIR_EXPANSION_VAR + "/stderr")
        );


    LocalResource applicationMasterJar =
        Records.newRecord(LocalResource.class);
```

```
        setupJarFileForApplicationMaster(new Path(args[1]),
    applicationMasterJar);
        applicationMasterContainer.setLocalResources(
                Collections.singletonMap("MasteringYarn.jar",
    applicationMasterJar)
        );

        Map<String, String> appMasterEnv = new HashMap<>();
        setupEnvironmentForApplicationMaster(appMasterEnv);
        applicationMasterContainer.setEnvironment(appMasterEnv);

        Resource resources = Records.newRecord(Resource.class);
        resources.setVirtualCores(1);
        resources.setMemory(100);
```

10. The final step is to submit the application to the ApplicationManager in the RM. The submission parameters are bundled in an ApplicationSubmissionsContext object. The YarnClientApplication class holds a reference to this context. The ApplicationSubmissionContext object is given the container specifications, the submission queue, a friendly name for the application, and the Resource object needed to bootstrap the container. The ApplicationSubmissionContext object also gives ApplicationId. This ApplicationId object can be used to reference the application in the management APIs. In the following example, we will set the application to be in the default queue with a friendly name, MasteringYarn. Finally, the YarnClient object is used to submit the application. Internally, the proxy is used to post the application request to the RM. The Scheduler then kicks in and schedules the application on the cluster. The Application Master is the first container that will be spawned:

```
ApplicationSubmissionContext submissionContext =
    yarnClientApplication.getApplicationSubmissionContext();
        submissionContext.setAMContainerSpec(applicationMaster
    Container);
        submissionContext.setQueue("default");
        submissionContext.setApplicationName("MasteringYarn");
        submissionContext.setResource(resources);

ApplicationId applicationId =
    submissionContext.getApplicationId();
```

```
System.out.println("Submitting " + applicationId);
yarnClient.submitApplication(submissionContext);
System.out.println("Post submission " +
    applicationId);
```

Once the submission of the application finishes, the progress of the application can be monitored using the `getApplicationReport` method on the `YarnClient` object. The `ApplicationReport` object contains useful information about the application that can be used to determine the success or failure of the application. It also contains a diagnostic field that can help the developer gain insight in the case of failures.

The `ApplicationReport` object has the `getYarnApplicationState` method that gives the current state of the application. In the following code, we poll the application state every 1 second and see whether it is terminated. An application is terminated if it is in the `KILLED`, `FINISHED`, or `FAILED` state. The `getDiagnostics` function is used to print diagnostic information in the event of failures:

```
ApplicationReport applicationReport;
YarnApplicationState applicationState;

do{
            Thread.sleep(1000);
            applicationReport =
                yarnClient.getApplicationReport(applicationId);
            applicationState =
                applicationReport.getYarnApplicationState();

            System.out.println("Diagnostics " +
                applicationReport.getDiagnostics());

    }while(applicationState != YarnApplicationState.FAILED &&
            applicationState != YarnApplicationState.FINISHED
            &&
            applicationState != YarnApplicationState.KILLED );

    System.out.println("Application finished with " +
        applicationState + " state and id " + applicationId);
}
```

A couple of helper methods complete the client. The first method, `setJarFileForApplicationMaster`, sets up the Application Master JAR file with appropriate properties, most of which are self-explanatory. Similarly, all the necessary environment variables are packaged in the `setEnvironmentForApplicationMaster` method. This method also illustrates the use of `YarnConfiguration` to read off of the `yarn-site.xml` file. Finally, the main driver method instantiates the `DistributedShellClient` object and calls the run method on it:

```
    private void setupJarFileForApplicationMaster(Path jarPath,
        LocalResource localResource) throws IOException {
    FileStatus jarStat = FileSystem.get(conf).getFileStatus(jarPath);
        localResource.setResource(ConverterUtils
            .getYarnUrlFromPath(jarPath));
        localResource.setSize(jarStat.getLen());
        localResource.setTimestamp(jarStat.getModificationTime());
        localResource.setType(LocalResourceType.FILE);
        localResource.setVisibility(LocalResourceVisibility.PUBLIC);
    }


    private void setupEnvironmentForApplicationMaster(Map<String,
        String> environmentMap) {
        for (String c : conf.getStrings(
            YarnConfiguration.YARN_APPLICATION_CLASSPATH,
            YarnConfiguration.DEFAULT_YARN_APPLICATION_CLASSPATH))
    {
            Apps.addToEnvironment(environmentMap,
                ApplicationConstants.Environment.CLASSPATH.name(),
                    c.trim());
        }
        Apps.addToEnvironment(environmentMap,
            ApplicationConstants.Environment.CLASSPATH.name(),
            ApplicationConstants.Environment.PWD.$() +
                File.separator + "*");
    }


    public static void main(String[] args) throws Exception {
    DistributedShellClient shellClient = new DistributedShellClient();
        shellClient.run(args);
    }
}
```

Writing the Application Master entity

Application Master is the leader of the application. This entity encapsulates all the logic for the application and requests for resources from the RM as and when it is appropriate. Unlike the Client, Application Master has to keep contact with the following two entities:

- **ResourceManager**: This is used for communications regarding the global state of the application. This is also known as **ApplicationMasterProtocol**.

- **NodeManager**: This is used for communications regarding containers allocated to the application. This protocol is also called **ContainerManager**.

Writing the Application Master is similar to writing a client. We start off creating a `YarnConfiguration` object. To facilitate communication with the RM, `AMRMClient` is created. This client encapsulates the proxy object that is needed to talk to the RM. Again, the proxy can be explicitly created, though this is a simpler and recommended way to do it. `AMRMClient` has many methods; the most important methods deal with the registration of the AM (`registerApplicationMaster`) and container allocation request (`addContainerRequest`) methods.

To communicate with the NM, an `NMClient` object is created that encapsulates the communication proxy. The important methods on `NMClient` are the `startContainer` and `stopContainer` methods that are used to launch and terminate containers on nodes. The following code snippet illustrates this:

```
package MasteringYarn;

import org.apache.hadoop.conf.Configuration;
import org.apache.hadoop.yarn.api.ApplicationConstants;
import
org.apache.hadoop.yarn.api.protocolrecords.AllocateResponse;
import org.apache.hadoop.yarn.api.records.*;
import org.apache.hadoop.yarn.client.api.AMRMClient;
import org.apache.hadoop.yarn.client.api.NMClient;
import org.apache.hadoop.yarn.conf.YarnConfiguration;
import org.apache.hadoop.yarn.exceptions.YarnException;
import org.apache.hadoop.yarn.util.Records;

import java.io.IOException;
```

```
import java.util.Collections;

public class DistributedShellApplicationMaster {


    public static void main(String[] args) throws YarnException,
IOException, InterruptedException {

        Configuration configuration = new YarnConfiguration();
int numberOfContainers = Integer.parseInt(args[1]);
        String command = args[0];

        System.out.println("Starting Application Master");

        AMRMClient<AMRMClient.ContainerRequest>
            resourceManagerClient = AMRMClient.createAMRMClient();
        resourceManagerClient.init(configuration);
        resourceManagerClient.start();


        System.out.println("Started AMRMClient");

NMClient nodeManagerClient = NMClient.createNMClient();
        nodeManagerClient.init(configuration);
        nodeManagerClient.start();

        System.out.println("Started NMClient");
```

Both the `AMRMClient` and `NMClient` classes have corresponding asynchronous versions. Asynchronous APIs are resource efficient as threads don't block themselves waiting for responses. After the method call is invoked, threads are free to take up some other task. When the results of the APIs are ready, registered callback handler methods are called based on the nature of the result.

The following code outline illustrates the usage of the `AMRMClientAsync` class for communication with the RM:

```
class AMRMClientCallbackHandler implements
AMRMClientAsync.CallbackHandler {
public void onContainersAllocated(List<Container>
containers) {
     //the container is allocated and relevant tasks
can
be executed.
}
public void onContainersCompleted(List<ContainerStatus>
statuses){
     //the container has completed. The application
status needs to be updated.
}
public void onNodesUpdated(List<NodeReport> updated) {}
     public void onReboot() {}
}
AMRMClientAsync asyncClient =   AMRMClientAsync.
createAMRMClientAsync(appId, 1000, new
AMRMClientCallbackHandler ());
//init the client with the configuration and start the
proxy.
asyncClient.addContainerRequest(container)
```

The `AMRMClientCallbackHandler` object is passed on async client creation. The appropriate methods on this handler are called whenever an event happens on the container. For example, when a container is allocated, the `onContainersAllocated` callback method is called. A similar API is present for the `NMClient` object as well.

The `AMRMClient` class is used to register the AM with the RM. On successful registration, the AM starts a heartbeat thread that periodically informs the RM that it is alive. The `registerApplicationMaster` method also supplies the host and port on which the Application Master is listening. Clients can use the AM's host and port to get information about the application.

Containers now have to be allocated based on the arguments specified when starting our DistributedShell application. The two important properties that need to be set is the priority of the container and the amount of resources to be allocated for the container.

The `Priority` class is instantiated to set the priority of the container. In the following example, we use the priority of 0. The `Priority` object is applicable within this particular application only.

As we did for the Application Master, we set the resource requirements for each worker container using the `Resource` class. To recall, the `setMemory` method sets the memory requirement of the container in MB, and `setVirtualCores` sets the number of cores required.

The `Priority` and `Resource` objects are then assigned to an `AMRMClient`. `ContainerRequest` object to be dispatched to the RM for resource allocation. The second and third parameters of the constructor are null. These correspond to any nodes and racks we would like the containers to be allocated on. This is particularly useful for applications such as MapReduce, where data locality needs to be exploited. The data type of these parameters is `String[]`. The racks corresponding to any nodes that are listed in the second parameter are automatically added to the list of racks.

The `ContainerRequest` objects are now added to the `AMRMClient` proxy object using the `addContainerRequest` method on the client:

```
resourceManagerClient.registerApplicationMaster("localhost",
    80010, "myappmaster");

        System.out.println("Registration done");

        // Priority for worker containers - priorities are intra-
            application
        Priority priority = Records.newRecord(Priority.class);
        priority.setPriority(0);

        // Resource requirements for worker containers
        Resource capability = Records.newRecord(Resource.class);
        capability.setMemory(128);
        capability.setVirtualCores(1);


        for(int i=0; i < numberOfContainers; i++){
```

```
    AMRMClient.ContainerRequest containerRequest = new
        AMRMClient.ContainerRequest(capability, null,
            null, priority);
    resourceManagerClient.addContainerRequest(containerReque
st);

        }
```

The `allocate` method on the `AMRMClient` class indicates to the RM to allocate containers. It also acts like a heartbeat to the RM. The return value of this method is an `AllocateResponse` object. This object contains information about newly allocated containers, completed containers, and cluster-related information. It also indicates the remainder resources that are available for this particular application within the cluster.

`AllocateResponse` also has `ResponseId` that can be used to disambiguate duplicate requests. The parameter in the `allocate` method is a progress indicator of the float type. The AM can indicate the progress of the application via this parameter.

In the following code snippet, we use the `getAllocatedContainers` method to get the entire `Container` object corresponding to the newly allocated containers. For each of these containers, we have to launch the shell command that was specified in the command line.

 Concurrent allocate request calls should be avoided. This might lead to request loss.

Container launch is always done using the `ContainerLaunchContext` object. It is very similar to the launch of the AM container where we specify the commands, environment variables, local resources, and other parameters that are needed by the program to execute in the container.

The container is then launched using the `NMClient` object. This informs `NodeManager` to launch the container and execute the relevant commands. The `startContainer` also takes in the `Container` object that was returned by the RM. The `Container` object contains identifiers, tokens, and the node where the container is allocated:

```
int completedContainers = 0;
int containerId = 0;
while(completedContainers < numberOfContainers){

    AllocateResponse allocateResponse = resourceManagerClient.
allocate(containerId);
```

```
containerId++;

for(Container container : allocateResponse.getAllocatedContainers())
{

    ContainerLaunchContext shellContainerContext = Records.newRecord(C
ontainerLaunchContext.class);
    shellContainerContext.setCommands(
    Collections.singletonList(command +
    " 1>"  +
    ApplicationConstants.LOG_DIR_EXPANSION_VAR + "/stdout "  +
    " 2>"  +
    ApplicationConstants.LOG_DIR_EXPANSION_VAR + "/stderr")
    );

    nodeManagerClient.startContainer(container,
shellContainerContext);

}
```

Once the containers are launched, the allocate call can be used to monitor the completed containers, as shown in the next code snippet. The `getCompletedContainersStatuses` method on the `AllocateResponse` object gives the status of each completed container. On completion, the AM can unregister from the RM by calling the `unregisterApplicationMaster` call using the `AMRMClient` object. The status of the application can be communicated to the RM. This in turn can be reported back to the client or any other process that monitors the application.

The `FinalApplicationStatus` enum has the FAILED, KILLED, SUCCEEDED, and UNDEFINED values. The unregister call also take in any diagnostic message that needs to be communicated and any new URL the client can use to get information about the Application Master on termination:

```
for(ContainerStatus containerStatus : allocateResponse.
getCompletedContainersStatuses()){
                completedContainers++;
                System.out.println("Completed Container " +
completedContainers + " " + containerStatus);

        }

        Thread.sleep(1000);
```

```
    }


        resourceManagerClient.unregisterApplicationMaster(FinalApplica
tionStatus.SUCCEEDED, "", "");


    }



  }
```

The application can now be executed using the following commands. The date command will be run on two containers in the cluster:

```
hadoop fs -copyFromLocal MasteringYarn-1.0-SNAPSHOT.jar
```

```
hadoop jar MasteringYarn-1.0-SNAPSHOT.jar
MasteringYarn.DistributedShellClient
hdfs://localhost/user/sandeepkaranth/MasteringYarn-1.0-SNAPSHOT.jar
date 2
```

Monitoring YARN

The RM provides a friendly web interface to view the cluster and its resources. The home page of this interface gives details about the cluster, such as the RM state, number of applications, the total memory available, total number of nodes, and node status, among other details. The next screenshot shows the home page.

On the left-hand side of the screen, there are links to navigate and get different kinds of details of the cluster.

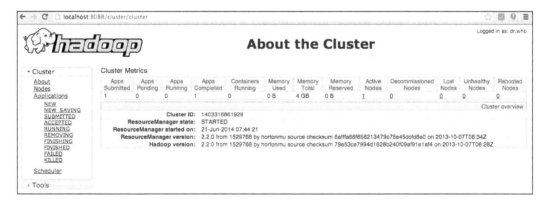

Clicking on the **Nodes** link on the left-hand pane gives the details of the nodes in the YARN cluster. The following screenshot shows an example of a single node cluster. For each node in the cluster, the screen gives details on the rack it belongs to, the node state, resource consumption (memory for now) on the node, HTTP address of the node, and last heartbeat details of the node, among other details.

The last-health update column in the nodes grid tells when the RM received the last heartbeat from the NM.

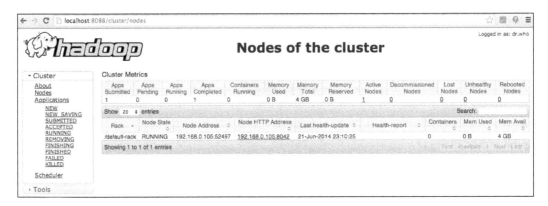

The **Applications** link on the left-hand pane gives details of all the applications, as shown in the following screenshot. Applications can be filtered based on the state they are in. The list of filters, such as **NEW, NEW_SAVING, SUBMITTED, ACCEPTED, RUNNING, REMOVING, FINISHING, FINISHED, FAILED**, and **KILLED** are present on the left-hand pane. By clicking on each filter, applications present in a particular state will be visible.

Application details such as the kind of application, the queue it belongs to, its state and final state, start and end times, and progress, among other details, are visible. Though the Web UI does not give any way to actually execute a command, the application ID can be used to execute commands using the YARN script.

We will look at some of the YARN commands to manipulate applications in the following sections in this chapter.

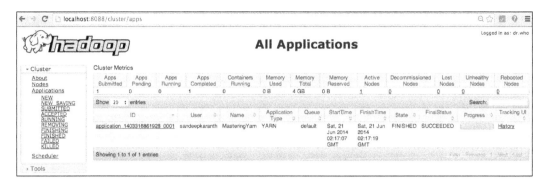

Clicking on the **Scheduler** link shows the details of the scheduler being used by the RM. The Web UI shows the hierarchy of queues and color-codes the capacity, maximum capacity, used capacity, and used capacity (over capacity) for each queue. The next section on scheduling gives a better sense of these application queues.

The details of any running applications are also given here. The heading of the page gives details on the states of applications that are shown on this page. Only **NEW**, **NEW_SAVING**, **SUBMITTED**, **ACCEPTED**, **RUNNING**, and **FINISHING** applications are shown.

The cluster metrics section is a common UI section across all the pages of the Web UI that RM exposes. The following screenshot shows an example scheduler page:

There is a **Tools** link on the left-hand pane, as shown in the following screenshot. On expansion, it has a few menu items. These are the tools that help an administrator and developer of a YARN cluster and application to debug.

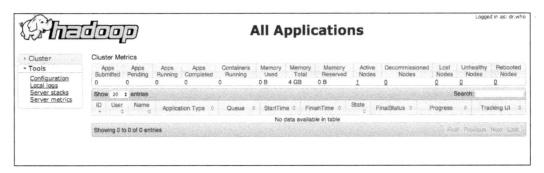

The **Configuration** hyperlink takes the user to the configuration that is used by YARN. This provides a quick-and-easy way to go through the values of different properties in the YARN cluster. The following screenshot shows the configuration page. The configuration is displayed in XML.

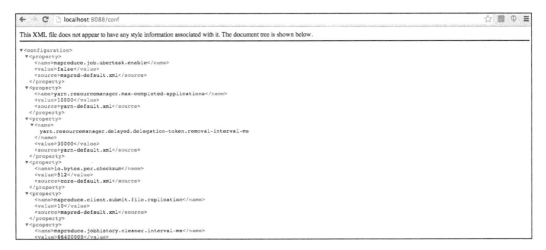

The **Local logs** link opens up the local log directory. Clicking on each log opens up the log in the browser. The following screenshot shows the local logs on a single machine cluster deployment:

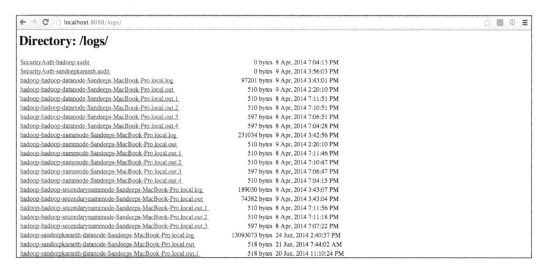

The **Server stacks** link opens up the exception stacks the server throws along with the threading information. The screenshot of the server stack link is as follows:

There is a **Server metrics** link that opens up the metrics page. Clicking on a node host takes the user to the **NodeManager** section. The left-hand pane of the page is now introduced with NodeManager-related links, as shown in the following screenshot. This screen gives the information of a particular node.

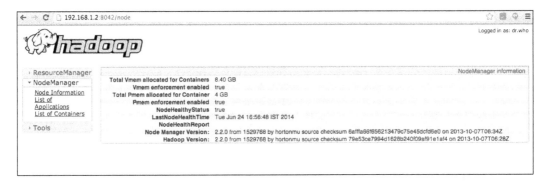

Clicking on the **List of Applications** link takes the user to a screen that looks something like the following one. Here, the list of applications running on this node is displayed with its application state.

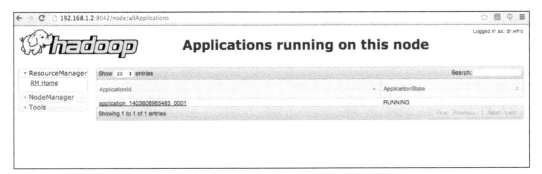

Clicking on the **List of Containers** link in the **NodeManager** menu item gives the details of the containers currently running on the NodeManager, with the state of each container. There is a link to open the logs directory as well.

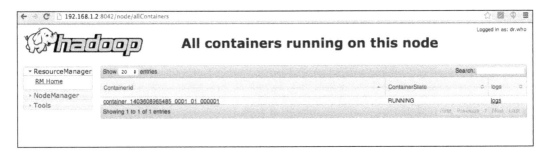

Job scheduling in YARN

Most cluster resources are multitenant in nature, that is, a number of teams or people share the cluster resources. Allocation of resources to satisfy the needs of all these tenants becomes important and is the responsibility of the scheduler. Individual clusters per team or person is not viable as they render poor utilization.

YARN provides a pluggable model to schedule policies. The initial versions of Hadoop had a simple **First in First Out** (**FIFO**) scheduler. However, FIFO was found to be inadequate in dealing with the complexities of multitenancy. We will discuss two other scheduling strategies that are used in Hadoop today, CapacityScheduler and FairScheduler.

CapacityScheduler

The concept behind CapacityScheduler is to guarantee a tenant-promised capacity on a shared cluster. If other tenants utilize less than the requested capacity, the scheduler allows the tenant to tap into these unused resources. The number one goal of CapacityScheduler is not to allow a single application or user to hog the cluster resources. The scheduler enforces strict limits on the resource usage of tenants sharing the cluster.

CapacityScheduler manages scheduling based on queues. Administrators configure these queues based on the requirements of the tenants. Hierarchical queues are used to share the underutilized part of the cluster. Hierarchies ensure that first preference is given to the tenant who has requested for the capacity before others can use it.

Each queue has a capacity that the administrator can configure. The sum of the capacities of all the queues in the cluster determines the cluster's capacity. The capacity of a queue is elastic, so the scheduler can transfer the unused capacity from one queue to another. This redistributed capacity can be reclaimed to satisfy the capacity guarantee made on a queue. A maximum capacity for a queue can also be enforced. In addition, each queue can also support per-user limits.

In addition to queues and their hierarchies, CapacityScheduler also has the following features:

- CapacityScheduler has a set of security features. Each queue has ACLs that authorize users to submit jobs into the queue. User jobs are isolated, preventing other users from modifying jobs other than their own. The scheduler also introduces the concept of per-queue and system administrator roles.

- CapacityScheduler is dynamic, that is, its properties, such as queue definitions and ACLs, can be changed at runtime. Delete operations on the queues are not permitted. Adding new queues is allowed.

- Administrators are allowed to stop queues, preventing new jobs from getting submitted onto the queue and its children queues. Existing jobs are allowed to continue, though without pre-emption. The administrator is allowed to start the queues once the jobs from the queue have drained.

- Applications that require higher resources such as multiple maps and reduce slots for a job, are allowed by CapacityScheduler. CapacityScheduler does a resource-based scheduling of the jobs as long as they do not exceed the capacity constraints that are set on the queues.

In YARN, CapacityScheduler can be plugged in using following methods:

- The ResourceManager can be directed to use CapacityScheduler by setting the `yarn.resource.manager.scheduler.class` property to `org.apache.hadoop.yarn.server.resourcemanager.scheduler.capacity.CapacityScheduler`. This setting is declared in the `yarn-site.xml` config file.

- Queues can be set up by adding entries to the `capacity-scheduler.xml` file. This is the configuration file of CapacityScheduler. A predefined queue called as the **root** is present. Any queue that is created is a child of the root queue.

- The `yarn.scheduler.capacity.root.queues` property is used to define additional queues. Queues are specified as comma-separated lists of queue names. Queue paths specify hierarchies of queues. Queue paths are special property names that start from the root queue and list the tree path using a dot notation. The following configuration file snippet describes two levels of queues. The x, y, and z queues are under the root queue. The x1 and x2 queues are under the x queue. The queue path for x1 and x2 is given by `root.x`:

```
<property>
<name>yarn.scheduler.capacity.root.queues</name>
<value>x,y,z</value>
<description>The queues at the this level (root is the root
  queue).   </description>
</property>
<property>
<name>yarn.scheduler.capacity.root.x.queues</name>
<value>x1,x2</value>
<description>The queues at the this level (root is the root
  queue).   </description>
</property>
```

- The resource allocation characteristics for each queue is characterized by the following properties:

  - `yarn.scheduler.capacity.<queue-path>.capacity`: This property is used to set the capacity of each queue as a percentage of the cluster capacity. The property is of the `float` type. At each level in the queue hierarchy, these queue values must add up to be a 100 percent. This is a soft limit. If unused capacity is available, the jobs in the queue can use it, providing elasticity to the queue.

  - `yarn.scheduler.capacity.<queue-path>.maximum-capacity`: This property is used to set a hard limit on the capacity used by a queue. This hard limit on the queue capacity is a float value and limits the elasticity of the queue. The default value is -1, that is, there is no limit on the elasticity.

  - `yarn.scheduler.capacity.<queue-path>.minimum-user-limit-percent`: This is an integer value property that enforces the percentage of resources allocated to a single user in the queue. The limit kicks in only when there is a demand for resources. For example, if we set this value to 50, a single user can be allocated 100 percent of the capacity, and two users can be allocated 50 percent of the capacity. However, beyond two users, the scheduler waits for the existing user applications to complete before scheduling the next one. The default value for this property is 100.

  - `yarn.scheduler.capacity.<queue-path>.user-limit-factor`:This property dictates multiple queue capacities that can be used by the user. For example, if this property has a value 2, a user on this queue can be allocated twice as many resources as the queue capacity. This can happen only if the cluster has the capacity and is idle. This is a `float` value type and the default is 1.

- CapacityScheduler supports the following properties to control the properties of running applications:

  - `yarn.scheduler.capacity.maximum-applications`: This property determines the maximum number of active applications in the cluster. This is a hard limit and submissions of applications beyond this limit are not allowed. The default value is 10,000.

  - `yarn.scheduler.capacity.<queue-path>.maximum-applications`: This property is a per-queue override for the preceding property. Both these properties are of `integer` type.

- ° `yarn.scheduler.capacity.maximum-am-resource-percent`: This property determines the percentage of resources in the cluster that is allocated for Application Masters alone. The default value is 0.1, that is, Application Master containers can utilize 10 percent of the cluster resources.

- ° `yarn.scheduler.capacity.<queue-path>.maximum-am-resource-percent`: This property is a per-queue setting for resources allocated to AMs.

- CapacityScheduler supports the following properties that help in setting cluster authorization and queue runtime parameters:

  - ° `yarn.scheduler.capacity.<queue-path>.state`: This property sets the queue state. It can be in the **RUNNING** or **STOPPED** state. In the **STOPPED** state, application submissions to this queue or any of its child queues are not allowed. In the **STOPPED** state, existing applications are allowed to execute and finish.

  - ° `yarn.scheduler.capacity.<queue-path>.acl_submit_applications`: This property determines the users who can submit applications to the queue and all its children. ACLs are inherited from parent queues. ACLs are comma-separated lists of users or groups. A * wildcard can be used to specify anyone.

  - ° `yarn.scheduler.capacity.<queue-path>.acl_administer_queue`: This property determines the users who can administer the queue and all its children queues.

- The `yarn rmadmin` command can be used to refresh the ResourceManager (RM) with the new properties. The refresh happens without having to restart the ResourceManager.

FairScheduler

As the name suggests, the concept behind FairScheduler is to provide, on an average, equal resources to all running applications over time. FairScheduler organizes applications into pools or queues and shares time between the different application pools. Periodically, the scheduler checks each application for the compute time it has received in the cluster and the amount of time it would have received under ideal conditions.

The applications are sorted in descending order of deficits. The next application to be scheduled will be the one with the largest deficit. The concept of hierarchical pools exists in FairScheduler as well.

To configure FairScheduler in YARN, the following points needs to be considered:

- The RM can be made to use FairScheduler by setting the `yarn.resourcemanager.scheduler.class` property to `org.apache.hadoop.yarn.server.resourcemanager.scheduler.fair.FairScheduler`. This configuration value is set in the `yarn-site.xml` config file.

- The other properties can be set in two files:
  - The `yarn-site.xml` file is used to define global scheduler properties.
  - An allocation file is used to specify properties such as weights and capacities for each queue or pool. This file is loaded every 10 seconds. Changes to this file take effect whenever the file is loaded.

- The important global properties that can be placed in the `yarn-site.xml` file are as follows:
  - `yarn.scheduler.fair.allocation.file`: This property contains the path to the allocation file. This file is in the XML format and specifies the properties of each pool or queue. The value defaults to the `fair-scheduler.xml` file.
  - `yarn.scheduler.fair.use-as-default-queue`: This property has a Boolean value. If set to `true`, it uses the username associated with the allocation as the pool or queue name. If set to `false`, there is a shared queue called **default**, and all jobs are allocated to this queue. The default value is `true`.
  - `yarn.scheduler.fair.sizebasedweight`: This is a Boolean property that suggests whether all apps have to be given equal share. It defaults to `false`, that is, all apps are given equal share. If set to `true`, the applications are weighted by the logarithm to base two of one plus the requested memory of the application.
  - `yarn.scheduler.fair.locality.threshold.node`: This property is of the `float` type between 0 and 1. When requesting containers on specific nodes to exploit locality, the app might want to delay allocation if containers cannot be allocated on these specific nodes. This particular property value determines the amount of delay before allocating the container on a nonlocal node. The value is the fraction of the cluster size. It defaults to -1.0, indicating to the scheduler to allocate containers without any delay.
  - `yarn.scheduler.fair.locality.threshold.rack`: This property is very similar to the previous property. However, unlike the previous property, this one deals with the rack-local placement of containers.

- ° `yarn.scheduler.fair.allow-undeclared-pools`: This is a Boolean property that determines whether new queues can be created when the application is submitted to the RM. If it is set to `false`, any application that does not belong to a pool specified by the allocations file will reside in the default pool.

- The allocation file defines the pools or queues in the cluster. It is an XML manifest file that has the following elements:

Queue element	Description
`minResources`	This is the value is of the form `A mb, B vcores`, indicating the minimum number of resources for this particular queue. If this condition cannot be satisfied, resources from parent pools are reallocated.
`maxResources`	This is the value corresponding to this tag gives the maximum resources a queue can consume. No containers are allocated to the queue if it is deemed to use more resources.
`maxRunningApps`	This is the upper limit on the number of applications that can run simultaneously from this particular queue.
`weight`	This defines the proportion of resources this queue can use when compared to the default. The default is 1. If the weight is 2, it can use twice the number of resources when compared to the default.
`schedulingPolicy`	The allowed values are `fifo`, `drf`, or `fair`.
`aclSubmitApps`	This is the ACL for the users and groups that can submit jobs to this queue. The ACL format is the same as in the case of CapacityScheduler.
`aclAdministerApps`	This is the ACL description for the list of users and groups that can do administrative functions on this queue.
`minSharePreemptionTimeout`	In conditions where the queue is not given its due share of resources (`minResources`), it waits for the time defined by this property. After this timeout, it pre-empts containers from other queues.

User Element	Description
maxRunningApps	This is the upper limit on the number of applications that can be run by a single user in the queue.

queuePlacementPolicy element	Description
rule	This particular node in the XML file contains the rules on how a submitted application should be placed within the queue. There can be a number of rules, and each rule is executed in the order of declaration. For example, the rule specified places the application in the queue that was specified during submission. If no queue is specified, it is placed in the default queue. The "user" rule places the app in the queue with the username.

The outline XML of the allocation file is given as follows:

```
<?xml version="1.0"?>
<allocations>
  <queue name="">
    <minResources></minResources>
    <maxResources>A mb, B vcores</maxResources>
    <maxRunningApps></maxRunningApps>
    <weight>1.0</weight>
    <schedulingPolicy>fair</schedulingPolicy>
    <queue name="sub_queue_name">
      <aclSubmitApps>username</aclSubmitApps>
    <!—other queue properties can appear à
   </queue>
  </queue>

  <user name="username">
    <maxRunningApps></maxRunningApps>
  </user>
<queuePlacementPolicy>
    <rule name="specified" />
    <rule name="user" />
    <rule name="primaryGroup" create="false" />
    <rule name="default" />
    <rule name="reject" />
  </queuePlacementPolicy>
</allocations>
```

YARN commands

Like Hadoop, YARN has a script that provides commands to manage YARN.
The commands are of the following two kinds:

- **User commands**: These are commands for the cluster user

- **Administration commands**: These are commands for the cluster administrator

In Hadoop deployment, the YARN script is found in the same directory as the
Hadoop scripts. The general syntax of the YARN script is as follows:

```
yarn [--config <config directory>] command [options]
```

The -config option can be used to override the default configuration. The
default configuration directory is picked up from the environment variable
$HADOOP_PREFIX/conf.

User commands

The following are the important user commands in YARN:

- The jar command is used to run a custom, user-built JAR file. In the
  previous distributed shell example, we use the following command
  to run the YARN job. The syntax for the command is:

  ```
  yarn jar <jar file path> [main class name] [arguments...]
  ```

- The application command is used to manipulate a running application in
  YARN. It has three verbs: to list all the running applications in the cluster,
  to get the status of the application, and to kill a running application. The list
  verb can be filtered on the application state and application type:

  ```
  yarn application -list [-appStates <state identifiers> | -
  appTypes <type identifiers>] | -status <application id> | -
  kill <application id>
  ```

- The node command is used to report the status on the nodes in a cluster. It has
  two verbs: to list all the status and to find the status of a particular node. The
  list command can also be used to filter nodes that are in particular states:

  ```
  yarn node -list [-all | -states <state identifiers> | -status
  <node id>
  ```

- The `logs` command is used to dump logs of completed applications. It has two verbs: to dump logs of a particular user or to dump based on container identifier and node address values. The application ID is the mandatory parameter:

```
yarn logs -applicationId <application Id> -appOwner <appOwner>
| (-nodeAddress <node address> & -containerId <container Id>)
```

Administration commands

The important administration commands in YARN are as follows:

- The `resourcemanager`, `nodemanager`, and `proxyserver` parameters start the respective daemons:

```
yarn resourcemanager | nodemanager | proxyserver
```

- The administrator can manipulate the ResourceManager by using the `rmadmin` command. This command has the following verbs:

  - `-refreshQueues`: This refreshes all the queue ACLs, states, and scheduler properties

  - `-refreshNodes`: This refreshes node-specific information in the ResourceManager

  - `-refreshUserToGroupMappings`: This refreshes all mappings about user memberships in groups

  - `-refreshSuperUserGroupsConfiguration`: This refreshes superuser-specific mappings

  - `-refreshAdminAcls`: This refreshes ACLs, determining the RM administrator access

  - `-refreshServiceAcl`: This reloads the authorization file in the RM

- The administrator uses the `daemonlog` command to get and set the log levels of the YARN daemons:

```
yarn [-getLevel <daemon host:port> <name>| -setLevel <daemon
host:port> <name> <level>]
```

Summary

YARN has opened up the Hadoop ecosystem to a wide range of applications. It has not only alleviated scaling bottlenecks that were present in traditional MapReduce-based Hadoop but also aided in improving infrastructure efficiency in an organization. This was made possible by:

- Separating out application-specific logic from resource management. The ResourceManager is solely responsible for cluster resource management and is agnostic of any application.

- Providing common and generic abstractions for resource specifications. Resources are specified in terms of cores and memory.

- Maintaining backward compatibility with existing Hadoop APIs. Existing Hadoop programs work on YARN on recompilation, without any code changes.

- Providing a variety of pluggable scheduling policies such as FairScheduler and CapacityScheduler. Pluggable policies make it easy for other paradigms to come onboard.

Development of newer computing paradigms on Hadoop is as simple as implementing a client and Application Master. These components interact with the ResourceManager and NodeManager to achieve their goals. Like MapReduce, applications such as Spark and Storm aspire to become first-class citizens in the Hadoop ecosystem. YARN has made this aspiration a reality.

In the next chapter, we will look at Storm and how it can be integrated with Hadoop. Storm is a real-time stream processing cluster-based engine that can operate on streaming data.

7
Storm on YARN – Low Latency Processing in Hadoop

Hadoop MapReduce builds on the concept of moving computation to data. Data is significantly larger than the instructions to manipulate it. The network is the slowest component in any distributed data processing system, so it is natural to move the smaller piece around, that is, the program itself. With assistance from the NameNode, Hadoop knows exactly how the data resides in a cluster of computers. It uses this data locality information to schedule tasks on appropriate nodes, putting in the best effort to locate the task very close to the data needed by the task.

In this chapter, we will discuss the opposite paradigm, that is, moving data to the compute, also known as the **streaming** paradigm. There are many frameworks that facilitate streaming, Apache Storm being a popular one. Apache Storm integrates with Hadoop YARN, bringing the streaming paradigm to Hadoop. In this chapter, we will cover the following topics:

- Comparing and contrasting a batch-processing paradigm such as MapReduce with the streaming paradigm
- The key concepts of Apache Storm
- Walking through application development using Apache Storm
- Walking through Apache Storm installation on Hadoop by running YARN

Batch processing versus streaming

MapReduce is a batch-processing model. The data is allowed to accumulate before processing is done on it. This leads to larger turnaround times. It can also lead to pressures on storage, memory, and compute resources of the system. A batch of data needs to be staged till analysis begins and ends, thus occupying storage resources. Analyzing a large piece of data will mean a peak load for a short amount of time on the nodes of the compute cluster.

Batch models also lead to poor utilization of the cluster resources. During data accumulation, the cluster compute and memory are idle. However, during analysis, they have peak load. Provisioning of the cluster must cater to the peak load.

The disadvantages of batch-processing systems are overcome by using **streaming computation models**. Instead of moving the computation to the data, data is streamed through computation nodes. Each compute node operates on the data point or a small window of data to analyze and output a result or update its internal state. The computation nodes form a topology that can be viewed as a continuously executing query. The turnaround time is now smaller because analysis is not done at the end of the batch, but continuously. Also, the analysis is done on very small sets of data. These systems provide near real-time analysis, that is, analysis as soon as the data is received by the system.

Let's illustrate this with an example. Let's say we are given a task to bucket vehicles passing at a point on the interstate based on the color of the vehicle and report the count of vehicles per color in one hour. In the batch approach, this will involve stopping all the vehicles that come in during the hour and parking them in a chartered parking lot nearby. At the end of one hour, we get to the parking lot and take the count of the vehicles for each color.

By contrast, the streaming approach will involve determining the color of the vehicle passing by and incrementing a counter based on the color. At the end of the hour, we have the counts per color. On the downside, if we make an error in counting or determining the color, we cannot recover from it. In the batch approach, we have the opportunity to double-check our computation.

Streaming systems thrive in applications where low latency is one of the primary goals. However, they come with a set of tradeoffs when accomplishing this goal. The ability to make decisions by seeing a few points makes accuracies of the results suffer. Also, not every analysis algorithm can be implemented using the streaming model. Streaming models are not suitable for algorithms that make multiple passes over the data and cannot be used if a decision can be made only by looking at the entire dataset.

The following diagrams contrast batch and stream processing of data. The first diagram shows batch processing:

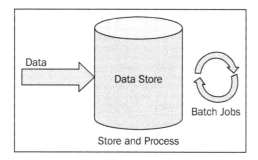

The following is a figure for stream processing of data:

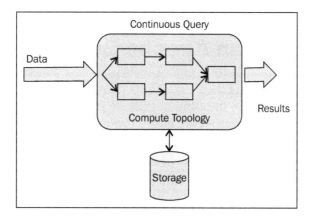

Apache Storm

Apache Storm is one of the most popular open source streaming engines and provides real-time analytics on unbounded streams of data. It is a distributed framework that can work on multiple nodes, providing both fault tolerance and horizontal scalability. Another primary feature of Apache Storm is that it provides guaranteed event processing, that is, every event that enters the system is processed without a loss of events. Apache Storm applications can be deployed with any programming language of the developer's choice, making it extremely attractive for usage in low-latency analytics.

MapReduce provides the Map and Reduce function primitives to build batch applications. Similarly, Storm provides its own set of primitives to support real-time analytics. If a framework such as Apache Storm is not available, writing real-time applications will mean a lot of complexity. It will involve adding and maintaining processing queues to guarantee processing of all events in the system. It will also involve writing worker programs that can read off the queue, do processing, and then enqueue the program elsewhere for downstream processing. Failure handling and synchronization between the workers and queues will be the onus of the developer.

Maintaining queues and workers will involve much greater effort than the data processing logic itself. Partitioning of the data stream when the throughput is extremely high will add additional overhead on the developer's time and effort, posing a threat on the scalability of the system. Providing fault tolerance is not an easy task too. Apache Storm tries to abstract these complexities and provide features that improve the reliability and availability of a real-time system.

Architecture of an Apache Storm cluster

A Storm cluster runs long-standing queries instead of jobs. Batch-processing systems, on the other hand, have jobs as their basic units. The key difference is that jobs finish executing eventually, but long-standing queries do not finish (unless explicitly killed). These long-standing queries are called **topologies**.

These are the two different kinds of nodes in a Storm cluster:

- **Master node**: This runs the Nimbus daemon, similar in function to a JobTracker in Hadoop MRv1
- **Worker node**: This runs the Supervisor daemon, similar in function to a TaskTracker in Hadoop MRv1

The Master node is the central node that takes care of three key functions. They are as follows:

- Distributing the code across the different worker nodes in the cluster for execution
- Scheduling by assigning tasks to available worker nodes within the Apache Storm cluster
- Monitoring for failures within the cluster and taking actions on them

The Supervisor daemon is present per node in the cluster. Its responsibilities are as follows:

- Listening to directions from the Master Nimbus daemon
- Starting and stopping worker processes based on the directions from Nimbus; each worker process executes a subset of the topology

The actual coordination between the Nimbus and Supervisor daemons happens through a Zookeeper cluster.

 Zookeeper is an open source service that takes care of configuration management, synchronization of nodes, and naming services within a distributed system. Though it was under the Hadoop project initially, it is now a top-level project within the Apache Software Foundation.

The following diagram shows a high-level view of an Apache Storm cluster:

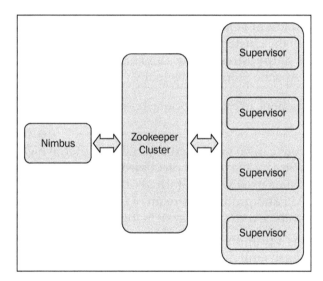

Computation and data modeling in Apache Storm

The computation is modeled as topologies, a graph of computations. Each node in this graph of computations contains logic to process data. The links between these compute nodes in the topology indicate the nature of data transfers between the nodes.

Topologies are defined as Thrift structs. In *Chapter 5, Serialization and Hadoop I/O*, we saw that Avro schemas can be defined in a data definition language such as JSON, making it agnostic to any programming language. Similarly, Thrift allows for topologies to be defined using its own **Interface Definition Language** (IDL), making the Apache Storm language agnostic.

Data abstraction used in Apache Storm is known as a **stream**. A Stream is a sequence of tuples that is unbounded. The Apache Storm cluster takes in one Stream and produces another Stream. For example, if a vehicle passing along the interstate is encoded as a tuple, in the example we used to compare batch and stream processing, the input stream contains a sequence of vehicle tuples. The output stream is a set of tuples giving us the count of vehicles per color. The output stream is unbounded, but the tuples come out of the cluster every hour. The Storm cluster transforms the input stream to produce an output stream. The number of streams that are ingested or egested to and from Apache Storm can be many.

There are three abstractions in Storm: spouts, bolts, and topologies, which are explained as follows:

- **Spouts**: A spout can be visualized as a data adapter, which converts the data source into a Stream that can be processed by Storm. A spout is the source for all the streams used within Storm. For example, a spout can connect to the Twitter API and produce a stream of tweets, or it can connect to a Kafka queue and produce a stream of system logs where each log entry is a tuple.

- **Bolts**: A bolt is a primitive that consumes multiple streams from the spouts and other bolts to emit new streams of data. A single topology in a Storm cluster might require a number of interconnected bolts to achieve the desired transformation. Bolts can do many kinds of transformations such as filtering, aggregation, stream joins, writing to data stores, or simple function execution. A bolt can subscribe to a set of streams from spouts or other bolts. This subscription sets up the links in the topology.

- **Topology**: A topology represents a network of spouts and bolts, with each edge in the network representing a bolt subscribing to the output stream of some other spout or bolt. A topology is an arbitrarily complex multistage stream computation. Topologies run indefinitely when deployed.

The following diagram illustrates a possible topology. **Bolt A** subscribes to **Spout A** and **Bolt C** subscribes to **Bolt A**. **Bolt B** is an example of a bolt subscribing to two streams, one stream from **Spout B** and another from **Bolt A**. Again, **Bolt D** subscribes to streams from **Bolt C** and **Bolt B**:

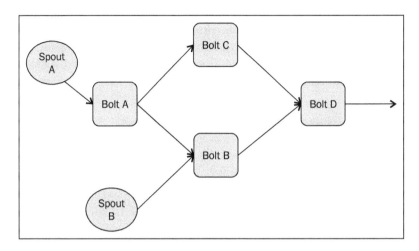

Use cases for Apache Storm

Streaming frameworks such as Apache Storm has a number of use cases. Some of the practical ones are as follows:

- **Algorithmic trading in stock markets**: Algorithmic trading requires low-latency decisions based on the performance of the stock, the market, and even external conditions such as events. Storm can parallelize decision-making and deliver distributed low-latency results.

- **Analytics from social network feeds**: Social networks such as Twitter and Facebook have a continuous stream of updates flowing into the system. A lot of analysis needs to be done at real time. For example, trending topics from Twitter feeds are low-latency applications. Trends change quickly and need to be reported as it happens.

- **Smart advertising**: Advertising is a major revenue generator for Internet companies and search engines. Advertisements have higher click-through rates if they are relevant to the user's browsing context. Smart selections and placements of advertisements is another application where frameworks such as Apache Storm can add a lot of value. Smart ads involve inferring the users' intent in real time.

- **Location-based applications**: A user's location can be used to target advertising, promotions, and services. This is a low-latency application as the target user might be at a location briefly. Storm can gather location data and make targeting happen in real time.

- **Sensor network-based applications**: Explosions of sensors in areas such as manufacturing, disaster monitoring, security, and so on has made it necessary to react and respond to anomalous events in real time. A sensor that can sense a disaster, such as an earthquake, can notify officials in real time, which can help save lives by timely evacuations and safety measures.

Developing with Apache Storm

Now, let's develop an Apache Storm topology using Java. Let's take `worldcitiespop.txt`, a CSV file containing city information along with the country code, population, and latitude/longitude information of each city. Though the example might not be an ideal streaming application, as the stream is bounded, it illustrates two patterns of stream filtering and grouping:

1. Let's develop a simple spout that reads each line from the `worldcitiespop.txt` CSV file and emits records as a stream of tuples. All spouts implement the `IRichSpout` interface. The abstract class, `BaseRichSpout`, also implements this interface. We will extend this class and override the abstract methods, as shown in the following code snippet. The three main methods to be overridden are:

   ° `open`: This method is used to initialize and start the spout. In our case, we open the file and store a handle to the output collector. The `SpoutOutputCollector` object is used to emit the tuples into the output stream. The key feature of the `SpoutOutputCollector` object is that the messages can be tagged with IDs to acknowledge or fail the messages. The configuration information is also available in this method.

   ° `nextTuple`: This method is called repeatedly to request the spout to emit tuples. This is a nonblocking call, that is, if there is no tuple to be emitted, the call will return. In the following example, we read one line of the file and emit it to the `SpoutOutputCollector` object. A `Values` object is used to package the tuple.

○   declareOutputFields: This method is used to specify the schema and IDs for the message. In the following example, we indicate that our tuple has a single field, city, through the Fields object:

```
package MasteringStorm;

import backtype.storm.spout.SpoutOutputCollector;
import backtype.storm.task.TopologyContext;
import backtype.storm.topology.OutputFieldsDeclarer;
import backtype.storm.topology.base.BaseRichSpout;
import backtype.storm.tuple.Fields;
import backtype.storm.tuple.Values;

import java.io.BufferedReader;
import java.io.FileReader;
import java.util.Map;


public class ReadCitySpout extends BaseRichSpout {

    private SpoutOutputCollector spoutOutputCollector;
    private BufferedReader cityFileReader;

    @Override
    public void open(Map map, TopologyContext
        topologyContext, SpoutOutputCollector
            spoutOutputCollector) {
      this.spoutOutputCollector = spoutOutputCollector;

        try{
            cityFileReader = new BufferedReader(new
                FileReader((String)map.get("city.file")));
        }
        catch(Exception ex){
            ex.printStackTrace();
        }

    }

    @Override
    public void nextTuple() {

        String city = null;
```

```
if(cityFileReader != null){

    try {
        city = cityFileReader.readLine();
    }
    catch(Exception ex){
        ex.printStackTrace();
    }

}


if(city != null){
    spoutOutputCollector.emit(new Values(city));
}

}

@Override
public void declareOutputFields(OutputFieldsDeclarer
    outputFieldsDeclarer) {
        outputFieldsDeclarer.declare(new Fields("city"));
}
}
```

2. Now that we have a stream of city tuples, we want to filter tuples that contain a valid population entry. If the worldcitiespop.txt file is observed closely, many cities do not have a population entry. We will filter out these records using bolts. The preceding code snippet illustrates the filtering pattern.

   All bolts have to implement the IRichBolt interface. The abstract BaseRichBolt class is extended, and three methods are overridden here too, which are as follows:

   ○ prepare: This method is used to initialize the bolt and make it ready to accept streams. We store the OutputCollector object so that we can write to the output stream.

   ○ execute: This method is the override where all the processing logic for the tuple goes. In the preceding code, we extract the city field from the tuple and split it on the comma character. We check for the population field of the record. If it is empty or throws NumberFormatException, we discard the tuple by not emitting anything.

○   declareOutputFields: This method is again used to specify the schema of the output tuple. This time, our tuple has two fields, countryCode and city. The former contains the country code, and the latter contains the entire city record.

```
package MasteringStorm;

import backtype.storm.task.OutputCollector;
import backtype.storm.task.TopologyContext;
import backtype.storm.topology.OutputFieldsDeclarer;
import backtype.storm.topology.base.BaseRichBolt;
import backtype.storm.tuple.Fields;
import backtype.storm.tuple.Tuple;
import backtype.storm.tuple.Values;

import java.util.Map;

public class FilterCityBolt extends BaseRichBolt {

    OutputCollector collector;

    @Override
    public void prepare(Map map, TopologyContext
        topologyContext, OutputCollector outputCollector) {
         this.collector = outputCollector;
    }

    @Override
    public void execute(Tuple tuple) {

        String city = tuple.getString(0);

        String[] tokens = city.split(",");

        //Filter cities that have a population number.
        if(tokens != null && tokens.length >= 7 &&
            tokens[4] != null && tokens[4].length() > 0){

            try {
                Long population =
                    Long.parseLong(tokens[4]);
            }
            catch(NumberFormatException ex){
                city = null;
            }

            if(city != null)
```

```
                              collector.emit(new Values(tokens[0],city));
            }

        }

        @Override
        public void declareOutputFields(OutputFieldsDeclarer
            outputFieldsDeclarer) {
            outputFieldsDeclarer.declare(new
                Fields("countryCode","city"));

        }
    }
```

3. Our next bolt is one that sums up all the city populations to get the country's population. The following code snippet exhibits this. As before, we extend the `BaseRichBolt` abstract class. In the `prepare` method, we initialize `HashMap` to store intermediate population values for each country. The `execute` method updates these intermediate population values and emits a tuple with the country code and the intermediate population value:

```
package MasteringStorm;

import backtype.storm.task.OutputCollector;
import backtype.storm.task.TopologyContext;
import backtype.storm.topology.OutputFieldsDeclarer;
import backtype.storm.topology.base.BaseRichBolt;
import backtype.storm.tuple.Fields;
import backtype.storm.tuple.Tuple;
import backtype.storm.tuple.Values;

import java.util.HashMap;
import java.util.Map;


public class SumPopulationForCountryBolt extends
    BaseRichBolt {

    private HashMap<String, Long> countryCodePopulationMap;
    private OutputCollector outputCollector;


    @Override
    public void prepare(Map map, TopologyContext
        topologyContext, OutputCollector outputCollector) {

        this.outputCollector = outputCollector;
```

```
        this.countryCodePopulationMap = new HashMap<>();
    }

    @Override
    public void execute(Tuple tuple) {

        String countryCode = tuple.getString(0);
        String city = tuple.getString(1);
        String[] tokens = city.split(",");
        Long population = Long.parseLong(tokens[4]);

        if(countryCodePopulationMap.containsKey(countryCode)) {
            Long savedPopulation =
                countryCodePopulationMap.get(tokens[0]);
            population += savedPopulation;
            countryCodePopulationMap.remove(countryCode);
        }

        countryCodePopulationMap.put(countryCode,
            population);
        outputCollector.emit(new Values(countryCode,
            population));

    }

    @Override
    public void declareOutputFields(OutputFieldsDeclarer
        outputFieldsDeclarer) {
        outputFieldsDeclarer.declare(new
            Fields("countryCode", "population"));

    }
}
```

4. Now that we have a spout that emits tuples, a bolt to filter out bad tuples, and an aggregation bolt that sums up the population, let's build a topology. As we saw previously, building a topology is to set up links between the spouts and bolts. The following code illustrates the way to construct and submit a topology of spouts and bolts.

    The topology is built using the `TopologyBuilder` object. It has the methods `setSpout` and `setBolt` to set the spouts and bolts in the topology. The names of the spouts and bolts can be specified. The `setBolt` method returns a `TopologyBuilder.BoltGetter` object. This object permits different kinds of groupings. Groupings can be thought off as stream-partitioning directives.

In the preceeding code snippet, we use the `shuffleGrouping` method to link `FilterCityBolt` to `ReadCitySpout`. However, we use the `fieldsGrouping` method to link `SumPopulationForCountryBolt` to `FilterCityBolt`. This is because we want to aggregate the population by country and will like tuples of the same country to arrive at the same bolt task.

The `StormSubmitter` helper class is then used to submit the topology to the Apache Storm cluster. We use the `Config` object to specify any additional configuration values. In this case, we set `debugging` and the filename that we got from the command line.

These are the following seven stream-partitioning schemes that are native to Apache Storm:

- **Shuffle grouping**: Each tuple is randomly distributed to the Bolt tasks. This scheme tries to guarantee that each Bolt task gets an equal number of tuples.
- **Fields grouping**: Based on the value of a particular field, tuples will be sent to a single Bolt task. In the code used in this section, we group based on the `countryCode` field, which guarantees that tuples that share the same country code are sent to the same task.
- **All grouping**: Every generated tuple is duplicated and sent to all the Bolt tasks.
- **Global grouping**: The entire stream goes to a single Bolt task. This is useful when calculating global metrics.
- **None grouping**: This defaults to Shuffle grouping for now. In the future, this will give a provision to push down to execute in the same thread of the Bolt or Spout.
- **Direct grouping**: In this case, the Bolt or Spout generating the tuple decides the Bolt it goes to.
- **Local or Shuffle grouping**: If the Bolt receiving the tuple happens to have some tasks in the same worker process as the producer, the tuples will be shuffled in-process. If this is not the case, it will fallback to the Shuffle grouping.

```
package MasteringStorm;

import backtype.storm.Config;
import backtype.storm.StormSubmitter;
import backtype.storm.topology.TopologyBuilder;
```

```
import backtype.storm.tuple.Fields;

public class MasteringStormTopology {

    public static void main(String[] args){

        Config config = new Config();
        config.setDebug(true);

        if(args != null){
            System.out.println(args.length);
        }

        System.out.println(args[0]);
        config.put("city.file", args[0]);

        TopologyBuilder topologyBuilder = new
            TopologyBuilder();

        topologyBuilder.setSpout("cities", new
            ReadCitySpout(), 3);
        topologyBuilder.setBolt("filter", new
            FilterCityBolt(), 3).shuffleGrouping("cities");
        topologyBuilder.setBolt("group", new
            SumPopulationForCountryBolt(),
                3).fieldsGrouping("filter", new
                    Fields("countryCode"));

        try {
            StormSubmitter.submitTopology("test-filtering-
                storm", config,
                    topologyBuilder.createTopology());

        }
        catch(Exception ex){
            ex.printStackTrace();
        }

    }


}
```

The topology can be submitted into a Storm cluster using a command line similar to the following:

```
storm jar MasteringStormOnYarn-1.0-SNAPSHOT-jar-with-dependencies.jar
MasteringStorm.MasteringStormTopology worldcitiespop.txt
```

> If you use Maven to build your topology JAR file, use the `<scope>provided</scope>` tag when specifying the Apache Storm dependency. If this is not used, the Apache Storm JAR files and `default.yaml` file are packaged into the JAR file. This leads to duplicate `default.yaml` files, which results in a runtime error. The following code snippet shows the dependency section in `pom.xml`:
>
> ```
> <dependencies>
>     <dependency>
>         <groupId>storm</groupId>
>         <artifactId>storm-core</artifactId>
>         <version>0.9.0</version>
>         <scope>provided</scope>
>     </dependency>
> </dependencies>
> ```

Apache Storm 0.9.1

Apache Storm 0.9.1 was released in February, 2014. It brings in a number of enhancements when compared to the older versions of Storm. The latest releases of Apache Storm can be found at `http://storm.apache.org/downloads.html`. The important enhancements are as follows:

- **Netty-based transport**: Previously, Apache Storm came with 0MQ as its transport. 0MQ needed native binaries to be installed on the cluster, which was tedious. Netty is a Java-based transport that ensures good portability across nodes in the cluster. It also comes with superior performance characteristics, providing almost two times more improvement in message throughput.

- **Windows support**: Apache Storm can now be run on the Windows platform. This is significant for the number of clusters running on Windows.

- **Apache Software Foundation**: Apache Storm is an incubator project within the Apache Software Foundation. This ensures greater community reach and provides distribution and licensing structure to the software.

- **Maven Integration**: Apache Storm is primarily written in a JVM-based Lisp language called Clojure. Leiningen used to be a popular build tool for Clojure and Storm builds as they used to be based on Leiningen. However, as Apache Storm moved as an incubator project within the Apache Software Foundation, the choice of build tool became an important feature for release management. Apache Storm now uses the Maven build system, which makes it easy to release early and often.

Storm on YARN

In *Chapter 6, YARN – Bringing Other Paradigms to Hadoop*, we built a YARN application that executes distributed shell commands. Storm is one such application that has been brought to YARN by Yahoo!. Any Hadoop cluster running YARN can now execute streaming workloads for low-latency real-time applications. The Application Master and client program to execute Storm are available for deployment. It is open sourced on GitHub at `https://github.com/yahoo/storm-yarn`.

Installing Apache Storm-on-YARN

Apache Storm-on-YARN can currently be installed from GitHub. This section assumes that the Hadoop 2.2.0 cluster is available.

Prerequisites

The following prerequisites are necessary to install Storm-on-YARN:

- Java 7
- Maven: This needs to be installed on the gateway machine to help compile and deploy the Storm-on-YARN Application Master and client:
    - `wget http://mirror.symnds.com/software/Apache/maven/ maven-3/3.1.1/binaries/apache-maven-3.1.1-bin.tar.gz`
    - `tar -zxvf apache-maven-3.1.1-bin.tar.gz`
    - `mkdir -p /usr/lib/maven`
    - `mv apache-maven-3.1.1 /usr/lib/maven`
    - `vi ~/.bash_profile and add $PATH=$PATH:/usr/lib/maven/ bin`

Installation procedure

Perform the following steps for installation:

1. A copy of the Storm-YARN repository can be downloaded from GitHub. If you have Git installed, the repository can be cloned locally:

   ```
   wget https://github.com/yahoo/storm-yarn/archive/master.zip
   ```

2. The downloaded `master.zip` file needs to be decompressed:

   ```
   unzip master.zip
   ```

3. Now, the Maven config file, `pom.xml`, has to be edited to reflect the Hadoop version being used. We are using 2.2.0, so mention it in the `hadoop.version` XML tag:

   ```
   <properties>
           <storm.version>0.9.0-wip21</storm.version>
           <hadoop.version>2.2.0</hadoop.version>
           <!--hadoop.version>2.1.0.2.0.5.0-67</hadoop.version-->
   </properties>
   ```

4. The Storm-YARN project comes with Storm binaries in the `lib` directory of the downloaded project files:

   ```
   mkdir ~/working-dir
   ```

5. Go to the `storm-yarn-master` directory:

   ```
   cd storm-yarn-master
   cp lib/storm.zip ~/working-dir
   ```

6. The `storm.zip` file has to be placed within HDFS so that it can be deployed on all the nodes of the Hadoop cluster. For now, this path is hardcoded to `/lib/storm/<storm-version>` within the Storm-YARN AM:

   ```
   hadoop fs -mkdir /lib
   hadoop fs -mkdir /lib/storm
   hadoop fs -mkdir /lib/storm/0.9.0-wip21
   hadoop fs -put storm.zip /lib/storm/0.9.0-wip21
   ```

7. The `storm.zip` file has to be unpacked in the working directory and added to the path:

```
unzip storm.zip
vi ~/.bash_profile
```

8. Add the `storm-yarn-master` and `storm` bin paths into the PATH environment variable:

```
export STORM_HOME="<your path>/working-dir/storm-0.9.0-wip21"
export STORM_YARN_HOME="<your path>/storm-yarn-master"
export PATH=$PATH:$STORM_HOME/bin:$STORM_YARN_HOME/bin
```

9. Go to `storm-yarn-master` and execute the Maven package command:

```
cd storm-yarn-master
mvn package
```

10. The Maven package command will build the Application Master and Client. Additionally, it will run tests to verify that everything went well. It is highly recommended that tests be run to catch any issues early. You can skip tests by running the following command:

```
mvn package -DskipTests
```

11. As we saw in the section on Storm architecture, Zookeeper is used to coordinate communication between the Nimbus and Supervisor daemons. It is important to install a Zookeeper cluster before starting off on Storm:

```
wget
http://www.gtlib.gatech.edu/pub/apache/zookeeper/zookeeper-
3.4.6/zookeeper-3.4.6.tar.gz
```

12. You need to unzip and untar the package and store it in a location of your choice:

```
tar zxvf zookeeper-3.4.6.tar.gz
```

13. Zookeeper stores all configuration information on disk. Go to the `conf` folder of the Zookeeper installation, create a `zoo.cfg` file from the template that is given to you, and check the settings. Most importantly, the directory pointed by the `dataDir` setting must exist:

```
cd conf

cp zoo_sample.cfg zoo.cfg

vi zoo.cfg
```

The Zookeeper configuration on my machine is given as follows:

```
# The number of milliseconds of each tick
tickTime=2000
# The number of ticks that the initial
# synchronization phase can take
initLimit=10
# The number of ticks that can pass between
# sending a request and getting an acknowledgement
syncLimit=5
# the directory where the snapshot is stored.
# do not use /tmp for storage, /tmp here is just
# example sakes.
dataDir=/data/zookeeper
# the port at which the clients will connect
clientPort=2181
```

To start Zookeeper, go to the `bin` folder and execute the following command:

```
cd bin

./zkServer.sh start
```

Once Zookeeper is started, it is time to submit the Apache Storm application to our Hadoop YARN cluster. This can be done using the following command:

```
storm-yarn launch
```

It can take a few minutes to launch. To check if all the necessary services are running, you can execute the `jps` command:

```
jps
```

The following screenshot shows all the necessary services that need to run:

The **QuorumPeerMain** service is the Zookeeper service. Since the cluster I am running on has a single node, we see a single supervisor. The Nimbus daemon is also visible. The MasterServer is the Application Master for Storm. It is the container that spawns Nimbus. There are a number of worker processes. These are the actual topologies that run in Storm. We will shortly see how to run a topology. For now, you might not be able to see the worker processes.

You can check to see the application ID within YARN using the following command:

```
yarn application -list
```

The following screenshot gives the output of the list command from YARN RM. The application ID for the Storm application is application_1404566721714_0004 in this case:

You can also check the application ID by connecting to the RM web UI, as shown in the following screenshot:

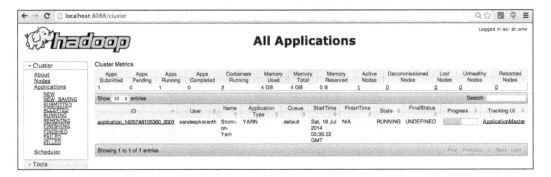

The Apache Storm configuration can be stored with the `.storm` directory in the user's home. In this way, whenever topologies are submitted to the cluster, Storm can automatically pick the configuration from this place:

```
storm-yarn getStormConfig -appId <appId from YARN> -output ~/.storm/
storm.yaml
```

The `storm.yaml` file has the configuration of the Apache Storm cluster. It is important to review it for the correct information. For example, the `nimbus.host` property shows the host where the Nimbus daemon is running. All the Zookeeper configurations, timeouts, and other properties can be set in this config file.

Now that the Apache Storm cluster is up and running, it is time to submit some topologies for testing. Storm YARN comes with a couple of test topologies, such as `storm.starter.WordCountTopology` and `storm.starter.ExclamationTopology`. These can be run to check whether the cluster is deployed correctly.

To run the topologies, use the following command:

```
storm jar storm-starter-0.0.1-SNAPSHOT.jar
storm.starter.WordCountTopology
```

Also run the following command:

```
storm jar storm-starter-0.0.1-SNAPSHOT.jar
storm.starter.ExclamationTopology
```

Apache Storm comes with its Web UI to monitor topologies. The web endpoint is on the gateway machine at port 7070. The following screenshot shows a Storm cluster running both topologies.

The `jps` command execution on each node can be used to check whether worker processes are running on the nodes.

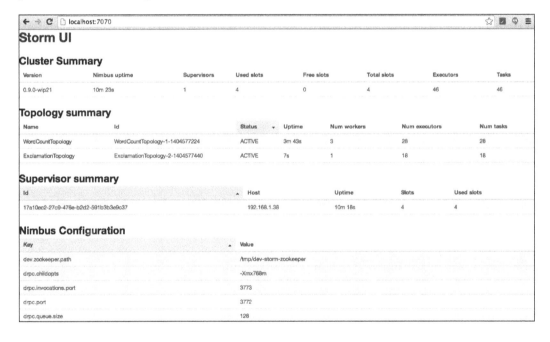

Clicking on a particular topology gives us its details. The following screenshot gives the details of ExclamationTopology running on the cluster. It provides the details of the number of bolts and spouts that are running. Actions can be taken on a particular topology as well. The currently permitted actions are to activate/deactivate, kill, and rebalance the topology.

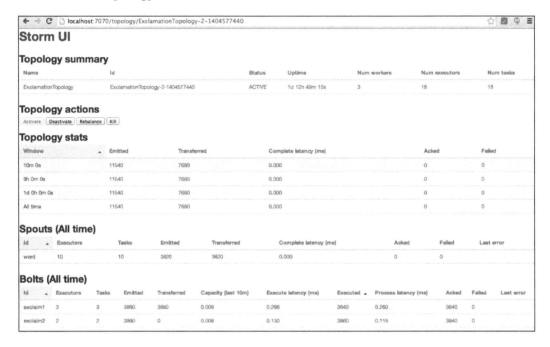

The following screenshot gives a snapshot of the logs from `ExclamationTopology`. These logs were gathered from a container that was running the topology. `ExclamationTopology` adds the string `!!!` to every word that was generated by the spout. The spout, in this case, selects a word randomly from a list of words and sends it to the bolts. The `exclaim1` bolt adds the three exclamation marks to the word and forwards it to the `exclaim2` bolt that adds three more marks.

In the logs, the `exclaim1` output always has three exclamations, while the `exclaim2` output has six exclamations. The word `spout` emits the word randomly from a set of words defined in the spout.

There are Apache Storm commands to kill a topology instead of using the Web UI. The killing process takes place in several steps. First, the spouts in the topology are deactivated. Then, Apache Storm waits for a timeout before it can terminate the workers and clean up all the states. During this interval, workers can complete processing the tuples they have received. The -w flag can be used to vary this particular timeout:

```
storm kill <topology-name> [-w wait_for_seconds]
```

Similarly, Apache Storm provides other commands to manage the topologies. We previously encountered the jar command that can be used to instantiate topologies within the cluster. The key here is that it automatically picks up the Storm configuration from the .storm directory within home.

The entire Apache Storm application can be stopped on the cluster using the Storm-YARN shutdown command. The usage is given as follows:

```
storm-yarn shutdown -appId <application id>
```

Both Apache Storm and Storm-YARN have many other commands. The Apache Storm commands manage a deployed instance of Storm, while the Storm-YARN command talks to the RM to manage the Storm application with YARN.

A comprehensive set of Apache Storm commands is given using the following command:

```
storm help [command]
```

For a comprehensive set of Storm-YARN commands and options, you can run the following command:

```
storm-yarn help
```

Some important Storm commands are as follows:

- `activate`: This command activates a spout. It is analogous to turning on a faucet at a sink to get a stream of water. Activating a spout starts the stream of tuples.
- `deactivate`: This command deactivates a spout. It is analogous to turning off the faucet. This command stops the stream of tuples.
- `dev-zookeeper`: This particular command can be used to instantiate a `Zookeeper` cluster during development, debugging, and testing. It is used when we do tests on the Storm-on-YARN package. The properties of this transient cluster are given by the `dev.zookeeper.path` property that specifies the path for the Zookeeper data directory and the `storm.zookeeper.port` property that specifies the port of the Zookeeper process.
- `drpc`: This command launches a distributed RPC daemon. The distributed RPC is a special pattern that is possible via Storm. RPC calls that are intensive can be parallelized using an Apache Storm topology. The function name and arguments form the tuple in the input stream.
- `list`: This command lists the topologies running in the Apache Storm cluster.

- `localconfvalue`: This command prints out the configuration value for a specified property. This value is taken from the `storm.yaml` file in the `.storm` directory merged with the properties from the `default.yaml` file.
- `logviewer`: This command launches a web endpoint from where logs can be viewed.
- `nimbus`: This command launches a Nimbus daemon.
- `rebalance`: Addition of nodes to the cluster might call for redistributing the workload in the cluster. This can be done in two ways; the first is to kill and restart the topology, and the second is to use the `rebalance` command. The `rebalance` command first deactivates the spouts in the system, then redistributes the workload and activates the spouts. The `rebalance` command can also be used to modify the parallelism of the workers in the cluster.
- `remoteconfvalue`: This command prints the configuration value for a property on a cluster machine. The path to the `storm.yaml` file is `$STORM-PATH/conf/storm.yaml`. Again, it merges the properties with the `default.yaml` file.
- `supervisor`: This command launches the supervisor daemon.
- `ui`: This command launches the UI daemon. The port number of the endpoint is given in the `storm.yaml` file.

Summary

The number one goal of the streaming paradigm is to cater to low-latency applications. The Storm-on-YARN project has brought this paradigm to Hadoop. Stakeholders can now multiplex streaming and batch processing on a single Hadoop cluster and cater to different kinds of applications.

There are a number of streaming frameworks available, such as Microsoft SQL Server StreamInsight, S4, and Apache Storm, among others. Apache Storm is open source, part of the Apache Software Foundation, Hadoop integrated, and has a large community behind it, making it attractive for distributed stream processing.

Some key takeaways from this chapter are as follows:

- The basic data model in Apache Storm is an unbounded sequence of tuples called Streams.
- Long-standing queries are modeled as computational topologies. The data stream flows through these topologies.
- Apache Storm provides the following primitives:
  - Spouts: They convert input data into streams
  - Bolts: They take an input stream, do some processing on the stream, and output another stream
- Apache Storm provides guaranteed message delivery and fault tolerance in a distributed setting.
- Apache Storm uses Thrift to specify topologies, making it language-agnostic.
- Storm-on-YARN is an open source under-development project initiated by Yahoo! to bring Apache Storm to Hadoop clusters running YARN.

In the next chapter, we will look at Hadoop's cloud support, particularly the one by Amazon, which is one of the biggest cloud vendors.

8
Hadoop on the Cloud

Cloud computing is the paradigm that has made computing a utility. Just like electricity grids and water supply channels bring electricity and water, to individual homes, cloud computing allows individuals and businesses—small, medium, and large—to tap into pooled computing resources connected via a network to execute desired tasks and run their applications.

In this chapter, we will be:

- Looking at the characteristics and advantages of cloud computing
- Comparing and contrasting the *Hadoop on the cloud* offering by Amazon AWS and Microsoft Azure, two of the leading players in the cloud computing space
- Delving into the details of Amazon's managed Hadoop service called **Elastic MapReduce (EMR)**
- Looking at how to provision an EMR cluster within minutes and run MapReduce jobs

Cloud computing characteristics

The **National Institute of Standards and Technology (NIST)** (www.nist.gov) defines the following five important characteristics as the essence of cloud computing:

- **On-demand self service**: Consumers of computing utility can provision and deprovision resources on the fly. The provisioning action can happen unilaterally in a self-serve manner without any human intervention with the service provider. For example, cloud computing has made it possible for an organization to provision a Hadoop cluster of a desired configuration from a console in their office, without having to call Amazon and letting them know about it.

- **Broad network access**: The self-service part of cloud computing is facilitated via the Internet, allowing heterogeneous clients ranging from mobile phones to desktop computers to interact with the cloud computing service. Standard communication protocols such as HTTP are used to allow communication between these diverse sets of clients and the service provider.

- **Resource pooling**: The entire setup is multitenant, that is, a number of consumers operate their workloads on a pooled set of computing resources of the service provider. Dynamic adjustments of physical resources among the consumers happen as the demand varies.

- **Rapid elasticity**: The resources utilized by a single consumer can be scaled outward and inward as demanded in a very short amount of time. Most cloud computing providers also provide an auto-scaling feature, where the resources scale outwards or inwards based on a set of conditions defined by the consumer. A feeling of infinite capacity is given to the consumer using the cloud-based service.

- **Measured service**: The cloud service provider measures, monitors, and reports the usage of each of its tenants. The measurement is transparent to the consumer and is used for billing. The cloud computing service always follows a pay-as-you-go model, where the consumer pays only for what has been used. For example, if a consumer provisions a Hadoop cluster of three nodes, runs a MapReduce job for one hour, and turns the cluster off once the job is done, the cloud computing service provider bills the consumer only for one hour of compute time on three nodes.

The reasons why the cloud makes sense to run Hadoop clusters are as follows:

- **Lower costs**: Operationalizing analytic workloads in an organization is always the last step in the data processing pipeline. Before operationalizing, iterations of refinements happen in the analyses and trials on different datasets. During the pre-operationalization phase, it is not prudent to provision an in-house Hadoop cluster, which involves a huge capital expenditure. Any in-house cluster that is provisioned will either be overprovisioned or underprovisioned at this stage. With the cloud, this situation is alleviated as organizations can lease out clusters based on their needs, without having to pay for the capital costs of the cluster. Also, traditionally, it will take months to set up the hardware and software for such a cluster. With the cloud model, this can happen in minutes.

- **Elasticity**: Experimentation and prototyping involves variable workloads. The cloud infrastructure is known for its elasticity. Hadoop clusters of different sizes can be provisioned, and nodes added or removed based on the requirement of the job. The inward or outward expansion of the cluster can be done dynamically too.

- **Administration**: The self-service model of the cloud makes it easy to administer and maintain a cluster. This has significant bearing not only in terms of administrative costs but also in terms of time taken to recover from failures.

Cloud-based software can be categorized into three service models:

- **Infrastructure as a Service (IaaS)**: This cloud service provider provides physical or virtual machines as a service.

- **Platform as a Service (PaaS)**: This cloud service provider provides a computing platform as a service. A computing platform can be an execution runtime, a database, a Hadoop cluster, or a web server.

- **Software as a Service (SaaS)**: This cloud service provider provides a software application as a service.

As we move from IaaS to SaaS, the flexibility of application configuration decreases with the decreasing cost of service. Hadoop on the cloud is a PaaS offering. It is sometimes termed **Hadoop as a Service** (**HaaS**). This distributed computing framework along with HDFS is available for a consumer as a service.

Hadoop on the cloud

All major cloud service providers have Hadoop as a PaaS offering. Amazon with Elastic MapReduce, Microsoft with their HDInsight offering, and Google with their Hadoop on the Google Cloud platform are the frontrunners in this space. The first to offer Hadoop on the cloud, way back in 2009, was Amazon.

We will briefly compare and contrast EMR and HDInsight in the following table:

Amazon AWS EMR	Microsoft Azure HDInsight
It was released in 2009. It has more than five years of service and technology maturity.	It was released in 2012. It has around two years of service and technology maturity.
The popularity of AWS makes the learning curve less steep for a new user. EMR is integrated with the popular AWS console.	Microsoft Azure is picking up, but it's not yet as popular as AWS. HDInsight is also integrated with Microsoft Azure dashboards.
It has the ability to deploy clusters with the MapR Hadoop distribution.	Hadoop distribution is limited to Microsoft's distribution in partnership with Hortonworks.
No Microsoft Windows support is available.	Hadoop distribution is tailored to run on Microsoft Windows.

Amazon AWS EMR	Microsoft Azure HDInsight
It is marginally less expensive.	It is slightly more expensive when compared to EMR.
It lags behind in end-user tooling.	It integrates better with the Microsoft Office suite. For example, it provides a Hive ODBC driver and Hive Excel add-on for frontend analysis and visualization.
It provides native support for Java, Pig, and Hive. Other executables/scripts can be executed using Hadoop Streaming.	It provides native support for C#, Java, Javascript, Pig, and Hive. Other executables/scripts can be executed using Hadoop Streaming.

Amazon Elastic MapReduce (EMR)

Amazon AWS offers Hadoop as a PaaS. Organizations and individuals can provision Hadoop clusters on the fly, run their workloads, and download results. Provisioning a Hadoop cluster using EMR takes a few minutes and is a few clicks away.

 Usage of any Amazon Web Service requires an Amazon account. Visit `http://aws.amazon.com` and register for a free account. A credit card is mandatory to register for an Amazon account. However, it will be charged only on usage beyond the free tier offered by Amazon. The registered e-mail is subsequently used as the username.

The general steps to create and run workloads on EMR are as follows:

1. The application is developed locally in Java using Hadoop's MapReduce APIs, Hive, Pig, or a language of the user's choice. Non-Java-based languages can be executed in a Hadoop cluster using Hadoop Streaming. A developer guide can be found at `http://docs.aws.amazon.com/ElasticMapReduce/latest/DeveloperGuide/emr-what-is-emr.html`.

2. The application and relevant data are stored in Amazon S3. S3 is a scalable storage service provided by Amazon. There are many ways of placing data in Amazon S3. A number of clients for data upload are available, or a web interface can also be used. Data can directly be written to HDFS on the EMR cluster as well.

3. Using the management console, the cluster configuration is specified and launched. The cluster configuration includes the kind of machines in the cluster, the version of Hadoop to use, and additional applications that need to be installed on the cluster. The actions to be performed once the cluster is provisioned are also part of this step.

4. The cluster is then launched, the data processing is done, and the results are either moved into S3 or can be read directly off HDFS on the cluster.

Provisioning a Hadoop cluster on EMR

To provision a Hadoop cluster on EMR, perform the following steps:

1. Once you have procured an Amazon account, visit `https://console.aws.amazon.com` and log in with your Amazon account credentials. The following screenshot shows an AWS console page. It lists all the different cloud services Amazon has to offer. The services of interest to us will be S3, a scalable storage service on the cloud, and Elastic MapReduce, a managed Hadoop service.

2. Clicking on the **Elastic MapReduce** link takes the user to the EMR service management page. The following screenshot shows the EMR page. It gives you a brief introduction to EMR and the main steps to launch a cluster. The **Create cluster** button is used to launch the Hadoop cluster wizard.

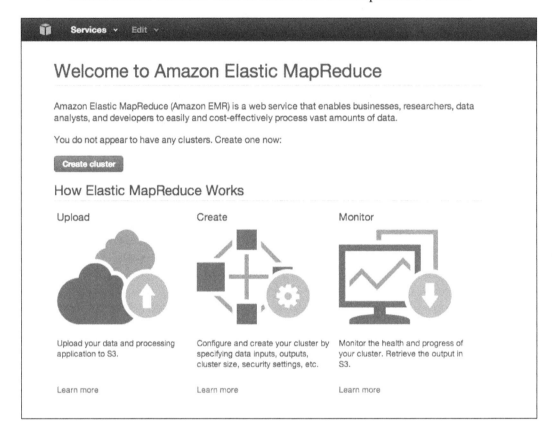

3. Before launching the cluster, we have to upload the data and corresponding application onto S3. Using the **Services** dropdown on the top navigation bar, a user can quickly navigate to the management console of any of Amazon's cloud services. S3 can be chosen to go to the S3 management console. The following screenshot shows the S3 management console:

4. It is mandatory to have a bucket in S3 before any file can be uploaded. Files can be uploaded to S3 using the **Upload** button once a particular bucket is selected. There is a button to create folders within the bucket. The **Actions** dropdown lists many other actions, such as copy, move, download, and setting access control on the file or folder. The files display metadata properties such as size, its storage class, and the last modified date and time of a particular file. It must be noted that the folders do not have these metadata properties as they do not have any underlying structure. Files can be uploaded to S3 using a number of file manager programs available for S3, or via the web interface shown in the following screenshot:

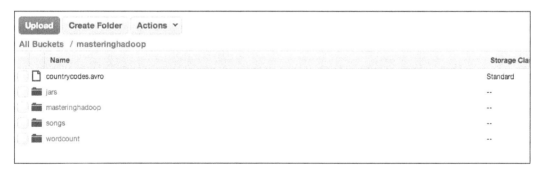

S3 stores files in containers called **buckets**. A bucket can be part of a single account and needs to be unique. Buckets can be assigned to different regions to cater to low-latency serving of files for users close to the region.

Buckets can contain folders and files. Folders are pseudo-structures and are used to prefix the filenames. A bucket is a flat container and does not contain any folder hierarchies. The following screenshot shows the MasteringHadoop bucket with folders and files in an S3 account.

Amazon EMR provides a number of sample jobs that can be run on the provisioned clusters. One such JAR is a Hadoop Streaming program for word count. The program is written in Python and counts the words in a document. The files whose words need to be counted, and the program, are already on a public bucket on S3 and can be used by anyone to test out EMR.

Hadoop Streaming is a utility that comes with every Hadoop distribution. It can be used to run Hadoop jobs with any executable or script. The executable can be written in any language of the developer's choice. Hadoop Streaming is particularly useful for executing legacy applications in a Hadoop environment. Hadoop Streaming should not be confused with the Stream computing paradigm we saw in the previous chapter.

5. We will start off by going back to the EMR console using the **Services** navigation dropdown. The next step is to click on the **Create cluster** button on the console.

   The **Create Cluster** page has multiple sections. Each section configures a particular aspect of the cluster.

6. The first section is the **Cluster Configuration** section where the cluster properties are mentioned. The next screenshot shows this section on the **Create Cluster** page. Some of the properties are as follows:

   ○ **Cluster name:** This is a friendly name for the cluster. This name will help identify and manage a cluster based on the name. In the example, it has been set to MasteringHadoopWordCount.

- ◦ **Termination protection:** This is set to **Yes**, as shown in the next screenshot. When turned on, it prevents the cluster from terminating when failures are encountered. If the cluster needs to be terminated, it has to be explicitly set to **No** before termination. It is recommended to turn on this property as it might be necessary to back cluster instance data before terminating the cluster. All cluster instance data will be lost otherwise.

- ◦ **Logging:** Logging can be turned on and a S3 path can be specified to dump the logs. Logs are written on the `/mnt/var/log` directory of the Master Node. These are copied onto S3 at intervals of 5 minutes.

- ◦ **Debugging**: By enabling debugging, an index of the logfiles is created in SimpleDB.

7. The next section is the **Tags** section. Up to 10 key-value strings can be associated with the EMR cluster. These tags are persisted in the underlying EC2 instances that run the Hadoop cluster. Tags can be powerful metadata that can help classify and manage EMR clusters and EC2 instances.

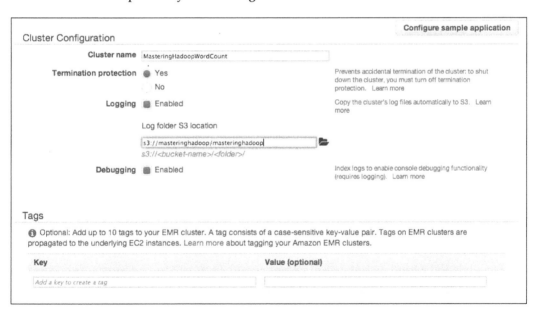

8. The next sections configure the software and hardware of the EMR cluster we want to provision. The next screenshot shows the page with both these sections.

In the **Software Configuration** section, the fields are as follows:

   ° **Hadoop distribution**: The Hadoop distribution to be used in the cluster can be set here. Amazon has its own Hadoop distribution. This distribution is optimized to run on Amazon's EC2 instances. It also supports MapReduce's Hadoop distribution. The **AMI version** dropdown gives the versions of Hadoop that are present within the distribution. Hadoop versions 2.4.0, 2.2.0, 1.0.3, and 0.20.205 are present. Each version of Hadoop has different AMIs corresponding to it. In the preceding screenshot, we choose Hadoop 2.2.0 that is installed on AMI Version 3.0.4 to be consistent throughout the book.

   ° **Additional applications**: Additional applications can be added to the cluster. By default, Hive and Pig are installed. If it is not required for your workloads, they can be removed. HBase, Impala, and Ganglia are three other applications that are available with this version of Hadoop.

In the **Hardware Configuration** section, the fields are as follows:

   ° **Network**: A **Virtual Private Cloud (VPC)** can be used to connect to a private cloud to process sensitive data. As shown in the next screenshot, we will choose a default VPC.

   ° **EC2 Subnet**: The EC2 subnet can be chosen using the dropdown. All subnets available within your region are shown. There is an option to choose a random subnet, as shown in the next screenshot.

   ° **Instance Information**: There are three types of EC2 instances that can be specified:

   ° **Master**: This EC2 instance is responsible for assigning tasks to the different cores and task nodes. There mandatorily has to be one master instance.

- ° **Core**: These are the nodes that execute tasks as well as the ones that act as data nodes. In the example, we set the number of **Core** instances to **2**. We choose the smallest possible VM, **m1.medium**. Amazon offers many other VMs with different CPU and memory parameters.

- ° **Task**: These are nodes that can only execute tasks. They do not have the DataNode component, and therefore, are not part of the HDFS.

9. The next section is the **Security and Access** section. It allows the user to set access control on the cluster and specify the keys for access. If you want to securely log in into any of the EC2 instances, it requires an Amazon EC2 key pair. The PEM file associated with this key pair is used when connecting to EC2 via ssh. The instructions on how to set up a key pair are given at `https://docs.aws.amazon.com/ElasticMapReduce/latest/DeveloperGuide/emr-plan-access-ssh.html`. In the example, we use the `MasteringHadoop` key pair to access the cluster via ssh. Also, we don't allow access to any other AWS user by selecting **No Other IAM users** in the **IAM user access** subsection. EMR allows role-based access control, and there are two access control grants that can be specified.

10. Setting a role in the **EMR role** dropdown allows the application using this role to access other AWS services such as EC2. Similarly, setting a role in **EC2 instance profile** allows EC2 instances within EMR to access other AWS services:

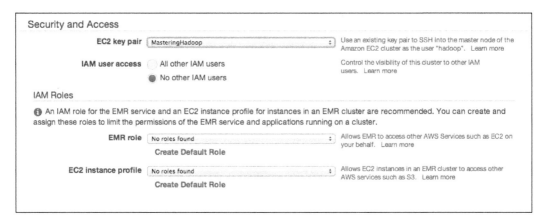

11. The next section shows how to set **Bootstrap Actions** for the cluster. The next screenshot shows an image of this section. Setup scripts can be specified here to instruct any special configuration that will be required before starting the cluster. The Bootstrap action dropdown has options to configure Hadoop, configure daemons, execute scripts on predicates, or conduct some custom actions. In the example, we will omit having any bootstrap actions.

12. The final section is the **Steps** section. This is the section where jobs can be submitted to the Hadoop cluster. In the example, the dropdown has options to execute a Hive program, Pig program, Streaming program, Impala program, or a custom MapReduce Java JAR file. We will see how we can add a streaming program from the AWS EMR samples that are already available. This section also has an autoterminate action that terminates the cluster once the last step has been executed. In the example, we set the **Auto-terminate** radio button to **No** as we wish to explicitly terminate the cluster.

In the example, let's select a Hadoop Streaming program step by choosing it from the dropdown. Clicking on the **Configure and add** button opens up the **Add step** wizard, as shown in the following screenshot. We enter a friendly name for the step. The Mapper task is set to the Python program given by the S3 path, `s3://us-west-2.elasticmapreduce/samples/wordcount/wordSplitter.py`.

The **Reducer** field is set to `aggregate`. This is a built-in reducer that sums the values corresponding to each key. The folder containing the files on which we run the word count is given by the S3 path, `s3://us-west-2.elasticmapreduce/samples/wordcount/input`. This is specified in the **Input S3 location** path. The output S3 path is specified by the `s3://masteringhadoop/wordcount/output/2014-07-15/15-28-19` path. The word count output is put in this folder. Any additional arguments can be specified in the **Arguments** box. We can also specify the steps to be undertaken if a failure is encountered. In the example, we have chosen to terminate the cluster on any failure. The other options are to continue executing subsequent steps or cancel and wait for user intervention. We then click on the **Save** button. We are now ready to review the cluster before running it.

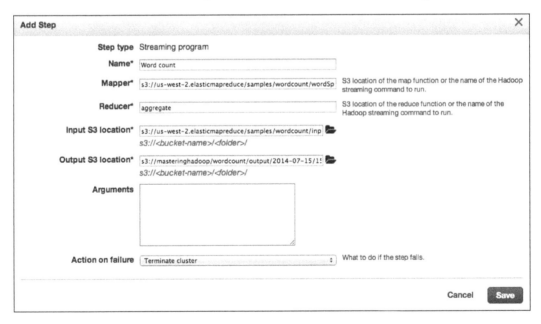

13. The **Steps** section now looks similar to what is shown in the following screenshot. Clicking on the **Create cluster** button starts provisioning the cluster:

14. The EMR dashboard now shows the list of clusters that are running. Clicking on a cluster of interest shows the details of the cluster. The following screenshot shows the status of the executing cluster. The configuration status and state of each cluster component are given. In the screenshot, the Master Node is **Bootstrapping** while the two core nodes are in the **Provisioning** state.

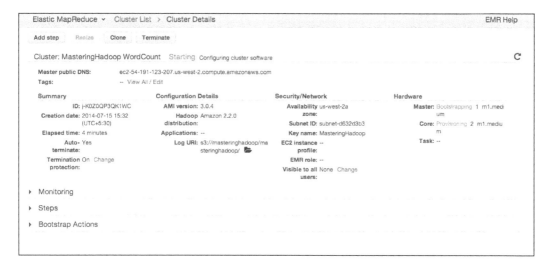

15. The page has expandable sections that can be expanded to see the details of each section. When we expand the **Steps** section, the details are as shown in the following screenshot. It can be seen that the Hadoop setup step is completed, and word count streaming is currently being executed.

16. The link to the right gives details on the jobs being executed in the step. Clicking on the **View jobs** link of the currently executing step shows the details of the job and its tasks, as shown in the following screenshot. Three Reduce tasks were executed along with twelve Map tasks to complete the program. The attempts by the tasks can be analyzed by clicking on the **View attempts** link. The status of each task is also given.

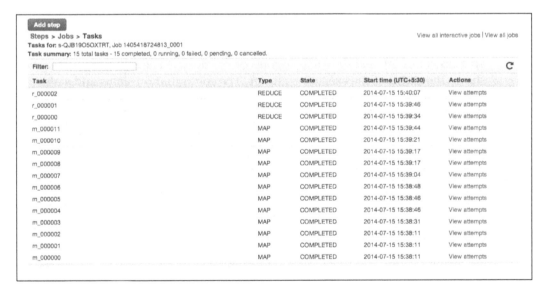

17. Expanding the cluster information on the EMR dashboard can give a quick summary of the cluster. Details such as elapsed time are given here. A step-by-step breakdown of the elapsed time is also visible. The following screenshot gives this view:

18. Finally, when the job is complete, the output files can be seen in S3. The output folder was specified when initiating the job. The following screenshot shows the output folder in S3. We had three Reduce tasks in the job, and it promptly has three output files in S3, one file per Reduce task.

We can also run Hive and Pig scripts via the management console. The scripts need to be uploaded in S3. During the software configuration step, we need to specify the install of Hive and/or Pig, based on the requirement. The following screenshot shows the **Software Configuration** section of a cluster with Hive and Pig installed. Based on the AMI chosen, an appropriate version of Hive and Pig are available:

We will look at how to run Hive and Pig interactively on EMR, instead of a batch mode, via the management console. Once the cluster is provisioned with Hive and Pig installed, we can securely log in to the Master Node. To reiterate, it is very important to get a key-value pair from Amazon and assign it to the cluster. If this is not done, it is not possible to securely log in to the cluster.

The following screenshot shows how to securely log in to the cluster. The DNS name of the Master Node can be copied from the cluster status page. In the example, the Master Node DNS name is `ec2-54-191-39-199.us-west-2.compute.amazonaws.com`.

It is also important to provide a username when logging in. All Hadoop services run under the `hadoop` user.

```
Sandeeps-MacBook-Pro:Mastering Hadoop sandeepkaranth$ ssh ec2-54-191-39-199.us-west-2.compute.amazonaws.com -i MasteringHadoop.pem
The authenticity of host 'ec2-54-191-39-199.us-west-2.compute.amazonaws.com (54.191.39.199)' can't be established.
RSA key fingerprint is 5f:c4:fd:b5:33:74:65:80:82:cf:5b:a6:13:76:45:71.
Are you sure you want to continue connecting (yes/no)? yes
Warning: Permanently added 'ec2-54-191-39-199.us-west-2.compute.amazonaws.com,54.191.39.199' (RSA) to the list of known hosts.
Permission denied (publickey).
Sandeeps-MacBook-Pro:Mastering Hadoop sandeepkaranth$ ssh hadoop@ec2-54-191-39-199.us-west-2.compute.amazonaws.com -i MasteringHadoop.pem


       _|  _|_|  )
      _|  (   /    Amazon Linux AMI
     _|\___|___|

https://aws.amazon.com/amazon-linux-ami/2013.09-release-notes/
46 package(s) needed for security, out of 254 available
Run "sudo yum update" to apply all updates.
Amazon Linux version 2014.03 is available.
-------------------------------------------------------------------

Welcome to Amazon Elastic MapReduce running Hadoop and Amazon Linux.

Hadoop is installed in /home/hadoop. Log files are in /mnt/var/log/hadoop. Check
/mnt/var/log/hadoop/steps for diagnosing step failures.

The Hadoop UI can be accessed via the following commands:

  ResourceManager    lynx http://localhost:9026/
  NameNode           lynx http://localhost:9101/
```

Providing the respective program names on the command line of the Master Node can start the Hive and Pig (Grunt) shells. The following screenshots illustrate this:

```
[hadoop@ip-172-31-5-27 ~]$ hive
14/07/19 05:10:03 INFO Configuration.deprecation: mapred.input.dir.recursive is deprecated. Instead, use mapreduce.input.fileinputformat.input.dir.recursive
14/07/19 05:10:03 INFO Configuration.deprecation: mapred.max.split.size is deprecated. Instead, use mapreduce.input.fileinputformat.split.maxsize
14/07/19 05:10:03 INFO Configuration.deprecation: mapred.min.split.size is deprecated. Instead, use mapreduce.input.fileinputformat.split.minsize
14/07/19 05:10:03 INFO Configuration.deprecation: mapred.min.split.size.per.rack is deprecated. Instead, use mapreduce.input.fileinputformat.split.minsize.per
.rack
14/07/19 05:10:03 INFO Configuration.deprecation: mapred.min.split.size.per.node is deprecated. Instead, use mapreduce.input.fileinputformat.split.minsize.per
.node
14/07/19 05:10:03 INFO Configuration.deprecation: mapred.reduce.tasks is deprecated. Instead, use mapreduce.job.reduces
14/07/19 05:10:03 INFO Configuration.deprecation: mapred.map.tasks.speculative.execution is deprecated. Instead, use mapreduce.map.speculative
14/07/19 05:10:03 INFO Configuration.deprecation: mapred.reduce.tasks.speculative.execution is deprecated. Instead, use mapreduce.reduce.speculative
14/07/19 05:10:05 WARN conf.Configuration: org.apache.hadoop.hive.conf.LoopingByteArrayInputStream@320bdadc:an attempt to override final parameter: mapreduce.
job.end-notification.max.retry.interval; Ignoring.
14/07/19 05:10:05 WARN conf.Configuration: org.apache.hadoop.hive.conf.LoopingByteArrayInputStream@320bdadc:an attempt to override final parameter: mapreduce.
job.end-notification.max.attempts; Ignoring.

Logging initialized using configuration in file:/home/hadoop/.versions/hive-0.11.0/conf/hive-log4j.properties
Hive history file=/mnt/var/lib/hive_0110/tmp/history/hive_job_log_hadoop_3530@ip-172-31-5-27.us-west-2.compute.internal_201407190510_1469366415.txt
hive>
```

```
[hadoop@ip-172-31-5-27 ~]$ pig
2014-07-19 05:11:47,772 [main] INFO  org.apache.pig.Main - Apache Pig version 0.11.1.1 (reported) compiled Feb 17 2014, 22:18:48
2014-07-19 05:11:47,773 [main] INFO  org.apache.pig.Main - Logging error messages to: /mnt/var/log/apps/pig.log
2014-07-19 05:11:47,807 [main] INFO  org.apache.pig.impl.util.Utils - Default bootup file /home/hadoop/.pigbootup not found
2014-07-19 05:11:48,797 [main] INFO  org.apache.pig.backend.hadoop.executionengine.HExecutionEngine - Connecting to hadoop file system at: hdfs://172.31.5.27:
9000
2014-07-19 05:11:48,814 [main] INFO  org.apache.hadoop.conf.Configuration.deprecation - fs.default.name is deprecated. Instead, use fs.defaultFS
2014-07-19 05:11:48,816 [main] INFO  org.apache.hadoop.conf.Configuration.deprecation - mapred.used.genericoptionsparser is deprecated. Instead, use mapreduce
.client.genericoptionsparser.used
2014-07-19 05:11:51,709 [main] INFO  org.apache.hadoop.conf.Configuration.deprecation - fs.default.name is deprecated. Instead, use fs.defaultFS
grunt>
```

Interactive commands can now be executed at these prompts. File locations can be specified with the `s3://<bucket name>/<folder name>` paths to read them from S3.

Summary

Cloud is a cost-efficient and effective way of developing pre-operationalized analytics. The self-serve, pay-as-you-go, and elastic deployment features of the cloud are reasons for the cost benefits. Many companies such as Yelp and Netflix run massive analytic workloads using the cloud infrastructure. Apache Hadoop is available as a PaaS offering on all major cloud service providers.

Some key takeaways from this chapter are as follows:

- Amazon's Hadoop offering is called Elastic MapReduce (EMR), and it has been around since 2009. Microsoft launched its Hadoop offering in 2012, which is known as HDInsight on Microsoft Azure.

- Using an AWS account, a Hadoop cluster can be launched in a matter of minutes. The number of EC2 instances in the Hadoop cluster is currently limited to 20. For more instances, a special request needs to be mailed to Amazon. Here's a word of caution for you: remember to terminate your Hadoop EMR cluster after use. If this is not done, charges will be incurred even if the cluster is idle.

- EMR provides many Hadoop versions, the latest being 2.4. It also provides the MapR Hadoop distribution.

- For now, in EMR, a custom JAR, Hive queries, Pig scripts, and Hadoop Streaming programs can be run. The input and the MapReduce program are generally stored in S3, the scalable storage offering from Amazon AWS.

- EMR provides granular access control to Hadoop clusters. Roles can be defined and assigned appropriately.

In the next chapter, we will see how HDFS can be replaced with other filesystems. With HDFS replacement strategies, the file load time before job execution can be brought down significantly, thus bringing down the latency of the job.

9
HDFS Replacements

The parallelism and scalability of the MapReduce computing paradigm are greatly influenced by the underlying filesystem. HDFS is the default filesystem that comes with most Hadoop distributions. The filesystem automatically chunks files into blocks and stores them in a replicated fashion across the cluster. The information of the distribution pattern is supplied to the MapReduce engine that can then smartly place tasks so that movement of data over the network is minimized.

However, there are many use cases where HDFS may not be ideal. In this chapter, we will look at the following topics:

- The strengths and drawbacks of HDFS when compared to other POSIX filesystems.

- Hadoop's support for other filesystems. One of them is Amazon's cloud storage service known as **Simple Storage Service** (S3). Reading and writing files from and to the S3 services is permitted within Hadoop.

- Hadoop HDFS has extensibility features. Extending the framework can be of two kinds: by providing a new object storage interface or by providing a drop-in replacement for HDFS. The former would mean changing the MapReduce layer by providing the ability to read via the new interface, while the latter requires no change to existing jobs.

- How to extend HDFS to support S3's native filesystem.

HDFS – advantages and drawbacks

HDFS has its advantages and drawbacks. Some of its advantages are as follows:

- HDFS is inexpensive because of two reasons. Firstly, the filesystem relies on commodity storage disks that are much less expensive than the storage media used for enterprise grade storage. Secondly, the filesystem shares the hardware with the computation framework as well, in this case, MapReduce. Also, HDFS is open source and does not levy licensing fee on the user.

- HDFS has been around for more than 7 years and is considered mature technology. There is a large community behind it and a broad range of organizations that are storing petabytes of data on HDFS.

- HDFS is optimized for MapReduce workloads. It provides very high performance for sequential reads and writes, which is the typical access pattern in MapReduce jobs.

But, HDFS does not cater to all the data needs that may arise in an enterprise. The main drawback of HDFS is that it is not POSIX compliant. This means:

- HDFS is immutable, that is, files cannot be modified. They rather need to be created from scratch. The **append** action is the only action possible on the files and was introduced much later in the evolution of HDFS.

- HDFS is not mountable. Unlike POSIX-compliant filesystems, HDFS cannot be mounted and operated upon. This eliminates the employment of many familiar and popular filesystem tools that are used to search, browse, and manipulate data.

- HDFS is optimized for streaming reads and not for random access of files. This feature of HDFS in combination with the preceding two properties makes it tedious for the user to get a holistic view of the files in HDFS.

- Though HDFS is optimized for MapReduce jobs, Hadoop has moved on to become a generic cluster compute framework with the introduction of YARN. Other computing paradigms might have different expectations from the underlying filesystem, and HDFS falls short of meeting these expectations.

Amazon AWS S3

S3, short for Simple Storage Service, is Amazon's storage as a service offering. It provides reliable storage for data by providing redundancy. The consumer is charged for storage of data on S3 based on the amount of storage used. Any download of data from S3 is also charged, but data upload and transfer of data between AWS properties are free of charge. This makes it extremely attractive for the user to run EMR (Elastic Map Reduce) on AWS and have data stored on S3.

S3 can be used as the input and output data store for MapReduce jobs. The intermediate files can be stored on local disks or the HDFS of the EMR cluster. This also allows easy sharing of input and results among different people in the organization without fearing data loss, with high data security. If an EMR cluster gets terminated accidentally, all of the HDFS data will be lost unless it is moved out. Using S3 for input and output mitigates such risks.

However, S3 is significantly slower because it does not provide data locality and should be used wisely. The best practice is to get the initial dataset for MapReduce jobs from S3 and move the final results back to S3. All intermediate output from the cascaded MapReduce job should be kept within HDFS.

Hadoop support for S3

Hadoop supports transfers to and from a cluster and S3. Two kinds of file storage support are provided by Hadoop, which are as follows:

- **S3 native filesystem (s3n)**: The native S3 filesystem object within Hadoop allows reading and writing of files as S3 objects. The files are stored in S3's native form. This makes it possible to read files using other S3 tools. However, S3 imposes a limit of 5 TB on the file objects.

- **S3 block filesystem (s3)**: This is similar to how a file is stored in HDFS. The file is broken into blocks and all the blocks are stored using S3. S3 is purely a storage layer for the file blocks. Though the block-based filesystem on S3 allows storage of files greater than 5 TB, it imposes a requirement of dedicating an entire bucket as the Hadoop store. Storage of other non-block-based file types is not permitted. Unlike the S3 native filesystem, it does not allow reading data from other standard S3 tools.

The S3 block filesystem comes close to being a drop-in replacement for HDFS. However, it has some limitations. The biggest limitation other than data locality is the problem of eventual consistency that is inherent to a distributed store. Changes made to the filesystem might not be visible immediately and might take an indefinite time to converge.

A few configuration changes such as providing the credentials for the S3 bucket are needed to connect and move files to and from the S3 bucket using the mentioned filesystem drivers. The `core-site.xml` file in the Hadoop `conf` directory can be modified as shown in the following XML snippet:

```
<property>
  <name>fs.s3n.awsAccessKeyId</name>
  <value><Your access id></value>
```

```
      </property>

      <property>
        <name>fs.s3n.awsSecretAccessKey</name>
        <value><Your secret key></value>
      </property>
```

The preceding code tells Hadoop's S3 native filesystem driver to use the specified credentials to connect to S3. If the S3 block-based filesystem driver is being used, the property names change to `fs.s3.awsAccessKeyId` and `fs.s3.awsSecretKeyId`.

Any HDFS command can now be executed with the `s3` or `s3n` scheme in the URL to conduct file operations on the specified S3 path. For example, the following command lists all the files in the `masteringhadoop` AWS bucket:

hadoop fs -ls s3n://masteringhadoop/

The output of this command is as follows:

```
Found 10 items
-rw-rw-rw-   1   43736787 2014-07-31 16:44
s3n://masteringhadoop/HDFSReplacements-1.0-SNAPSHOT-jar-with-
dependencies.jar
-rw-rw-rw-   1      3875 2014-06-08 20:06
s3n://masteringhadoop/countrycodes.avro
-rw-rw-rw-   1      3787 2014-07-19 10:18
s3n://masteringhadoop/countrycodes.txt
drwxrwxrwx   -          0 1970-01-01 05:30
s3n://masteringhadoop/jars
drwxrwxrwx   -          0 1970-01-01 05:30
s3n://masteringhadoop/logs
drwxrwxrwx   -          0 1970-01-01 05:30
s3n://masteringhadoop/masteringhadoop
drwxrwxrwx   -          0 1970-01-01 05:30
s3n://masteringhadoop/songs
drwxrwxrwx   -          0 1970-01-01 05:30
s3n://masteringhadoop/user
drwxrwxrwx   -          0 1970-01-01 05:30
s3n://masteringhadoop/wordcount
```

The key part to note here is that Hadoop is able to connect to S3 out of the box because the S3 credentials were specified in the `core-site.xml` file. The S3 filesystem is addressed by a scheme, `s3n`, indicating that we are using Hadoop's S3 native filesystem driver. The scheme can be changed to `s3` if we use the S3 block filesystem driver.

Instead of specifying the access and secret key in `core-site.xml`, it can be directly specified in the path of the file as follows:

```
s3n://AWS-ACCESS-ID:AWS-SECRET-KEY@masteringhadoop/
```

The AWS secret key and access key can be obtained in the accounts section of the AWS management console.

Implementing a filesystem in Hadoop

Based on the situation, it might be a necessity to replace HDFS with a filesystem of your choice. Hadoop provides out-of-the-box support for a few filesystems such as S3. HDFS replacement can be done either as a drop-in replacement or, as in the case with S3, seamless integration with the S3 file store for input and output.

In this section, we will re-implement the S3 native filesystem and extend Hadoop. The code in this section illustrates the steps on how HDFS replacement can be done. Error handling and other features related to S3 have been omitted for brevity.

The major steps in implementing a filesystem for Hadoop are as follows:

1. The `org.apache.hadoop.fs.FileSystem` abstract class needs to be extended and all the abstract methods need to be overridden. There are out-of-the-box implementations for `FilterFileSystem`, `NativeS3FileSystem`, `S3FileSystem`, `RawLocalFileSystem`, `FTPFileSystem`, and `ViewFileSystem`.

2. The `open` method returns an `FsDataInputStream` object. A backing `InputStream` object that can read from the underlying filesystem whose support the user wishes to incorporate in Hadoop needs to be created.

3. The `create` and `append` methods return an `FsDataOutputStream` object. A backing `OutputStream` object that can write to the underlying filesystem whose support the user wishes to incorporate within Hadoop needs to be created.

4. An `org.apache.hadoop.fs.FileStatus` object needs to be created whenever the status of a particular file given by a `Path` object is specified.

5. The JAR file containing this implementation has to be placed in the `$HADOOP_HOME/share/hadoop/hdfs/lib` directory so that it can be picked up when the distributed filesystem is started. The `core-site.xml` file must have the `fs.<scheme>.impl` property value set to the fully-qualified class name for the filesystem implementation. Additional properties can also be provided to configure the filesystem.

Implementing an S3 native filesystem in Hadoop

Let's first create `InputStream` and `OutputStream` for the filesystem. In our example, we have to connect to the AWS to read and write files to S3.

Hadoop provides us with the `FSInputStream` class to cater to custom filesystems. We extend this class and override a few methods in the example implementation. A lot of private variables are declared along with the constructor and helper methods to initialize the client as illustrated in the following code snippet. The `private` variables contain objects that are used to configure and retrieve data from the filesystem. In this example, we use objects such as `AmazonS3Client` to call REST web APIs on AWS, `S3Object` as a representation of the remote object on S3, and `S3ObjectInputStream` representing the object stream to perform the read operation. All the AWS-related classes are present in the `com.amazonaws.services.s3` and `com.amazonaws.services.s3.model` packages. There are a few other private variables such as the S3 bucket name and the S3 key. The Hadoop `Configuration` object is passed to help read any configuration properties the user might have defined.

The constructor ensures that all the private variables are correctly initialized. In the example, we open the S3 object stream lazily. Therefore, there are no stream initialization calls in the constructor. To lazily initialize the object and the object stream, we have the `openObject` and `openS3Stream` calls. If the object is not initialized, `openObject` calls `openS3Stream` by setting the stream to the beginning of the file. The `openS3Stream` call aborts any open stream and reinitializes a new object and stream:

```java
private class S3NFsInputStream extends FSInputStream{

    private AmazonS3Client s3Client;
    private Configuration configuration;
    private String bucket;
    private String key;
    private long length;

    private S3ObjectInputStream s3ObjectInputStream;
    private S3Object s3Object;
    private long position;

    public S3NFsInputStream(AmazonS3Client s3, Configuration
        conf, String bucket, String key, long length) {
        super();

        this.s3Client = s3;
```

```
            this.configuration = conf;
            this.bucket = bucket;
            this.key = key;
            this.length = length;

            this.s3Object = null;

        }

        private void openObject(){

            if(s3Object == null){
                openS3Stream(0);
            }

        }

        private void openS3Stream(long position){

            if(s3ObjectInputStream != null){
                s3ObjectInputStream.abort();
            }

            GetObjectRequest objectRequest = new
                GetObjectRequest(this.bucket, this.key);
            objectRequest.setRange(position, length - 1);
            this.s3Object =
                this.s3Client.getObject(objectRequest);
            this.s3ObjectInputStream =
                this.s3Object.getObjectContent();

            this.position = position;

        }
```

In the preceding example, we go ahead and implement the methods that mandatorily
have to be overridden. The code snippet that follows gives the override methods
and their implementations. The `read` override method is used to read a byte from
the input stream. The position of the input stream is incremented. The `read` override
is overloaded with another variant that fills a byte buffer and returns the number
of read bytes. All these methods call the `openObject` call before reading from
`S3ObjectInputStream` to lazily initialize the stream.

The `close` method is used to clean up and the `seek` method is used to get to a particular position in the file. We do not support any markers in this simple implementation. You can recall markers as points in the file that can be used for splittable compression:

```
@Override
public int read() throws IOException {

    openObject();
    int readByte = this.s3ObjectInputStream.read();

    if(readByte >= 0){
        this.position++;
    }

    return readByte;
}

@Override
public int read(byte[] b, int off, int len) throws
IOException {

    openObject();
    int readByte = this.s3ObjectInputStream.read
        (b, off, len);

    if(readByte >= 0){
        this.position+=readByte;

    }
    return readByte;
}

@Override
public void close() throws IOException {
    super.close();

    if(s3Object != null){
        s3Object.close();
    }
}


@Override
```

```
public boolean markSupported() {
    return false;
}

@Override
public void seek(long l) throws IOException {

    if(this.position == l){
        return;
    }
    openS3Stream(l);

}

@Override
public long getPos() throws IOException {
    return this.position;
}

@Override
public boolean seekToNewSource(long l) throws IOException
{
    return false;
}


}
```

Next, we will implement the output stream to write files to the object. We extend the `java.io.OutputStream` package and override the abstract methods. As with the input stream, we have a bunch of private variables such as `AmazonS3Client`, the Hadoop `Configuration`, and the backing `OutputStream` object. The strategy here is to write to a local file, and when the stream is closed, the file is uploaded onto S3. To facilitate writing to the local file, we create the `BufferedOutputStream` and `LocalDirAllocator` objects.

When the client writes to this `OutputStream` object, a temporary file is created and written into using the `BufferedOutputStream` object. The file is created in a local directory based on the specification in the configuration. We use the temporary directory given by the value `hadoop.tmp.dir` in the configuration. The example code is for illustrating the concepts behind extending HDFS and cannot be used as is in production. For example, cleanup of the temporary directories has to be done manually. Also, we use the same backing filename, `temp`, which may lead to thread safety issues in multithreaded environments.

A constructor is used to create the temporary file in the local directory. BufferedOutputStream is also initialized. The write and flush overrides are operations on BufferedOutputStream. The close method override is where we upload the file from the local store to S3. The PutObjectRequest S3 class is used to specify the properties of the object that needs to be uploaded to S3. The AmazonS3Client object is then used to upload the local file:

```
private class S3NFsOutputStream extends OutputStream{

    private OutputStream localFileStream;
    private AmazonS3Client s3Client;
    private LocalDirAllocator localDirAllocator;
    private Configuration configuration;
    private File backingFile;
    private BufferedOutputStream bufferedOutputStream;
    private String bucket;
    private String key;


    public S3NFsOutputStream(AmazonS3Client s3, Configuration
        conf, String bucket, String key) throws IOException{
        super();
        this.s3Client = s3;
        this.configuration = conf;
        this.localDirAllocator = new
            LocalDirAllocator("${hadoop.tmp.dir}/s3mh");

        this.backingFile =
            localDirAllocator.createTmpFileForWrite("temp",
                LocalDirAllocator.SIZE_UNKNOWN, conf);
        this.bufferedOutputStream = new
            BufferedOutputStream(new
                FileOutputStream(this.backingFile));
        this.bucket = bucket;
        this.key = key;
    }


    @Override
    public void write(int b) throws IOException {
        this.bufferedOutputStream.write(b);
    }

    @Override
    public void write(byte[] b) throws IOException {
```

```
                this.bufferedOutputStream.write(b);
        }


        @Override
        public void write(byte[] b, int off, int len) throws
            IOException {
            this.bufferedOutputStream.write(b, off, len);
        }


        @Override
        public void flush() throws IOException {
            if(this.bufferedOutputStream != null){
                this.bufferedOutputStream.flush();
            }
        }


        @Override
        public void close() throws IOException {

            if(this.bufferedOutputStream != null){
                this.bufferedOutputStream.close();
            }


            try {
                PutObjectRequest putObjectRequest = new
                    PutObjectRequest(bucket, key, backingFile);
                putObjectRequest.setCannedAcl(CannedAccessControlList.
Private);

                s3Client.putObject(putObjectRequest);
            }
            catch(AmazonServiceException ase){
                ase.printStackTrace();
            }


        }
    }


}
```

Now we can extend the `FileSystem` class and implement the override methods. The following code snippet gives the class declaration and the `initialize` method override. The `initialize` method takes in the `URI` of the file or directory and the Hadoop `Configuration` object. It then constructs the `AmazonS3Client` based on the access and secret keys present within the configuration. To recall, the configuration values are taken from `core-site.xml` and its override files.

We define `fs.s3mh.access.key` as the property name that contains the access key and `fs.s3mh.secret.key` as the property name whose value contains the secret key. We use the `BasicAWSCredentials` object to encapsulate the credentials before constructing the `AmazonS3Client` object.

The `getScheme` and `getUri` methods are overridden. We use the scheme for our filesystem implementation as `s3mh`. Our filesystem class itself is called `S3NFileSystem`, indicating that we will use the Amazon S3 native object model:

```
package MasteringHadoop;

import com.amazonaws.AmazonServiceException;
import com.amazonaws.auth.BasicAWSCredentials;
import com.amazonaws.services.s3.AmazonS3Client;
import com.amazonaws.services.s3.model.*;
import org.apache.hadoop.conf.Configuration;
import org.apache.hadoop.fs.*;
import org.apache.hadoop.fs.permission.FsPermission;
import org.apache.hadoop.util.Progressable;

import java.io.*;
import java.net.URI;
import java.util.ArrayList;

public class S3NFileSystem extends FileSystem {

    private URI uri;
    private AmazonS3Client s3Client;
    private Configuration configuration;
    private String bucket;

    public S3NFileSystem(){
        super();
    }

    @Override
```

```
public void initialize(URI name, Configuration conf) throws
    IOException {

    super.initialize(name, conf);
    this.uri = URI.create(name.getScheme() + "://" +
        name.getAuthority());

    String accessKey = conf.get("fs.s3mh.access.key");
    String secretKey = conf.get("fs.s3mh.secret.key");

    System.out.println("Access Key: "  + accessKey);

    s3Client = new AmazonS3Client(new
        BasicAWSCredentials(accessKey, secretKey));

    this.bucket = name.getHost();

    if(!s3Client.doesBucketExist(this.bucket)){
        throw new IOException("Bucket " + this.bucket + " does
            not exist!");
    }

    this.configuration = conf;


}

@Override
public String getScheme() {
    return "s3mh";

}

@Override
public URI getUri() {
    return uri;
}
```

Next, we override the open, create, and delete methods. We do not support append and rename. In S3, rename is implemented by doing a copy followed by the delete operation. The open method returns the FSDataInputStream object, whose class implementation we saw previously. S3 has a concept of folders, but folders do not translate into actual objects in the filesystem and will have a length of 0. The length parameter for the custom implementation of the FSDataInputStream object is obtained from the getFileStatus method. The delete method deletes a file object from S3. For directories, the delete call is ignored, as they are pseudo-objects:

```
@Override
public FSDataInputStream open(Path path, int i) throws
    IOException {
    FileStatus fs = getFileStatus(path);
    return new FSDataInputStream(new
        S3NFsInputStream(this.s3Client, this.configuration,
            this.bucket, pathToKey(path), fs.getLen())));
}


@Override
public FSDataOutputStream create(Path path, FsPermission
    fsPermission, boolean b, int i, short i2, long l,
        Progressable progressable) throws IOException {
    String key = pathToKey(path);
    return new FSDataOutputStream(new
        S3NFsOutputStream(this.s3Client, this.configuration,
            this.bucket, key), null);
}


@Override
public FSDataOutputStream append(Path path, int i,
    Progressable progressable) throws IOException {
    throw new IOException("Append functionality is not
        supported");
}


@Override
public boolean rename(Path path, Path path2) throws
    IOException {
    throw new IOException("Rename is copy followed by
        delete");
}


@Override
```

```
public boolean delete(Path path, boolean b) throws IOException
    {

    FileStatus fs = getFileStatus(path);

    if(b){
        throw new PathIOException("Recursive delete is not
supported");
    }

    if(!fs.isDirectory()){
        s3Client.deleteObject(this.bucket, pathToKey(path));
    }

    return false;
}
```

The listStatus override lists all the objects at a given path as illustrated in the following code snippet. A ListObjectRequest object is created and AmazonS3Client is used to retrieve the object summaries. The metadata is extracted and then stored in a FileStatus object before it is returned. AWS can list objects in batches. In this example, we use a batch file of size 1,000. If the number of objects is greater than this number, the first 1,000 objects are fetched. In actual production code, all objects are retrieved in batches.

The other important override method is the getFileStatus method. It takes in a path and returns a single FileStatus object for that path. The path can be a folder or a file. Helper methods are also used, such as pathToKey, which returns keys from a path object, and isADirectory, which checks whether an object is a directory or not based on its name and size:

```
@Override
public FileStatus[] listStatus(Path path) throws
    FileNotFoundException, IOException {

    ArrayList<FileStatus> returnList = new ArrayList<>();
    String key = pathToKey(path);
    FileStatus fs = getFileStatus(path);
    if(fs.isDirectory()){

        if(!key.isEmpty()){
            key = key + "/";
        }
```

```
            ListObjectsRequest listObjectsRequest = new
                ListObjectsRequest(this.bucket, key,
                    null, "/", 1000);
            ObjectListing objectListing =
                s3Client.listObjects(listObjectsRequest);

            for(S3ObjectSummary summary :
                objectListing.getObjectSummaries()){

                FileStatus fileStatus;
                if(isADirectory(summary.getKey(),
                    summary.getSize())){
                    fileStatus = new FileStatus(summary.getSize(),
                        true, 1, 0, 0, new Path("/" + key));
                }
                else{
                    fileStatus = new FileStatus(summary.getSize(),
                        false, 1, 0, 0, new Path("/" + key));
                }

                returnList.add(fileStatus);

            }

        }
        else{
            returnList.add(fs);
        }

        return returnList.toArray(new
            FileStatus[returnList.size()]);
    }


    @Override
    public void setWorkingDirectory(Path path) {}
@Override
    public Path getWorkingDirectory() {return null; }
    @Override
    public boolean mkdirs(Path path, FsPermission fsPermission)
        throws IOException { return false;}
    @Override
    public FileStatus getFileStatus(Path path) throws IOException
    {
```

```
            String key = pathToKey(path);
            System.out.println("Key : " + key);
            System.out.println("Bucket : " + this.bucket)   ;
            if(key.isEmpty()){
                throw new IOException("File not found.");
            }
            ObjectMetadata objectMetadata =
                s3Client.getObjectMetadata(this.bucket, key);
            if(isADirectory(key, objectMetadata.getContentLength())){
                return new FileStatus(0, true, 1, 0, 0, path);
            }
    return new FileStatus(0, false, 1, 0,
        objectMetadata.getLastModified().getTime(), path);
        }


        private String pathToKey(Path path) {
            return path.toUri().getPath().substring(1);
        }

        private boolean isADirectory(String name, long size) {
            return !name.isEmpty()
                    && name.charAt(name.length() - 1) == '/'
                    && size == 0L;
        }
```

Once all the code snippets are compiled and made into a JAR file, the JAR file can be placed in the HDFS library directory. The following snippet shows the configuration information that needs to go into the `core-site.xml` file in order to indicate the JAR file for the filesystem driver, as well as other credential information required by the implementation. Any HDFS command can now be executed, with the path indicating the `s3mh` scheme used to invoke this `FileSystem` implementation:

```
<!-- omit for IAM role based authentication -->
<property>
  <name>fs.s3mh.access.key</name>
  <value><!-- Your Amazon AWS key --></value>
</property>

<!-- omit for IAM role based authentication -->
<property>
  <name>fs.s3mh.secret.key</name>
```

```
    <value><!—Your Amazon AWS Secret à</value>
  </property>

  <!-- necessary for Hadoop to load our filesystem driver -->
  <property>
    <name>fs.s3mh.impl</name>
    <value>MasteringHadoop.S3NFileSystem</value>
  </property>
```

Summary

HDFS is a great filesystem for MapReduce workloads. But its sequential access pattern and non-compliance with POSIX interfaces make it tedious to work with in certain situations. Hadoop allows its users to extend HDFS or provide drop-in replacements. The key takeaways from this chapter are as follows:

- There are a number of implementations that extend or provide drop-in replacements for HDFS. CephFS, MapRFS, GPFS from IBM, and Cassandra by DataStax are some examples of such extensions.

- Interface to the Amazon S3 storage service is available out of the box in Hadoop. Both a native-storage S3 filesystem interface and a block-storage filesystem interface are available.

- Extending Hadoop to incorporate other filesystems is done by extending the FileSystem abstract base class. The FSDataInputStream and FSDataOutputStream objects are used to wrap the input and output streams of the underlying filesystem respectively.

- The security and access control mechanisms of the underlying filesystem can be left intact within Hadoop by allowing configurations to be specified via the Hadoop Configuration files and classes.

In the next chapter, we will continue our study of HDFS by looking at the federation aspects of HDFS and how it changed when it moved from Hadoop 1.X to 2.X.

10
HDFS Federation

The NameNode component of HDFS was the central point of failure in the initial versions of Hadoop. In the later versions, a secondary NameNode was introduced as a backup for the primary NameNode. Until Hadoop 2.X, the NameNode component could only handle a single namespace, making it less scalable and difficult to isolate in a multitenant HDFS environment. Scalability and isolation were the two most desired requirements for Hadoop enterprise deployments. Most organizations shared infrastructure among their different teams with varying degrees of availability and authorization aspirations.

HDFS Federation is a feature that enables Hadoop to have multiple namespaces, making it easy to use for shared cluster scenarios. This feature brings about a separation between the storage and namespace management. Similar to YARN, this separation helps onboard other applications and use cases on to HDFS, making Hadoop move away from a MapReduce-only platform to a more generic cluster-computing platform.

In this chapter, we will be:

- Looking at the necessity behind HDFS Federation
- Studying HDFS Federation and its architecture
- Understanding the steps to deploy federated NameNodes
- Understanding backup and recovery options for the active NameNode
- Studying the strategies and commands that support NameNode high availability
- Looking into some useful tools and commands in HDFS
- Looking into HDFS block placement strategies in the MapReduce environment

Limitations of the older HDFS architecture

The older HDFS architecture had two main components, which are as follows:

- **Namespace**: This is the HDFS component that handles building blocks such as directories, files, and the actual file blocks. The Namespace component supports the create, delete, list, and update/modify operations on these building blocks. The Namespace component is within the NameNode daemon.

- **Block Storage Service**: This is the HDFS component that handles file block management. The block storage component is divided between the NameNode and DataNode. The DataNode part of the block storage service takes care of block storage on the local machine in a cluster. It provides read and write services for the blocks. The NameNode part of the block storage performs the following actions:

    ○ Taking care of DataNode registrations, monitoring, and health reports.

    ○ Digesting block reports from DataNodes and storing the location of the file blocks in memory.

    ○ Dealing with the create, delete, list, and update operations at the block level. As we saw earlier, at the file level, the Namespace component performs these operations.

    ○ Facilitating replica placement algorithms and heuristics. It can manage the placement of replicated blocks. It can also replicate underreplicated blocks and delete overreplicated ones.

The following diagram illustrates the older HDFS architecture:

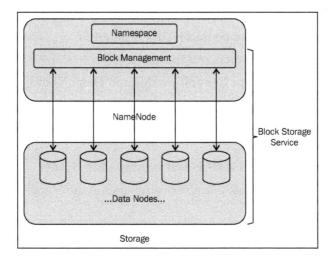

This architecture has a number of limitations, which are as follows:

- From the figure, it is apparent that the block storage service component intrudes into the NameNode. This leads to tight coupling between the Namespace and Block Management Service components. All block management functions need to go through the NameNode. The DataNodes are not capable of being an independent block storage service.

- The architecture allows for a single NameNode. This NameNode stores all directories, files, and block-level metadata in memory. Unlike the DataNodes, the NameNode cannot be scaled horizontally. It has to be scaled vertically by adding more memory to the machine where the NameNode runs. The memory of the NameNode becomes the limiting factor behind the scalability of the cluster.

- With a single NameNode, about 60K tasks can be managed within the cluster. However, with changes in the Hadoop stack and the introduction of YARN, this can go up to 100K tasks and beyond. This kind of task explosion puts a lot of pressure on the request servicing capabilities of the NameNode. A single NameNode might not be able to handle so many requests without adversely affecting the performance of the tasks.

- Larger organizations require a certain degree of isolation between the different teams within them. The reasons for isolation can be for confidentiality, performance, or availability reasons. A single Namespace will not satisfactorily guarantee any of the three reasons. A shared Namespace requires rigorous security measures. Performance and availability depend a lot on the other workloads that are already running on the cluster.

The preceding limitations call for the separation of the Namespace from the Block Storage service component. They also call for a capability to run many instances of the NameNode, particularly in multitenant environments. Horizontal scaling of the NameNode will also help in performance by load balancing.

Architecture of HDFS Federation

The crux of the HDFS Federation feature is that it allows for multiple NameNodes to run on a cluster. These NameNodes are independent and do not have any dependency on each other. However, the DataNodes are shared between all the NameNodes in the system. The NameNodes are said to be federated because they can be run independently without coordination.

Each DataNode sends heartbeats and block report information to all the NameNodes in the cluster. DataNodes also receive instructions from all the NameNodes. They are the common shared storage resource in the cluster and still run on commodity hardware. However, they cater to different NameNodes, and in turn, facilitate different Namespaces. These independent Namespaces provide isolation guarantees in a multitenant environment. By running many NameNodes, the cluster can be horizontally scaled and requests can be load-balanced among these NameNodes.

The following diagram shows the architecture of a federated HDFS cluster:

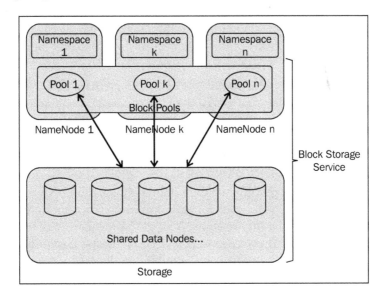

A concept called **block pools** is used to provide block federation. A block pool is a set of blocks that belong to a single NameNode. DataNodes store blocks that can potentially belong to different block pools. Each block pool is independent and management of one block pool does not affect any other block pools. The Namespace based on its block pool can independently generate Block IDs.

A Namespace, along with its block pool, is termed as the **Namespace Volume**. When a NameNode is decommissioned or a Namespace is deleted, DataNodes delete all the blocks related to the block pool that belongs to the Namespace Volume.

Another parameter, **ClusterId**, is used to identify all the nodes in the cluster. Any new NameNode joining the cluster is given a Cluster ID to correctly identify the cluster to which it belongs. This parameter can either be specified manually or generated automatically. The default behavior is to automatically generate this ID.

Benefits of HDFS Federation

HDFS Federation overcomes the limitations of a single NameNode and provides the following benefits:

- The most important benefit is the horizontal scalability it provides for the NameNode. Clusters with a large number of smaller files benefit immensely from this. Every file occupies memory in the NameNode to store its metadata. The Namespace can now be divided into many Namespaces, either based on function or organizational divisions. The load can now be distributed across many NameNodes rather than a single NameNode.

- Read-and-write throughput scaling is a benefit that is hindered with a single NameNode. Organizations can now divide the Namespace among different NameNodes and keep the throughputs at a desirable level. Information about the kind of workloads that run on the cluster can be used to determine the number of NameNodes that will be required in a federated HDFS deployment.

- Having different NameNodes and Namespaces makes it natural and easy for isolation. Organizations can now isolate different organizational datasets. NameNodes can also be divided based on functions such as development, test, or production. All of the data can be multiplexed onto a bunch of DataNodes promoting efficient sharing. The isolation property ensures that the NameNode does not become the performance bottleneck when jobs of varying needs are executed on the cluster. For example, a job that overloads the NameNode need not affect another job if the data required by them reside in different Namespaces.

- The Federation feature also makes it possible to treat the Block Storage Service as a generic block store. The block pool abstraction can be used to build newer filesystems or HDFS APIs with different characteristics. This generic nature of storage can save costs for the enterprise by increasing the efficiency of existing hardware in their clusters.

- A side effect of the HDFS Federation architecture's simplicity is the backward compatibility of the feature. Existing single-NameNode deployments do not break. They are a special case of the federated approach. Most of the code that change to the Hadoop implementation to support this feature actually happened on the DataNode. This helped in keeping the entire NameNode stable from a Hadoop testing perspective. The DataNode has an additional level of indirection, indicating the block pool where the block belongs.

Deploying federated NameNodes

In this section, we'll see how to deploy multiple NameNodes. To try out these steps, you will need at least two machines with different addresses. The configuration for federated deployment is backward compatible. It supports previous installations with a single NameNode.

To support federation, **NameServiceId** is introduced. The secondary backup and checkpoint nodes belong to a particular NameServiceId. The NameServiceId is suffixed to all the properties of the NameNode and its associated components when specifying in the configuration.

The important configuration steps are as follows:

1. Specifying the NameServiceIds for the different NameNodes in a cluster. This is specified by adding the `dfs.nameservices` property to the configuration. The value of this property is a comma-separated list of all the NameServiceIds.

2. All the other properties that are specified for a particular NameNode should be prefixed with an appropriate NameServiceId. This should be one of the NameServiceIds specified in the `dfs.nameservices` property.

3. A NameNode can be formatted using `bin/hdfs namenode -format [-clusterid clustered]`. If no `clusterId` is specified, an ID is automatically generated.

4. All additional NameNodes can be formatted using the same command as the preceding one, but the `clusterid` parameter becomes mandatory. If the `clusterid` parameter is not specified, then the NameNodes will not be federated. Now, the command is `bin/hdfs namenode -format -clusterid <specify clusterid that was given in the previous step>`.

5. Older releases of Hadoop can be upgraded to the newer release. After upgrading, the NameNode can be started using `bin/hdfs namenode -config <new configuration directory> -upgrade -clusterid <clusterid>`.

6. Adding another NameNode to the system is simply adding the new configuration parameters for the new NameNode and propagating it throughout the cluster. The important parameters are the NameServiceIds and related NameNode properties using the NameServiceId suffix. The NameNodes are then started. Now, the DataNodes have to be informed about the new NameNode. This is done by the `bin/hdfs dfadmin -refreshNameNode <datanode host and port>` command. This command must be executed for all DataNodes that form the block storage layer for the new NameNode.

The following snippet shows a sample `hdfs-site.xml` configuration file that supports two NameNodes. The NameServiceIds are `ns1` and `ns2`:

```
<property>
  <name>dfs.namenode.name.dir.ns1</name>
  <value>[path to namenode store]</value>
  <description>Path on the local filesystem where the NameNode
      stores the namespace and transaction logs
          persistently.</description>
</property>
<property>
  <name>dfs.namenode.name.dir.ns2</name>
  <value>[path to namenode store]</value>
  <description>Path on the local filesystem where the NameNode
      stores the namespace and transaction logs
          persistently.</description>
</property>
<property>
  <name>dfs.nameservices</name>
  <value>ns1,ns2</value>
</property>
<property>
  <name>dfs.namenode.rpc-address.ns1</name>
  <value>[ip:port]</value>
</property>
<property>
  <name>dfs.namenode.http-address.ns1</name>
  <value>[ip:port]</value>
</property>
<property>
  <name>dfs.namenode.secondaryhttp-address.ns1</name>
  <value>[ip:port]</value>
</property>
<property>
  <name>dfs.namenode.rpc-address.ns2</name>
  <value>[ip:port]</value>
</property>
<property>
  <name>dfs.namenode.http-address.ns2</name>
  <value>[ip:port]</value>
</property>
<property>
  <name>dfs.namenode.secondaryhttp-address.ns2</name>
  <value>[ip:port]</value>
</property>
```

HDFS high availability

NameNodes are the heart of an HDFS Namespace. The availability of any cluster using HDFS is directly related to the availability of the NameNode.

Secondary NameNode, Checkpoint Node, and Backup Node

In Hadoop 1.X, the concept of a **Secondary NameNode** was introduced. The Secondary NameNode is a shield against disasters. On the failure of a NameNode, the Secondary NameNode can be used to recover the NameNode. The term Secondary NameNode is a misnomer. It is a cold standby and cannot service requests on its own. The NameNode can, however, read from the Secondary NameNode when encountered with failures.

The NameNode writes all HDFS updates to the `edits` log in the native filesystem. The log is written in an append-only fashion. The NameNode owns another file called the `fsimage` file that contains the image of HDFS. A NameNode starting up, reads the `edits` file and applies all the edits one by one to the `fsimage` file. During this time, no writes are allowed on HDFS. The NameNode is said to be in **Safe Mode**. The Safe Mode ends once the NameNode receives block reports from the DataNodes about the health of the blocks. Writes are allowed only after the NameNode is confident about the health of HDFS. Before starting normal service, the NameNode begins with an empty `edits` file and an updated `fsimage` file.

The longer a NameNode runs, the bigger its `edits` file. This directly translates to longer startup times for the NameNode when it is restarted. The Secondary NameNode periodically takes the `fsimage` and `edits` files and merges them. Generally, to maximize the probability of recovery from a disaster, the Secondary NameNode is run on a different machine. The NameNode can query the Secondary NameNode for the `fsimage` and `edits` files when recovering from a failure. The Secondary NameNode mimics the directory structure of the NameNode when storing checkpoints. This makes it easy for the NameNode to read data when recovering from failures.

The concept of a **Checkpoint Node** is also introduced. It is very similar in function to the Secondary NameNode, with an additional function. Periodically, the Checkpoint Node not only gets the `fsimage` and `edits` file updates from the NameNode, but also folds the edits into the `fsimage` file and uploads it back on to the NameNode. This helps the NameNode to recover fast from failures. The Checkpoint Node can be considered as the Secondary NameNode with a feature to upload the updates back to the NameNode. Again, the checkpoints are stored in the same directory structure as the NameNode.

The Checkpoint Node is started using the following command:

```
hdfs namenode -checkpoint
```

The `dfs.namenode.backup.address` and `dfs.namenode.backup.http-address` properties in the configuration are used to specify the location of the Checkpoint Node and its HTTP endpoint.

A **Backup Node** is more live than the Checkpoint Node and the Secondary NameNode. It streams in updates from the NameNode and updates its own copy of the `fsimage` and `edits` files. The Checkpoint Node and the Secondary NameNode, on the other hand, download the `fsimage` and `edits` files from the active NameNode. A Checkpoint Node is not allowed to run along with a Backup Node. The memory requirements of the Backup Node are the same as that of the NameNode as it stores all information that a NameNode would store.

The Backup Node is started using the following command:

```
hdfs namenode -backup
```

The configuration parameters for the Backup Node are the same as that of the Checkpoint Node.

High availability – edits sharing

In *Chapter 1, Hadoop 2.X*, we briefly saw how to provide NameNode high availability using the Quorum Journal Manager and the NFS strategy. Having a hot standby, a NameNode that can instantly switch over to becoming an active NameNode, is the key to ensure **High Availability (HA)**. The standby node maintains enough information about the active NameNode so that it can provide fast failover. The standby can also perform check-pointing to aid in disaster recovery.

The general strategy behind HA of the NameNode is to share the `edits` file between the active and standby NameNodes. The Quorum Journal Manager is a way to do this using an array of Journal nodes. An NFS share can also be used to achieve the same result.

Hadoop supports the following two failover modes:

- **Manual failover**: Here, the administrator of the Hadoop cluster can execute commands to make the standby active. Since this is a deterministic action, the time for the standby to become active is a matter of about 5 seconds. The command used is as follows:

```
hdfs haadmin -failover <standby-namenode> <active-namenode>
```

- **Automatic failover**: When there are systems in place to monitor the health of the active NameNode, the monitoring system might find enough evidence to do an automatic switch between the active and standby NameNodes. This is based on heuristics, and the failover process might take a few seconds longer (order of tens of seconds). Zookeeper is a tool that can help in automatic failover along with the ZKFailoverController module.

If there is a failure in the ZKFailoverController module, there is a possibility that both NameNodes, active and standby, will think that they are in the active state. This scenario is called the *split-brain* scenario. A split-brain scenario can leave the Namespace in an inconsistent state as both NameNodes can make conflicting changes. The solution to this problem is to have the active NameNode stop making changes to the system. The QJM strategy for failover has fencing built in as there is an array of Journal nodes that allow writing only from a single NameNode.

Useful HDFS tools

A number of useful tools are provided to check the health of HDFS. These tools are as follows:

- **Rebalancer**: The distribution of blocks among the DataNodes might not be uniform. These skews in distribution appear when new DataNodes are commissioned in the cluster. To help administrators view the distribution and redistribute the blocks, a `balancer` option is available in the Hadoop command, as shown:

```
hadoop balancer [-threshold threshold]
```

- **fsck**: Like the native filesystem, the `fsck` command goes through the files in the filesystem and provides a report on the health of the blocks and files. Unlike the `fsck` utility of the native filesystem, the Hadoop `fsck` tool takes no action. It is purely a reporting tool. Most of the errors in HDFS are generally taken care of by Hadoop:

```
hadoop fsck
```

- **Import checkpoint**: It is possible for the NameNode to import checkpoints from the Backup or Checkpoint Node. All these nodes store the checkpoints in the same directory structure as the NameNode. This can be achieved by configuring the `dfs.namenode.checkpoint.dir` property to the directory where the checkpoint resides, and using the `-importcheckpoint` flag when starting the NameNode.

Three-layer versus four-layer network topology

Traditionally, Hadoop topologies follow a three-layer architecture, as shown in the following diagram. The leaves of the hierarchy are the data nodes. Data nodes are combined into racks and racks form the data center. A Hadoop cluster can also span multiple data centers connected via a WAN.

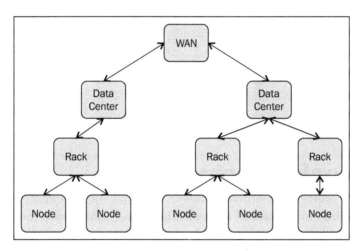

With the advent of virtualization, a single physical machine can now run multiple nodes as virtual machines. This leads to an additional layer in the Hadoop topology. This layer is called the Nodegroup layer. All virtual machines running on the same physical machine belong to a single Nodegroup. In other words, a Nodegroup is per hypervisor. Communication between nodes in a Nodegroup does not have to go through the network and can give rise to some interesting block placement policies. The following diagram illustrates the four-layer architecture:

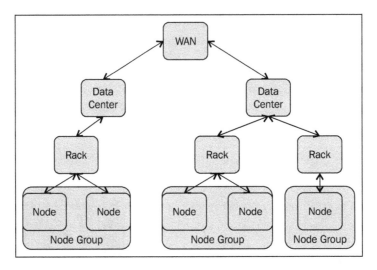

HDFS block placement

Replication is an important feature in HDFS; it ensures data reliability against loss and high availability in the face of failures. The default replication factor is 3, though this parameter can be tuned using the dfs.replication configuration parameter. HDFS does not replicate the file as a whole; rather, it chunks the file into fixed size blocks and stores it across the cluster.

The replication factor can be specified at file creation time. It can be changed as and when desired. The salient feature of HDFS is the smart placement of blocks, and this feature distinguishes it from other distributed filesystems. The placement policy is said to be rack-aware, that is, it is cognizant of the physical location of where the block resides. This not only aids in fault tolerance but can also be instrumental in making network bandwidth utilization efficient. Any computing paradigm running on HDFS can make use of this information to minimize the amount of data that needs to be moved across the network.

A rack is a bunch of machines stacked up. Generally, a single switch serves all the machines in a single rack. A data center is made of many such racks. The intra-rack network bandwidth is higher than the inter-rack network bandwidth. Therefore, it is potentially faster to move data within the same rack than between racks.

The NameNode is aware of the rack on which the DataNode resides. When placing replicas of a single block, the NameNode can decide which rack each block should reside in. To increase fault tolerance, the NameNode might decide to place each replica of a block in a separate rack. This helps in load balancing and data loss on rack failures. However, writing a block can take additional time as it has to span different racks.

The default rack placement policy, when the replication factor is 3, is to place a replica on a node in a rack, the second replica on a different node on the same rack, and the third replica on a node in a separate rack altogether. Generally, during a write, the first block is written on the same node as the client (for clients within the cluster). The next two blocks are written on the same random node off-rack. This helps in increasing write throughput as the writes are local. It does suffer a certain amount of skew as two-thirds of the replicas reside on the same rack. However, it again does not affect reliability and availability as the probability of rack failure is much less than the probability of a node failure. In the rare scenario of a rack failure, there is an additional copy on a different rack that can come to the rescue. If the client is not present on the cluster, a random first node is chosen to write the first copy of the block.

When a read is initiated, the NameNode tries to point the reader to the node that is closest to it. The hierarchy of selection in order of preference is to first try something on the same node as the reader first; if it is not present, it tries to get a read replica from the same rack as the reader. If it is not present in the same rack, it goes to another rack in the same data center, before moving on to another data center.

The block placement policies are now pluggable in Hadoop 2.X. This enhancement was done as a fix for ticket HDFS-385.

Pluggable block placement policy

HDFS now provides a pluggable block placement policy. This can be achieved by overriding the `BlockPlacementPolicy` abstract class in the `org.apache.hadoop.hdfs.server.blockmanagement` package. This abstract class has a few override methods. The `chooseTarget` override tells HDFS the placement choices. The `chooseReplicaToDelete` override is used to decide whether deleting a specific replica makes all the blocks conform to the block placement policy. There is a third override, `verifyBlockPlacement`, which verifies whether the block is present in `minRacks`. An `initialize` method is also provided to set up private variables of the `BlockPlacementPolicy` object.

Once the class derived by `BlockPlacementPolicy` is created, it is built into a JAR. The JAR can be placed in the Hadoop classpath. Hadoop then needs to be informed about the new block-placement policy. Introducing a property in the `hdfs-site.xml` file does this. A configuration property with the `dfs.block.replicator.classname` key is created, whose value contains the fully qualified class name of the `BlockPlacementPolicy` custom class, as shown in the following config file snippet:

```
<property>
    <name>dfs.block.replicator.classname</name>
    <value><Fully qualified class name of the custom block
        placement implementation class</value>
</property>
```

Out of the box, Hadoop has two block-placement-policy-derived classes that can be used. They are as follows:

- The `BlockPlacementPolicyDefault` class that provides a policy as discussed in this section
- The `BlockPlacementPolicyWithNodeGroup` class that deals with topologies that have the Nodegroup layer

Summary

Hadoop is made of the compute and storage layers. The compute layer has been replaced by YARN in Hadoop 2.X, helping other paradigms to co-exist on the Hadoop cluster hardware. The storage layer is making rapid progress towards a similar goal. Features such as HDFS Federation are one step closer in making the storage layer generic. By loosely coupling Block Storage from the Namespace, this can become a reality soon.

The key takeaways from this chapter are as follows:

- With HDFS Federation, it is possible to run multiple NameNodes. This not only helps in isolation, but it can also aid in performance by load balancing. Horizontal scaling of the NameNode is easier.

- Block pools are the abstractions that facilitate federation. Blocks from a single Namespace belong to a single pool. Each pool is given an identifier for addressability. The DataNodes remain shared among the different NameNodes.

- In Hadoop 2.X, there are a number of different options to ensure NameNode recovery from failures. Secondary NameNodes were the only option previously. Now, there are Checkpoint and Backup Nodes. All three strategies preserve the NameNodes directory structure and can be used by the NameNode to recover.

- The modern virtualized data center takes a four-layered approach for the Hadoop network topology. Communication between different nodes on the same physical hardware does not need to go over the network and can help optimize block placements.

- HDFS allows for pluggable block-placement strategies by overriding the `BlockPlacementPolicy` abstract class.

Hadoop and data security are important aspects of Hadoop. In this chapter, we saw isolation as one way to ensure separation of concerns. However, this does not suffice in large organizations with regulatory compliance requirements on data. More rigorous data security safeguards are required. We will look at Hadoop security in the next chapter.

11
Hadoop Security

Data is an asset to any organization. In this millennium, large companies such as Google have shown that gathering data and analyzing it can in itself be a product that can lead to an extremely successful business. This demonstration led to an explosion in data-driven decision-making for businesses and personalized experiences for the consumer. Data essentially became a high-value property for an organization. Just like any other asset, data needs to be protected.

Data security is the area that looks into protection of data. Security threats to data can come from outside the organization or from within it. Data theft is one of the highest reported cyber crimes. Recent studies have shown that data security threats are more common from within the organization, either by disgruntled personnel or inadvertently by benign users. A security feature such as authorization has become a baseline security feature for any data product.

In this chapter, we will look at the following topics:

- The security pillars
- Authentication in Hadoop
- Authorization in Hadoop
- Data confidentiality in Hadoop
- Audit logging in Hadoop

The security pillars

The four pillars of data security are as follows:

- **Authentication**: This refers to challenging a system or user to prove their identity. Only authenticated identities are allowed to gain access into the data system. Authentication in Hadoop can be of two major kinds, simple authentication and pseudo-authentication. The former is a loose kind of security where trust is placed on the user's assertion about their identity. In the latter, systems such as Kerberos are used for authenticating a user. In the industry, the latter is recommended as a best practice. Hadoop even supports seamless integration with a number of user stores such as LDAP and Active Directory. With the help of these stores, Kerberos can be implemented as an authentication mechanism.

- **Authorization**: Authorization refers to granting authenticated users access to data resources. In a multitenant system, or a multiteam organization sharing a single data cluster, policies, compliance, and regulatory norms might prohibit one team from accessing data belonging to another team. In such situations, it is very important to fence sensitive data resources from inadvertent or malicious access. Hadoop supports authorization at different levels. In HDFS, Hadoop provides fine-grained access control at the file level. The access control is very similar to any UNIX-based filesystem. The MapReduce compute layer also has **Access Control Lists (ACLs)** at a resource level. Hadoop services are allowed to have their own authorization features. For example, Hive tables can be protected using coarse-grained access control mechanisms, as in SQL.

- **Auditing**: Auditing is a mechanism to look into the usage patterns of a data system. A fundamental requirement to conduct any audit is to provide an accounting feature. All accesses and manipulations need to be recorded in an audit log to audit at a later point in time. Auditing is important to ensure compliance within an enterprise. Routine audits are conducted to ensure compliance with data policies. Some situations might call for ad hoc auditing, particularly when a security breach has happened in the system. Auditing can reveal forensic information that can help penalize the guilty and estimate the extent of damage caused by the breach. At the platform level, Hadoop supports auditing. At a service level, services such as Hive record all user-related actions in the metastore.

- **Data protection**: Big data systems are distributed across a number of machines. This mandates for the movement of data from one node to another. It might also involve storing data in untrusted domains, such as the cloud, for example. These two scenarios can lead to compromises in privacy and confidentiality. During transit, a man in the middle can sniff out the data that is being sent across the wire. An extremely malicious attacker can even manipulate the data. At rest, an untrusted party can snoop the data or modify it. Protection against such attacks can be done through cryptographic techniques. Data can be encrypted during transit and when at rest. Digital signatures can be generated to protect the data against modifications. Hadoop transports can be encrypted to ensure confidentiality over the wire. OS-level encryption can be used to protect confidentiality of HDFS data when at rest.

Hadoop addresses all these pillars to a satisfactory extent. We will look at some of these pillars in depth.

Authentication in Hadoop

Authentication in Hadoop can either be simple or in Kerberos. Hadoop also allows you to have your custom authentication scheme. In this section, we will look at Kerberos authentication and how the HTTP Hadoop interfaces can be secured via authentication.

Kerberos authentication

Kerberos is a network authentication protocol. It uses cryptography to provide a highly secure authentication mechanism. This authentication mechanism is popular because of its features, which are as follows:

- **Mutual authentication**: Both the client and server can mutually authenticate each other before proceeding with a session.

- **Single login per session**: Once a login happens, tokens with certain time validities are issued for usage. The duration of token validity defines the maximum length of the session.

- **Protocol message encryption**: All protocol messages during authentication are encrypted. It is not possible to conduct any man-in-the-middle or replay attacks by an adversary.

The Kerberos architecture and workflow

Central to Kerberos is the Kerberos **Key Distribution Center (KDC)**. The KDC has the following two important components:

- The **Authentication Server (AS)**
- The **Ticket Granting Server (TGS)**

The Authentication Server is responsible for authenticating the validity of clients. The Ticket Granting Server is the one that issues tokens or tickets that are time-bound cryptographic messages, which can be used by the grantee to authenticate itself.

The following diagram shows the general protocol workflow when a client authenticates using Kerberos:

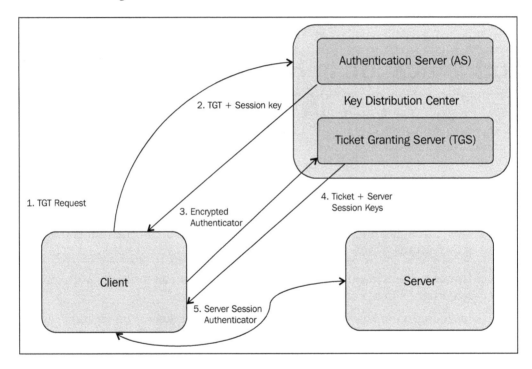

The authentication steps are as follows:

1. The protocol starts with the client requesting a **Ticket Granting Ticket (TGT)** with the AS in Kerberos.

2. The AS checks for the client in its database and sends back two messages. The first message is a session key, and the second is a TGT. Both messages are encrypted using the client's password as the key. The client can use the session key and the TGT only if the passwords match with what is stored by the AS.

3. A client wanting to access a service has to first go to the TGS with its identity. To prove its authenticity, the client has to send an authenticator encrypted by the session key that was received by it from the AS.

4. The TGS receives this request, decrypts it, and checks for validity of the client and request. On successful validation, the TGS grants a ticket with a validity period. A server session key is also returned to the client. The server session key comes in two copies—one encrypted with the client's secret and the other with the server's secret.

5. The client now presents the ticket, server session keys, and authenticator to the service that it needs access to. The server hosting the service validates the session key and grants access based on the result of the validation. If mutual authentication is desired, the server too sends back an authenticator that the client can check for validity. This is possible because the session key comes in two copies encrypted using the server and client secrets.

Kerberos authentication and Hadoop

An authenticating client within Hadoop requires a password to conduct the Kerberos authentication workflow. This might not be feasible for long-running MapReduce jobs that extend beyond the ticket validity time period. The `kinit` command can be used to initialize a client with a password in Hadoop. Though a ticket validity might be for a few hours, it is better to put the password in a `keytab` file for long-running jobs.

A `keytab` file can be created using the `ktutil` command. The `keytab` file can be given to the `kinit` command using the `-t` option. The `klist` command can be used to see the different tickets owned by a user. The `kdestroy` command can be used to expire tickets that are no longer in use.

Authentication via HTTP interfaces

By default, all HTTP web endpoints within a Hadoop cluster do not have authentication enabled. This means that anyone who knows the endpoint address can browse through the different services in the cluster. HTTP web interfaces can be explicitly configured to require Kerberos authentication using the HTTP SPNEGO protocol. This protocol is well supported on all major browsers.

Simple authentication can also be enabled. This involves appending the username in the web endpoint address as a query string parameter. The value of this parameter is the identity name of the user. Custom authentication schemes are also possible. All web endpoints within Hadoop support this extensibility as long as the `AuthenticatorHandler` class is overridden appropriately.

To configure HTTP authentication, the following properties in the `core-site.xml` file can be used:

- `hadoop.http.filter.initializers`: The `org.apache.hadoop.security.AuthenticationInitializer` class name needs to be put as the value of this property.

- `hadoop.http.authentication.type`: This property defines the authentication type. It can take the values `simple` or `kerberos`, or the class name of the custom `AuthenticatorHandler` derived class. By default, this is set to `simple`.

- `hadoop.http.authentication.token.validity`: The value of this property indicates the duration of validity of an authentication token. The value is in seconds, and the default is 36,000. After this duration, the token has to be renewed and presented.

- `hadoop.http.authentication.signature.secret.file`: The web endpoint secrets are kept in this file. The secret key is used to provide a digital signature for the authentication tokens.

- `hadoop.http.authentication.cookie.domain`: This is the whitelist of domains from where authentication tokens can be presented via cookies. There is no default value for this property.

- `hadoop.http.authentication.simple.anonymous.allowed`: This permits anonymous users to connect to the HTTP endpoint when set to `true`. The default value is `true`, and this works only when the authentication type is set to `simple`.

- `hadoop.http.authentication.kerberos.principal`: This value indicates the Kerberos principal name to be used when the authentication type is set to `kerberos`.

- `hadoop.http.authentication.kerberos.keytab`: This is the `keytab` file location for the Kerberos principal that is used in the HTTP endpoint.

Authorization in Hadoop

Authorization involves restricting access to resources. Hadoop provides authorization for both HDFS and all Hadoop services. In this section, we will look at how authorization can be enabled in Hadoop to secure shared resources against illegitimate access.

Authorization in HDFS

The HDFS authorization model is very similar to the authorization model in a POSIX system. In POSIX, each resource — files and directories — is associated with an owner user and a group. HDFS is similar to this. Permissions are given to each of these identities separately. There are separate permissions for:

- The owner of the resource
- The users of the group that are associated with the resource
- All other users within the system

There are two permissions levels, read and write. In contrast with POSIX, there is no execute permission on files in HDFS as files are not executables. Any user, or a user belonging to a group that has the read permission `r`, is only allowed to read the contents of a file from HDFS. Similarly, any user, or a user belonging to a group that has write permissions `w`, is allowed to write or append to existing files. A user or group can be given both read and write permissions `rw`.

For directories, the semantics change a bit. A read permission allows the user or users belonging to the group to list the contents of the directory. Write permissions allow the users or groups to create files and directories or append to files residing within the directory. Directories have a special execute permission `x`. This allows the user or group to access the children of a directory.

HDFS files do not have the concept of `setuid` and `setgid`, which are present in POSIX. Again, HDFS files are not executables, and it does not make sense to have these operations. In this case, even directories do not have `setuid` and `setgid`. HDFS directories do allow setting the sticky bit. This prevents any other user, other than the superuser, from manipulating the directory or its contents. However, setting the sticky bit on a file has no effect.

Like in any UNIX-based operating system, permissions are encoded as three octal numbers. The first octal number indicates the `rwx` bits for the owner, the second for the group, and the third for all other users. For example, the following command gives all permissions to the owner, read permissions to the group, and no permissions to other users in the system:

```
hadoop fs -chmod 740 masteringhadoop
```

The set of permissions for a file or directory is called a mode. It can be manipulated using the `chmod` command, which means change mode. When a process creates a file or directory in HDFS, it automatically assumes the identity of the process owner. However, the group is inherited from the parent directory.

A client operating on an HDFS file or directory presents the username and groups the user belongs to. HDFS first matches the username with the owner of the file or directory. If it matches, then a permissions check is done on the resource. If it does not match, a check is done to find out whether the user belongs to the group that is specified by checking the list of groups presented with the group associated with the resource. Again, a match makes a permission check against the requested operation. If both these matches fail, other permissions are checked for the user. If the permissions don't permit the operation in any of the three cases, the operation is rejected.

Identity of an HDFS user

As seen in the overview, Hadoop supports two mechanisms to authenticate a user. This is determined by the value in the `hadoop.security.authentication` property. The values can be of two kinds, which are as follows:

- `Simple`: This indicates that the identity of the user is determined and presented by the OS that runs the client process

- `kerberos`: This indicates that the identity of the user is determined by its Kerberos credentials

A key point to note is that HDFS cannot create, modify, or delete any identities. All identity management happens outside HDFS, either in the OS, as with simple authentication, or with Kerberos. HDFS simply uses the identity presented to it and performs authorization checks on the identity.

Group listings for an HDFS user

The user to group mapping services is determined by the value in the `hadoop.security.group.mapping` property. By default, this value is `org.apache.hadoop.security.ShellBasedUnixGroupsMapping`. When this particular implementation of the group mapping is used, the username is sent to a UNIX shell command to determine the list of groups the user belongs to. For example, with the bash shell, it is as follows:

```
bash -c groups
```

Enterprises can have their own user profile stores such as **Lightweight Directory Access Protocol (LDAP)** or **Active Directory**. In such cases, groups can be determined by asking these directory services for the group members. Hadoop has a built-in group-mapping service to connect to LDAP data stores to determine groups. Setting the `hadoop.security.group.mapping` property to the `org.apache.hadoop.security.LdapGroupsMapping` class does this.

The NameNode is responsible for invoking the appropriate API to determine the groups listing for a particular user. It is then presented to the data nodes. Also, all groups and usernames are stored as strings and not as numbers when compared to UNIX-based systems.

 Revoking permissions in the middle of a client operation lets the client access the blocks of the file that are already known to it.

HDFS APIs and shell commands

All HDFS APIs throw an `AccessControlException` exception on the failure of permission checks. The `FsPermission` class in the `org.apache.hadoop.fs.permission` package is used to encapsulate the necessary permission-related information for a file or directory. `FileStatus` includes the `FsPermission` object. The `getFileStatus` method can be used to get the status of the files.

Additionally, the `FileSystem` class provides a couple of methods to set the mode and owner/group of a file or directory. The signature of the `setPermission` method is given as follows:

```
public void setPermission(Path path, FsPermission permission)
    throws IOException
```

It takes in the `Path` object to the file or directory and the permissions that need to go on it. Similarly, the signature of the `setOwner` method is given as follows:

```
public void setOwner(Path p, String username, String group)
    throws IOException
```

The `setOwner` method takes in the owner and group that need to be set on the file or directory specified in the `Path` object.

A few Shell commands are also present to change the authorization parameters for files and directories. Consider the following command:

```
hdfs chmod [-R] <octal mode> <file path>
```

This command can be used to change the mode of the file or directory. The `octal mode` parameter is given to specify the desired permissions for the owner, group, and others. The `-R` flag can be used to recursively apply the mode on all descendent files and directories until the leaf files or directories. Strictly, the owner or superuser is allowed to change the mode of a particular file or directory.

Similarly, there is a `chown` command that can be used to set the owner or the group for a particular file or directories. The command is as follows:

```
hdfs chown [-R] [owner] [:[group]] <filepath>
```

The owner name and group can be specified along with the file path. The owner of the file can only be changed by the superuser and no one else. Again, the `-R` flag can be used to recursively change the owner of a directory and all its descendents.

The `chgrp` command can also be used to change the group a file belongs to. The command is specified as follows:

```
hdfs chgrp [-R] <group> <filepath>
```

Only an owner of the file or directory who belongs to the specified group is allowed to change the group. The superuser is also allowed to conduct this operation.

Specifying the HDFS superuser

In Hadoop, the HDFS superuser is the user under whom the NameNode runs. The superuser has ultimate privileges in HDFS. No permission checks fail for the superuser, and the superuser identity is allowed to execute all operations.

There is no permanent superuser identity. It is strictly determined by the identity that starts the NameNode service. It is not necessary for the superuser identity to be the administrator of the host that runs the NameNode though.

However, the administrator might also specify a group of users as superuser identities, though they might not be running the NameNode. Setting the configuration property `dfs.permissions.superusergroup` to the group of users that need to have superuser privileges does this.

HDFS provides a web interface to browse the filesystem. The web server hosting this interface runs under an identity. This identity is specified by the `dfs.web.ugi` configuration property. The value is a comma-separated list of the user and group that run the web interface. The user specified in this property can be the superuser as well. If the web server runs under superuser privileges, it has access to view the entire namespace. If it is set to a user and group that is not a superuser, access might be limited based on the permissions that are granted to the specified user or group. More than one group can also be specified in the comma-separated list.

Turning off HDFS authorization

The entire authorization feature is controlled by the `dfs.permissions` property. If it is set to `true`, all the permission-related rules and checks apply on each operation. If set to `false`, authorization is disabled. Turning off permissions does not alter the mode, user, or groups for the files and directories in the filesystem.

However, the `chmod`, `chown`, and `chgrp` commands that were discussed previously are not affected by turning permissions off. When these commands are executed, permissions are checked mandatorily.

Limiting HDFS usage

Even with adequate authentication and authorization setup, there is a possibility that a user or a group of users exceeds their fair share of resource usage. This can either be inadvertently due to faulty processes or through a compromised user trying to mount a denial of service on the Hadoop cluster.

HDFS provides quotas to limit usage. Quotas are imposed on the number of names and amount of space that can be used. These quotas are fixed at a directory level and applied to all files and directories that are descendants of the directory.

Name quotas in HDFS

The number of directories and filenames within a directory can be limited using the name quota. The name quota with a value 1 at a directory implies that no files or directories can be created below this particular directory. By default, a directory that has been created has no quota associated with it. The maximum quota that can be associated is `Long.Max_Value`. Setting a quota on a directory will succeed even if the directory violates the quota. The following command is used to set a quota on a directory or set of directories:

```
hdfs dfsadmin -setQuota <Quota> <dir1>….<dirn>
```

A quota can be removed from a directory or set of directories using the `-clrQuota` command. Its usage is as follows:

```
hdfs dfsadmin -clrQuota <dir1> ….. <dirn>
```

Space quotas in HDFS

The space usage under each directory can be limited using the space quota. The unit of space quota is in bytes. If the block allocation of a file within a directory exceeds this quota, the write fails. A zero quota allows a file to be created, but the file cannot be filled. This is because the metadata of files do not come under the quota. Even directories are exempt from being counted within space quotas. The maximum number of bytes that can be specified in the quota is the `Long.Max_Value` value.

File replications are accounted within quotas. A 1 TB file with a replication factor of three accounts for 3 TB of the quota. This has to be kept in mind when setting up quotas.

The space quotas in HDFS can be set using the following command:

```
hdfs dfsadmin -setSpaceQuota <Quota> <dir1>….<dirn>
```

Space quotas can be reset using the `-clrSpaceQuota` command, as shown:

```
hdfs dfsadmin -clrSpaceQuota <dir1>…. <dirn>
```

The `count` command on HDFS can be used with the `-q` switch to list all the quotas for the files and directories. If no quotas are set, the command displays `none` for the name quota value for this directory and `inf` (infinity) for the space quota value:

```
hdfs -count -q <dir1>…<dirn>
```

Service-level authorization in Hadoop

Hadoop has many services running in tandem, processing submitted applications and jobs. YARN has the Resource Manager (RM) that can run submitted applications. Application Masters (AMs) that take jobs as inputs and process them can be spawned. Similarly, HDFS has the NameNode service that provides a metadata store and directory service for HDFS. Authorization to access services is a mandatory security component in any framework.

In the Hadoop configuration directory, the `hadoop-policy.xml` file describes the authorization policies for service access. Authorization is defined by the use of ACLs that define the user or group and the type of access granted or denied to the user or group. These ACLs are checked at the beginning, much before the other authorization permission checks, such as the HDFS authorization.

Service-level authorization can be enabled by setting the `hadoop.security.authorization` property in the `core-site.xml` file to `true`. The Hadoop service-level authorization feature has a number of ACLs that can be defined to grant or restrict access to services. They are as follows:

- `security.client.protocol.acl`: This property determines the permissions on usage of the distributed filesystem client via the Hadoop APIs. A user or group who is granted access via an **access control entry** (**ACE**) can make calls to the NameNode service.

- `security.client.datanode.protocol.acl`: This property determines the users and groups who can access the DataNode within the Hadoop cluster. A user or group who is granted access via an ACE can call APIs on the DataNode. This is generally done in block recovery scenarios.

- `security.datanode.protocol.acl`: This property determines the ACEs that grant permissions for the DataNodes to communicate and access the NameNode.

- `security.inter.datanode.protocol.acl`: This property determines the ACEs that grant permissions for the DataNodes to communicate with other DataNodes. They are generally used to update generation timestamps. Generation timestamps are used in block write failure scenarios.

- `security.namenode.protocol.acl`: This property determines the kind of permissions the secondary NameNode has when communicating with the primary NameNode.

- `security.inter.tracker.protocol.acl`: This property determines the kind of permissions the task tracker has when communicating with the job tracker.

- `security.job.submission.protocol.acl`: This property determines the permissions job submission clients have. These clients are used to submit jobs or query job statuses.

- `security.task.umbilical.protocol.acl`: This property determines the permissions the Map or Reduce tasks have when communicating with the parent `TaskTracker` process.

- `security.refresh.policy.protocol.acl`: This property determines the permissions on the `dfsadmin` and `mradmin` commands for policy refresh.

- `security.ha.service.protocol.acl`: This property determines the permissions on the HAAdmin for active and standby NameNode management. This protocol ACL deals with NameNode high availability only.

Each ACL is a list of users followed by a list of groups. Each user list is comma separated. Each group list is comma separated as well. The user and group lists are separated by a space. For example, `u1, u2 g1, g2` represents an ACL for users `u1` and `u2` and groups `g1` and `g2`. A `*` can be specified as a wildcard for all users.

Any service-level authorization can be refreshed without having to restart the NameNode or any other daemons. Both the `dfsadmin` and `mradmin` commands have the `-refreshServiceAcl` option to reload the configuration.

The following XML is a snippet from a sample `hadoop-policy.xml` file:

```
<property>
    <name>security.job.submission.protocol.acl</name>
        <value>u1,u2 g1</value>
</property>
<property>
    <name>security.client.protocol.acl</name>
        <value>* </value>
</property>
```

The first ACL permits the users `u1` and `u2` to submit jobs in the cluster. In addition, all users belonging to group `g1` can also submit jobs. The second ACL grants all users to access HDFS.

Data confidentiality in Hadoop

Hadoop is a distributed system. All distributed systems are interconnected via a network. Networks are vulnerable to malicious sniffing of data. Data at rest can also be read if they are not protected via encryption.

Data confidentiality for data at rest is delegated to the OS that hosts the DataNode. Most modern OSes provide encryption schemes to protect data on disks under their purview. In this section, we will look at confidentiality over the wire and how to enable encryption when data is in transit.

HTTPS and encrypted shuffle

Encrypted shuffle is a feature that facilitates data confidentiality in the shuffle process. To recap, the shuffle step is where data moves from the Map to the Reduce tasks in a MapReduce job life cycle. The movement of data occurs across machines through the network. The transport used to move this data across the network is HTTP.

HTTP, by itself, sends data in clear text, that is, in an unencrypted form. This can lead to information leak when an adversary snoops in the network. HTTPS is the secure form of HTTP, where all packet payloads between the HTTP endpoints are encrypted using **Secure Socket Layer** (**SSL**). Hadoop allows for encrypted shuffle by facilitating HTTPS communication between the Map and Reduce task nodes.

Optionally, Hadoop also allows for client authentication. Encrypted shuffle comprises configuration settings to achieve:

- Switching off the shuffle process between HTTP and HTTPS
- Specification of a keystore and truststore to facilitate HTTP encryption
- Reload of trust stores when nodes are added or decommissioned

SSL configuration changes

The encrypted shuffle configuration requires SSL. To enable SSL, the changes required are as follows:

- In the `core-site.xml` file, the `hadoop.ssl.require.client.cert` property is set to `true` if client certificates are used. By default, this value is `false`.

- The `hadoop.ssl.hostname.verifier` property is used to specify the level of strictness when making an SSL connection. The `HttpsUrlConnection` class in Java uses this value to determine whether connections should be allowed to go through. The framework compares the identity of the server in the authentication scheme with the actual server identity to decide granting or rejecting the connection. This property can take the values `DEFAULT`, `STRICT`, `STRICT_I6`, `DEFAULT_AND_LOCALHOST`, and `ALLOW_ALL`. The default value is `DEFAULT`. `ALLOW_ALL` is the weakest form of verification. This value is specified in `core-site.xml`.

- The `hadoop.ssl.keystores.factory.class` property indicates the class name to be used to implement and manage keystores. By default, the value is `org.apache.hadoop.security.ssl.FileBasedKeyStoresFactory`. This value is specified in `core-site.xml`.

- The `hadoop.ssl.server.conf` property indicates the configuration file that is used to configure SSL on the server side. The default value is `ssl-server.xml`. This file is looked in the class path for availability. The values of this configuration file configure the keystore and other SSL properties. This value is specified in `core-site.xml`.

- The `hadoop.ssl.client.conf` property is similar to the preceding property, but defines the client-side SSL properties. The default value is `ssl-client.xml`, and it needs to be present in the class path.

All of the previous properties have to be marked as `final`, indicating that they cannot be overridden in any other configurations either by the framework or the user. The previous properties have to be set on all the nodes of the cluster.

The following configuration snippet shows a sample `core-site.xml` configuration:

```
<property>
    <name>hadoop.ssl.require.client.cert</name>
    <value>false</value>
    <final>true</final>
</property>
<property>
    <name>hadoop.ssl.hostname.verifier</name>
    <value>DEFAULT</value>
    <final>true</final>
</property>
<property>
    <name>hadoop.ssl.keystores.factory.class</name>
    <value>org.apache.hadoop.security.ssl
            .FileBasedKeyStoresFactory</value>
    <final>true</final>
</property>
<property>
    <name>hadoop.ssl.server.conf</name>
    <value>ssl-server.xml</value>
    <final>true</final>
</property>
<property>
    <name>hadoop.ssl.client.conf</name>
    <value>ssl-client.xml</value>
    <final>true</final>
</property>
```

The preceding properties set up SSL between the nodes so that HTTPS can be used as the transport for communication. To enable HTTPS in the encrypted shuffle process, the `mapreduce.shuffle.ssl.enabled` property can be set to `true` in `mapred-site.xml`. By default, this property is set to `false`. Again, this property is not overridable and has to be set as `final`. The following code snippet shows the default configuration for this property in `mapred-site.xml`:

```
<property>
    <name>mapreduce.shuffle.ssl.enabled</name>
    <value>true</value>
    <final>true</final>
</property>
```

Configuring the keystore and truststore

`FileBasedKeyStoreFactory` is the only keystore implementation available in Hadoop out of the box. The settings for truststores and keystores are in the files specified as values for the properties `hadoop.ssl.server.conf` and `hadoop.ssl.client.conf`.

Keystores and **truststores** have very similar structures. They are used to store private keys and certificates. Functionally, though, they serve different goals. A keystore is used to store credentials that need to be presented during an SSL connection. Generally, a keystore is used to store private keys and public key certificates that can be used to initiate a secure remote connection. If an SSL server is being launched or a server does client authentication, a keystore is a must to store the necessary keys and certificates.

A truststore, in contrast, is used to verify credentials when a connection is established. They generally contain third-party certificates such as root certificates or certificates that are signed by certificate authorities that identify and endorse endpoints.

The keystore and truststore can be the same file. However, generally, it is good practice to keep them separate.

The `ssl-server.xml` file can be configured with the properties listed in the following table:

Property name	Description
`ssl.server.keystore.type`	This is the type of keystore file. Java keystores are of type `jks`. The default value for this parameter is `jks`.
`ssl.server.keystore.location`	This is the location of the keystore file on the local node. The user running any MapReduce jobs needs at least read access to this file.
`ssl.server.keystore.password`	Each keystore and truststore file is password protected. The password for the keystore is specified here.
`ssl.server.truststore.type`	This is the type of truststore file. The default value is `jks`.
`ssl.server.truststore.location`	This is the file path of the truststore.
`ssl.server.truststore.password`	This is the truststore password.
`ssl.server.truststore.reload.interval`	This is the number of milliseconds after which a reload of the certificates must happen from the truststore. The default value is 1,000, indicating 10 seconds.

A sample `ssl-server.xml` configuration is given as follows:

```
<configuration>
<!-- Keystore Configurations -->
<property>
    <name>ssl.server.keystore.type</name>
    <value>jks</value>
</property>
<property>
    <name>ssl.server.keystore.location</name>
    <value>${user.home}/keystores/certstore.jks</value>
    </property>
<property>
    <name>ssl.server.keystore.password</name>
    <value><your keystore password></value>
</property>

<!-- Truststore configurations -->
<property>
```

```
    <name>ssl.server.truststore.type</name>
    <value>jks</value>
</property>
<property>
    <name>ssl.server.truststore.location</name>
    <value>${user.home}/keystores/castore.jks</value>
</property>
<property>
    <name>ssl.server.truststore.password</name>
    <value><your truststore password></value>
</property>
<property>
    <name>ssl.server.truststore.reload.interval</name>
    <value>10000</value>
</property>
</configuration>
```

The ssl-client.xml file can be configured with the properties in the given following table:

Property name	Comments
ssl.client.keystore.type	This is the type of keystore file. Java keystores are of type jks. The default value for this parameter is jks.
ssl.client.keystore.location	This is the location of the keystore file on the local node. A user running any MapReduce jobs needs at least read access to this file.
ssl.client.keystore.password	Each keystore and truststore file is password protected. The password for the keystore is specified here.
ssl.client.truststore.type	This is the type of truststore file. The default value is jks.
ssl.client.truststore.location	This is the file path of the truststore.
ssl.client.truststore.password	This is the truststore password.
ssl.client.truststore.reload.interval	This is the number of milliseconds after which a reload of the certificates must happen from the truststore. The default value is 1,000, indicating 10 seconds.

A sample `ssl-client.xml` configuration file is given as follows:

```
<configuration>
<!—Keystore configuration settings -->
<property>
    <name>ssl.client.keystore.type</name>
    <value>jks</value>
</property>
<property>
    <name>ssl.client.keystore.location</name>
    <value>${user.home}/keystores/clientcertstore.jks</value>
</property>
<property>
    <name>ssl.client.keystore.password</name>
    <value><your keystore password></value>
</property>
<!—Truststore configuration settings -->
<property>
    <name>ssl.client.truststore.type</name>
    <value>jks</value>
</property>
<property>
    <name>ssl.client.truststore.location</name>
    <value>${user.home}/keystores/clientcastore.jks</value>
</property>
    property>
    <name>ssl.client.truststore.password</name>
    <value><Your truststore password></value>
</property>
<property>
    <name>ssl.client.truststore.reload.interval</name>
    <value>10000</value>
</property>
</configuration>
```

Once the settings are in place, the encrypted shuffle can be activated by restarting all the `NodeManagers` (NMs) in the cluster. Encrypted shuffle will add processing overheads as the shuffle steps will have to do encryption and decryption in addition to its existing duties.

The SSL connections can be debugged on the Reduce task nodes. This is done by setting the `mapreduce.reduce.child.java.opts` property value to the `javax.net.debug=all` Java option. This can be done on a per-job basis or in `mapred-site.xml`, so all the jobs in the cluster can be debugged. The following snippet shows how this option can be set in `mapred-site.xml`:

```
<property>
    <name>mapred.reduce.child.java.opts</name>
    <value>-Djavax.net.debug=all</value>
</property>
```

The debug property should be used prudently only for debugging. When used, it slows down the job executing with this option. Debugging can also be enabled on the `NodeManager` by setting the following environment variable:

```
YARN_NODEMANAGER_OPTS="-Djavax.net.debug=all"
```

Audit logging in Hadoop

Audit logging is an accounting process that logs all operations happening in Hadoop. HDFS and the MapReduce engine logging are already present in Hadoop via the `log4j` properties. Audit logs use the same framework, but they log more events and give higher resolution into Hadoop operations. The file that is used to configure logging is the `log4j.properties` file.

By default, the `log4j.properties` file has the log threshold set to WARN. By setting this level to INFO, audit logging can be turned on. The following snippet shows the `log4j.properties` configuration when HDFS and MapReduce audit logs are turned on:

```
#
# hdfs audit logging
#
hdfs.audit.logger=INFO,NullAppender
hdfs.audit.log.maxfilesize=256MB
hdfs.audit.log.maxbackupindex=20
log4j.logger.org.apache.hadoop.hdfs.server.namenode.FSNamesystem
    .audit=${hdfs.audit.logger}
```

```
log4j.additivity.org.apache.hadoop.hdfs.server.namenode
    .FSNamesystem.audit=false
log4j.appender.RFAAUDIT=org.apache.log4j.RollingFileAppender
log4j.appender.RFAAUDIT.File=${hadoop.log.dir}/hdfs-audit.log
log4j.appender.RFAAUDIT.layout=org.apache.log4j.PatternLayout
log4j.appender.RFAAUDIT.layout.ConversionPattern=%d{ISO8601} %p
    %c{2}: %m%n
log4j.appender.RFAAUDIT.MaxFileSize=${hdfs.audit.log.maxfilesize}
log4j.appender.RFAAUDIT.MaxBackupIndex=${hdfs.audit.log
    .maxbackupindex}


#
# mapred audit logging
#
mapred.audit.logger=INFO,NullAppender
mapred.audit.log.maxfilesize=256MB
mapred.audit.log.maxbackupindex=20
log4j.logger.org.apache.hadoop.mapred.AuditLogger=${mapred.
    audit.logger}
log4j.additivity.org.apache.hadoop.mapred.AuditLogger=false
log4j.appender.MRAUDIT=org.apache.log4j.RollingFileAppender
log4j.appender.MRAUDIT.File=${hadoop.log.dir}/mapred-audit.log
log4j.appender.MRAUDIT.layout=org.apache.log4j.PatternLayout
log4j.appender.MRAUDIT.layout.ConversionPattern=%d{ISO8601} %p
    %c{2}: %m%n
log4j.appender.MRAUDIT.MaxFileSize=${mapred.audit.log.maxfilesize}
log4j.appender.MRAUDIT.MaxBackupIndex=${mapred.audit.log
    .maxbackupindex}
```

The `hdfs.audit.logger` and `mapred.audit.logger` properties are turned on by setting the level to `INFO`. These properties are then assigned to `log4j` properties such as `log4j.logger.org.apache.hadoop.hdfs.server.namenode.FSNamesystem.audit`. Other properties can be set appropriately to control the logging.

Summary

Security becomes a primary feature in a multitenant and distributed environment. Networks and resource sharing can potentially lead to information leaks via unauthorized access, malicious modifications, or even denial of service. Preempting attacks on Hadoop clusters can be done by enabling security features such as authentication, authorization, data protection, and data auditing.

The key takeaways from this chapter are as follows:

- Post 0.20, Yahoo! introduced Hadoop security-related features for compliance, confidentiality, and fair usage in shared enterprise clusters.

- Hadoop can now be configured for Kerberos-based authentication or simple authentication based on the topology and compliance requirements. User information can be retrieved from enterprise user stores such as LDAP or Active Directory.

- Hadoop has both service-level and resource-level authorization built in. HDFS authorization is very similar to the UNIX-based file authorization model.

- Hadoop provides data confidentiality by facilitating HTTPS in MapReduce shuffle and web endpoints. HTTPS can be turned on by tweaking a few parameters. Data confidentiality for data at rest is delegated to the node's operating system.

- Accounting is very important for compliance and forensics in an enterprise. Hadoop uses the log4j logging framework to provide audit logs.

In the next chapter, we will look at Hadoop applications, particularly in the field of big data analytics.

12
Analytics Using Hadoop

Hadoop has come to the fore because of its capability to aid in data analytics. As data grows in the dimensions of volume, velocity, and variety, there needs to be systems that are capable of analyzing this data efficiently and effectively. Vertically scaling hardware to handle this data is not viable because it is expensive and difficult to manage. Distributed computing and horizontal scaling are good options, and frameworks such as Hadoop automatically cater to the fault tolerance, scaling, and distribution needs of such a system.

Analytics is all about data. A question that frequently arises is when does Hadoop become overkill? Typically, it is recommended that you use Hadoop for datasets of 1 TB and upwards. However, when it becomes difficult to predict the rate of data growth, it may be a good idea to use Hadoop MapReduce because of its attractive "code once, deploy at any scale" characteristic.

There are organizations that use Hadoop to analyze a few hundreds of gigabytes of data as well. The smaller the dataset the better, since the user has to take into account latency costs due to long startup times and disk access associated with Hadoop jobs. The functional aspect of Hadoop MapReduce makes it easy to code and port over complex analytics functions. In some situations, when datasets are smaller and traditional SQL becomes unwieldy due to the nature of the analysis, it may be prudent to use Hadoop and directly interact with the filesystem.

In this chapter, we will look at the following topics:

- The workflow for data analytics
- A brief introduction to machine learning
- The basics of Apache Mahout
- Document analysis as a data analytics case study using Pig and Mahout

Data analytics workflow

Data analytics involves transforming and inspecting data to figure out the inherent meaningful information from it. The information extracted is used in decision making or suggesting conclusions. The analytics workflow is shown in the following diagram:

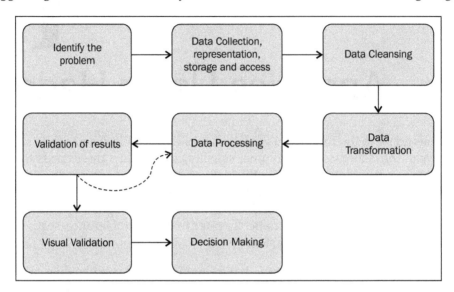

The steps involved in the analytics workflow are as follows:

1. The first step is to identify the problem to be solved. This is important as the decisions in the rest of the steps hinge on it. For example, the problem statement will dictate what kind of data to collect and what the important features that represent the solution to the problem are. A lot of domain expertise is required in data analytics, and a problem space where expertise is accessible is almost mandatory.

2. Once the problem is identified, appropriate data needs to be collected. The collected data needs to be represented in a format that optimizes on space without losing resolution in information. Enterprises now need to be aware of compliance and security. Access to the data might need to be restricted to authorized personnel and data could be confidential in some cases.

3. The stored data needs to be cleansed. Cleansing involves removal of outliers, missing values, and bad records. The result of the data analysis depends much on cleansing of the data. Data that is not cleansed might lead to skewed analysis.

4. The cleansed data is transformed into a representation that can be used for analysis. One example of transformation is normalization of data to a range between 0 and 1. Another example is changing the scale of the data to ease computation.

5. The transformed data is then analyzed using algorithms. Machine learning algorithms are a class of analysis algorithms that offer solutions based on previously known empirical evidence.

6. Once the data is transformed and results are obtained, they need to be validated. Validation can occur by either consulting with domain experts or by deploying it to a test set of users. Post-validation, if the results can be used to make meaningful decisions, it ends the process of analysis. Otherwise, the data scientist and associates get back to the drawing board and tweak the parameters in the pipeline.

7. The validated results are visually represented for the stakeholders (which could include users) to validate. The apt visual representation is decided at this stage.

8. Finally, the results are used to drive decisions.

Machine learning

Machine learning is about programming computers to optimize a function based on previous experience. The computer is given empirical data to analyze and build a model function that can predict the output on unseen data that it might encounter in the real world. The computer builds a function based on the parameters and the empirical data supplied to it. This function evolves as more empirical data is given or when there is a change in the data characteristics. When this function is applied on unseen data at a later point, it predicts the output based on the model function. The empirical data supplied to learn this function is termed as **training data**.

The following are the kinds of machine learning algorithms:

*   **Supervised learning**: The training data supplied to supervised learning methods is labeled. Each data point in the training dataset is a pair of objects, the actual data point representing the situation, which is generally a vector of values, and the desired output value for this situation. An expert who understands the domain of the data annotates the desired output value for the situation. This desired output is also called a **label** or a supervisory signal. The algorithm runs on the set of training data to infer a mathematical function. The function is as generalized as possible and is termed as a model. When this function is applied on any unseen data, it gives an output value. This model function's accuracy in prediction determines its strength.

- **Unsupervised learning**: The training data supplied to unsupervised learning methods is unlabeled. The learning algorithm is asked to determine the underlying structure in the data. Clustering is an example of an unsupervised learning method, where groups are determined from unlabeled data based on a distance metric between the data points.

- **Semi-supervised learning**: This takes a hybrid approach wherein unlabeled empirical data is given to the computer along with a few labeled data points.

The following diagram shows the machine learning process:

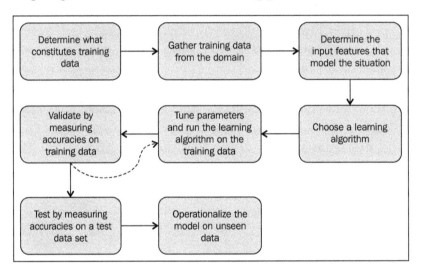

The steps in machine learning process are as follows:

1. The first step in machine learning is to determine a problem to be solved and what constitutes training data for the problem in hand. This involves figuring out how granular a training data point should be and also the number of points. Expertise in the domain of the problem can be very useful in determining the granularity and size of the training data set.

2. Once it is determined, the next step would be to actually gather the training data from the real world. Training data gathered may need to be annotated or labeled by an expert in the case of supervised learning. The optimal size of the labeled training data might become crucial in determining the accuracies of the modeling function. In general, getting an expert to label training data is very expensive and needs proper planning. Also, because of the manual nature of labeling, it does not scale well to a large number of data points. Semi-supervised techniques are becoming popular because of problems associated with getting labeled training data.

3. The training data point now needs to be broken down into a set of features. These are characteristics of the data point that accurately represent the situation when the data point was collected. Selection of the right features is critical to get good model functions. A lot of features could mean slower processing and too little features may lead to less accuracy.

4. The next step is to choose a good learning algorithm to learn the function. Depending on the nature of the problem, there are a number of algorithms. Classification algorithms output model functions that can determine the class to which a particular data point belongs. A clustering algorithm takes a set of data points and groups them into a number of groups based on a measure of distance.

5. Once a suitable algorithm is chosen, it is fed with the training data and parameters. The output of a learning algorithm is the model function. The learning parameters can be used to tune the characteristics of the model function. For example, a regularization parameter can be used to generalize the model function to solve the problem of **overfitting**. In a clustering scenario, a parameter can determine the number of clusters that need to be determined as the output of the learning algorithm.

6. Validation is one of the most important steps in machine learning workflows. It involves determining the strengths and weaknesses of the learned model. Using the learned model function to predict on random subsets of the training dataset itself does validation. In a supervised setting, since we know the labels beforehand, this information can be used to evaluate the accuracies of the learned model. If it is found to be less accurate, we can go back to step 4 or 5 to either change the algorithm or tune the parameters for a better model function.

7. A validated machine learning model is then used to predict the output on a test dataset. This is also a labeled dataset outside the training dataset. Operating parameters and characteristics of the model can be determined on this dataset. The operating parameters can then be used to predict unseen data points in the real world.

8. The final step is to deploy and operationalize the learned model so that it operates with the operating parameters determined in step 7. Unseen data is supplied to the learned model function and it is asked to predict the output. The predicted output can be used to drive business decisions.

9. Periodically, the models are updated either using newly gained knowledge from the field or in the form of feedback from users and stakeholders. Newer training data could be collected and steps 1 through 8 can be performed to update the model.

Often, the terms machine learning and data mining appear in the same context. **Data mining** is a field that involves discovering patterns from large sets of data. The differences between machine learning and data mining are as follows:

- Machine learning methods can be used as tools in the data mining process
- Machine learning solves specific tasks while data mining is exploratory in nature
- Machine learning deals with accurately identifying known information on unseen data, while data mining deals with discovering unknown information on data

Apache Mahout

Apache Mahout is a scalable machine learning library. It is an open source library under the Apache Software Foundation. It supports algorithms for clustering, classification, and collaborative filtering on distributed platforms. Apache Mahout welcomes contributors to contribute any algorithm to the library. The algorithm coded may not always be distributed and can run on a single machine as well.

As Apache Mahout allows developers to introduce single-machine algorithms, it is recommended that you study the implementation before running it on Hadoop.

Apache Mahout has a few algorithms that are implemented as MapReduce. These algorithms can be run in Hadoop to exploit the parallelism on a distributed cluster. Again, a word of caution for you is to study the implementation of an algorithm before using it in your Hadoop deployments. A non-MapReduce algorithm may not yield any speedup when run on a Hadoop cluster.

In a recent change, since April 2014, Mahout has stopped accepting algorithms that are programmed in the MapReduce model. However, Mahout has made a commitment to support all the algorithms that are already in its library and programmed using the MapReduce model.

The following is a list of use cases supported by Apache Mahout and the algorithms that can be run on Hadoop and exploit the parallelism provided by any Hadoop cluster categorized by the use case:

- **Classification**: This is a supervised method that learns how to place data points in different classes. Unseen data is then put into one of these classes. In the classification use case, Mahout supports parallelized implementation for the Bayesian classifier and the Random Forest classifier. The Bayesian classifier uses the Bayes rule and conditional probabilities to do binary classification. The Random Forest classifier is a decision-tree-based classifier at its core, but uses a collection or ensemble of decision trees.

- **Clustering**: This is an unsupervised method that categorizes training data points into coherent groups. Mahout supports distributed implementations of many clustering algorithms. K-means, a very popular clustering algorithm, has an implementation that is parallel and distributed. The core of K-means is to group data points such that the mean distance between the points is minimum. The fuzzy k-means clustering algorithm is also compatible with Hadoop. In this clustering method, the clusters are soft and allow multiple cluster memberships for a particular data point. Hierarchical, **Latent Dirichlet Allocation (LDA)**, Mean shift, MinHash, Dirichlet Process, Canopy, and Spectral clustering have got distributed implementations in the Mahout library.

- **Collaborative filtering**: This makes recommendations based on the user data that is available. Distributed-item-based collaborative filtering and parallel-matrix-factorization-based collaborative filtering algorithms have Hadoop-compatible implementations. The former uses the user's preferences for other items to predict the preference for a similar item. The latter predicts the preference of the user from a matrix of unseen items.

- **Frequent itemset mining**: This is also called market-basket analysis where the algorithm analyzes which other item typically appears along with the item in hand. There is a parallel implementation of the Parallel FP growth algorithm to determine item associations.

Document analysis using Hadoop and Mahout

In this section, we will take an example of document analysis to illustrate analytics using Hadoop and Mahout. We will be using Pig as the higher-level abstraction for Hadoop MapReduce. We will be calculating the distance between documents using a score called **Tf-idf**. This distance metric is very popular in the field of information retrieval and text analytics. It is based on the statistics of words occurring in a document.

Tf-idf is used to rank documents based on query terms. It is extensively used in text search scenarios. The distance between the query terms and the document terms determines how close the query is with respect to the document. This distance can be used to rank documents.

For this particular example, we will be using the NSF grants abstracts that are available at `http://kdd.ics.uci.edu/databases/nsfabs/nsfawards.html`. The dataset consists of about 120,000 abstracts and comes in three parts. Each grant abstract is a separate text file.

Tf-idf stands for **Term Frequency – Inverse Document Frequency**. It is the product of two metrics: term frequency (*tf*) and inverse of the document frequency (*df*).

Term frequency

As the words suggest, term frequency is the number of times a word occurs in a particular document. The more the occurrences of a word in a document, the stronger the association of that word with the document. For example, if the word "Hadoop" appears 10 times in document A and 15 times in document B, document B is more relevant in the context of the word Hadoop. This simple intuition drives the calculation of the term frequency metric.

Documents may have varying numbers of words in them. A larger document, say of 1,000 words, may have the word "Hadoop" appear 10 times, while a smaller document, say of 100 words, may have it five times. It might be unfair to say that the term Hadoop is more relevant in the larger document, because the percentage of occurrences of the term Hadoop relative to all the terms in the smaller document is larger. Therefore, when the term frequency is calculated, dividing it by the number of terms in the document normalizes it.

In essence, the term frequency for a term t and document d is given by the following formula:

```
Term Frequency (t,d) = Number of times t appears in d / Number of
terms in d
```

Document frequency

Using the term frequency alone might not do justice in determining the importance of a term relative to a document. There are terms in the English lexicon that occur very frequently in documents. For example, terms such as "and", "the", and "in" occur very often compared to other words. These words are called stop words.

There could be other words that occur frequently based on where the document repository is coming from. For example, documents coming from an organization might have the name of the organization appearing all over them. These terms, like the stop words, do not contribute to any signal when comparing the importance of a set of terms with a document.

Document frequency is used to eliminate or reduce the effect of these frequently occurring terms from the calculation of the distance measure. Calculating the number of documents in which a term appears in the entire document corpus or repository does this. More the value, less is the signal the term adds in differentiating the document. Therefore, the inverse of the document frequency is taken to reduce the effect of such terms appearing very frequently within the document.

In essence, the inverse document is calculated as follows:

```
inverse document frequency (t) = log(number of documents in the
corpus/number of documents the term t appears in)
```

The document frequency is divided by the number of documents in the corpus to normalize the values and make it a number between 0 and 1. The logarithm of the entire score is taken to keep the value within a reasonable range as the number of documents could be huge, like in a web corpus.

Term frequency – inverse document frequency

The product of the term frequency and the inverse document frequency for a given term and document gives the importance of the term in that particular document:

```
Tf-idf for term t and document d = tf for term t and document d *
idf for term t
```

It is important to understand that there is a Tf-idf score for each term and each document of a document corpus. These Tf-idf scores are stored in inverted indexes of full-text search engines and are used to measure distances between the query terms and the documents. The inverted index stores these values in sparse format, that is, a Tf-idf score is associated with a document only if a term is present in it. A term not appearing in a document has a Tf-idf score of zero as the term frequency in the document is zero. These zero-valued Tf-idf scores are not stored within the index.

Tf-Idf in Pig

The following steps illustrate how to calculate Tf-idf for the NSF grants abstract document corpus that was described previously:

1. The prerequisites are loading all the documents into the HDFS. This can be done using the `hadoop fs -cp` command. The next step will be to load the files into a Pig relation so that we can run data calculations and transformations on the relation. The `PigStorage` class is used to read a document into a relation that has the filename and the sentence in the document as `chararray (file_and_sentence)`. We use the `-tagsource` directive to inform the `PigStorage` class to tag the filename along with the tuple in the relation. This is needed to identify a particular document. Since the Tf-idf scores are term and document dependent, the filename acts as the document identifier.

2. Once the relation is loaded, the next step is to tokenize the sentence into its words. These words are used as terms for further calculations. We use the `TOKENIZE` Pig function to split the sentence into words. A more sophisticated regular expression can also be used to tokenize the sentence. The output is another relation, `file_and_words`, that contains the filename and the terms associated with that sentence in the file. We will get a number of such tuples for a single file depending on the number of sentences that are present in that file.

3. These tuples are now passed through a `filter` statement to remove all words that don't contain alphanumeric characters. The regular expression \w+ is used to do this filtering. In reality, a stop words list is also used to filter out commonly occurring words.

4. Next, all the remaining terms are converted to lowercase strings so that the same terms are uniformly represented. This is a very simplistic kind of transformation on the terms. In practice, operations such as **stemming** and **lemmatization** that help in representing variants of a word as the same word or term are done at this stage. For example, swimmers or swimmer can be represented as a single word, that is, swimmer. There are many stemming algorithms, and most well-known natural language processing libraries have built-in stemmers. **Porter Stemmer** is a very popular stemmer:

```
/* This is a Pig template file to get tf-idf calculated for
all the NSF grants. Before starting off,
* 1) Unzip the zip file in your local directory
* 2) Use bin/hadoop fs -cp
* /

/* We have to load all the files in hdfs grants directory.
This can be done using the command below. *The nice thing
about the PigStorage class is that it helps us get the file
name along with the *sentence in the file. At the end of
this command, you will have (file_name, sentence) tuples to
go *further. Please take care to change the hdfs load
directory if necessary*/


file_and_sentence = load 'grants/*' using PigStorage('\t',
    '-tagsource') as (file_name: chararray, sentence:
        chararray);


/*We now split each sentence using the TOKENIZE Pig
function and flatten out the tokens we get from the split.
At the end of this step, we get (filename, word1,
word2,....). The tuple of words are broken down from the
sentence.
*/

file_and_words = foreach file_and_sentence generate
    file_name as file_name,flatten(TOKENIZE(sentence)) as
        words;


filtered_file_and_words = filter file_and_words by (words
```

```
matches '\\w+');
```

```
/*We now group each file and the words of the sentence that
it follows. A group operation in Pig gives us (group,
{members of the group}). A flatten on the group will
produce more tuples. Please refer to this document for the
details. We are doing the following step for us to get neat
tuples of the form (filename, word, count of
word). http://pig.apache.org/docs/r0.9.1/basic.html#flatten
*/
```

```
lowercased_file_and_word = foreach filtered_file_and_words
    generate file_name as file_name, LOWER(words) as word;
```

5. Once we have cleansed and transformed the data appropriately, the
    GROUP BY operator in Pig is used to group on filename and the term. This
    yields a grouping of all terms in a particular file. The key to this grouping
    is the filename and is represented by the relation file_and_words_groups
    in the following Pig code snippet.

6. We now take the term counts per document by counting the number of terms
    in the grouping. The file_and_word_and_count relation represents this.
    The relation has tuples that have the filename, the word, and the number of
    times the word appears in the file. These are the term frequencies.

7. By grouping file_and_word_and_count differently, that is, by the filename,
    we can get the number of terms in a particular document. Summing up
    the counts for the terms in each and every group does this calculation. The
    unnormalized_term_counts relation gives the number of terms or words
    in each file.

8. These term counts in each document can then be used to normalize and
    calculate the term frequencies. In the example, the term_frequencies
    relation represents the term frequencies. It is calculated by dividing the
    term frequency by the number of terms in the document:

```
file_and_words_groups = group lowercased_file_and_word by
    (file_name, word);
```

```
file_and_word_and_count = foreach file_and_words_groups
    generate flatten(group) as (file_name:chararray,
        word:chararray),
            COUNT_STAR(lowercased_file_and_word) as count;
```

```
/* Now that we have the data massaged in the form of
```

```
(filename, word, count). I will let you proceed with the
rest of the exercise*/


/* We can now group appropriately and get different
statistics. For example, we are getting the number of terms
per document using the Pig commands below. JOINS maybe
important things to take note of when trying to normalise
the tf or the idf scores*/

group_file_and_word_and_count = group
    file_and_word_and_count by file_name;


/* Add doc sizes to the term count tuple */
unnormalized_term_counts = foreach
    group_file_and_word_and_count generate group as
        file_name, flatten(file_and_word_and_count.(word,
            count)) as (word, count),
                SUM(file_and_word_and_count.count) as
                    doc_size;


/* Generate the tf scores */
term_frequencies = foreach unnormalized_term_counts
    generate file_name as file_name, word as term,
        ((double)count / (double)doc_size) as term_freq;
```

9. By grouping `term_frequencies` by each term and counting the number of elements in the group, we get the document frequency for that particular term. In the next code snippet, the relation `doc_term_count` represents the number of documents containing the term.

10. The document frequencies now have to be normalized by the number of documents in the corpus. Grouping the `file_and_sentence` relation by the filename does this. The count of the groups represents the number of files in the corpus.

11. The final Tf-idf scores are then calculated per term and per file using the formula discussed previously. We then order the scores to validate our calculations. The term-document pairs with the highest scores are the most relevant terms for the document:

```
/* Generate the document frequencies */
group_term_frequencies = group term_frequencies by term;

doc_term_count = foreach group_term_frequencies generate
    FLATTEN(term_frequencies) as (file_name, term,
```

```
        term_freq), COUNT_STAR(term_frequencies) as
            doc_freq;


    /* Generate the doc count in the corpus */
    doc_groups = foreach (group file_and_sentence by file_name)
        generate group as file_name;

    doc_count = foreach(group doc_groups all) generate
        COUNT(doc_groups) as n_docs;


    /* Generate the final tf-idf scores */
    scores = foreach doc_term_count generate file_name as
        file_name, term as term, term_freq *
            LOG((double)doc_count.n_docs/(double)doc_freq)
                as tf_idf;

    ordered_scores = order scores by tf_idf ;
```

Cosine similarity distance measures

In the previous section, we saw how Tf-idf scores are calculated. A document can be represented as a vector of Tf-idf scores for each term that occurs in it. For non-occurring terms, the Tf-idf score is zero. Given this vector representation of a document, a question arises as to how we can find the distance between two documents or, in the case of a search engine, the distance between a document and a query. The least distance between two documents or a document and a query deems them most similar or relevant.

There are many distance measures. A commonly used distance measure involves finding the **Euclidean** distance or the vector difference between the two documents or the document and the query. The resultant vector is dependent on the length of the two vectors involved in the subtraction. Euclidean distance leads to longer documents being closer to each other than documents of different sizes. This might not be a very accurate way of measuring distance between two documents, particularly in the text analytics setting:

```
|D1 - D2|
or
|D1 - Q|
```

By taking into consideration the angle between the two vectors, document distance can be represented more correctly. In text analytics, document distances are calculated as the cosine of the angle between the two Tf-idf document vectors. The same calculation is made for the distance between a query and a document as the query is treated as a small document.

From elementary trigonometry, we know that two documents are similar if the cosine of the angle between their vectors is large. The cosine of zero is one, representing documents that are the same or very similar. Documents represented by orthogonal vectors have a value close to zero as the cosine of 90 degrees is equal to zero.

The cosine of two vectors can be calculated by the inner product of the two vectors as shown in the following formula:

```
Cosine similarity of document i and j = d1i * d1j + d2i * d2j……. +
dki * dkj
```

Dividing it by the length of the two vectors normalizes the cosine similarity.

Clustering using k-means

k-means is a popular clustering algorithm. It is built into the Apache Mahout library and can be run on a Hadoop cluster. It is an unsupervised learning method that groups data points by minimizing their distance from the cluster center.

The k-means algorithm is as follows when it is specified that the points have to be put into k-clusters:

1. The first step is to initialize *k* cluster centers. These centers are generally initialized randomly. In some cases, if prior knowledge of the clusters is available, then these clusters can be placed intelligently to bring down the computation time of the algorithm.

2. Each data point—in our example, the Tf-idf vector for a document—is assigned the closest cluster center. This notion of closeness is via different distance or similarity measures. We studied two distance measures in the previous section—the Euclidean distance and the cosine similarity distance.

3. Once all the data points are assigned, the next step is to readjust the cluster centers. The cluster centers are readjusted by taking the average of all the points that were assigned to the cluster center in step 2.

4. The steps 2 and 3 are repeated till convergence is reached or a preset number of iterations happen.

K-means clustering using Apache Mahout

In this section, we will see how to run k-means clustering using Hadoop and Apache Mahout. We will be running it on the grant proposal extracts discussed in the previous section.

 Installing Apache Mahout involves downloading the binaries from the site http://mahout.apache.org. The downloaded archive file is extracted. The following environment variables are set to inform Mahout about the Hadoop installation:

```
export HADOOP_HOME=<Path to Hadoop installation folder>
export MAHOUT_HOME=<Path to Mahout installation folder>
export PATH=$PATH:$HADOOP_HOME/bin:$MAHOUT_HOME/bin
```

The Mahout binary has a number of interesting command-line options.

We will examine the different steps and options that are provided by Mahout by executing the following commands:

```
#Convert the grant proposals into a sequence file. It combines all
the files into a single file
bin/mahout seqdirectory -i /user/hadoop/grants -o
    /user/hadoop/grants-seqdir -c UTF-8 -chunk 5

#Use seqdumper to visualize the sequence files. Observe the
    combining of all the files
bin/mahout seqdumper -i /user/hadoop/grants-seqdir/part-m-00000


#Generate all statistics like tf, df and tf-idf from the corpus.
Generate ids for each term and construct the dictionary. All the
vectors are in a sparse format
bin/mahout seq2sparse -i /user/hadoop/grants-seqdir/ -o
    /user/hadoop/grants-seqdir-sparse --maxDFPercent 85 --
        namedVector

#Examine the tf-idf vectors
bin/mahout seqdumper -i /user/hadoop/grants-seqdir-sparse/tfidf-
    vectors/part-r-00000
# Examine the dictionary file termid to term mappings

bin/mahout seqdumper -i /user/hadoop/grants-seqdir-
    sparse/dictionary.file-0

# Run kmeans for 3 clusters with cosine of tf-idf as the distance
    metric
```

```
bin/mahout kmeans -i /user/hadoop/grants-seqdir-sparse/tfidf-
    vectors/ -c /user/hadoop/grants-kmeans-clusters -o
        /user/hadoop/grants-kmeans -dm
            org.apache.mahout.common.distance.CosineDistanceMeasure
                -x 10 -k 3 -ow --clustering

# Use cluster dump to get metrics about the cluster
bin/mahout clusterdump -i /user/hadoop/grants-kmeans/clusters-*-
    final -o clusterdump -d /user/hadoop/grants-seqdir-
        sparse/dictionary.file-0 -dt sequencefile -b 100 -n 20 --
            evaluate -dm
                org.apache.mahout.common.distance.
CosineDistanceMeasure -sp 0 --
    pointsDir /user/hadoop/grants-kmeans/clusteredPoints
```

The steps to run K-means clustering using Apache Mahout are as follows:

1. The Mahout binary has an option to create `SequenceFile` from a directory. The `seqdirectory` option can be used to create it. The `seqdirectory` command has many options such as the encoding to be used, the chunk size in MB, and the class name for file parsing. In the following example, we create a `grants-seqdir` sequence file using UTF-8 encoding and a chunk size of 5 MB.

2. The `seqdumper` command in the Mahout binary is a very useful tool for visualizing the sequence file. In the following example, we observe one of the parts of the sequence file. The filename forms the key of each record and the contents of the file form its value in the sequence file. An example grants proposal looks similar to the following snippet:

```
Key: /a9996416.txt: Value: Title       : Inverse Diffraction
Problems in Optics
Type       : Award
NSF Org    : DMS
Latest
Amendment
Date       : September 13,  1999
File       : a9996416
Award Number: 9996416
Award Instr.: Standard Grant
Prgm Manager: Deborah Lockhart

           DMS   DIVISION OF MATHEMATICAL SCIENCES

           MPS   DIRECT FOR MATHEMATICAL & PHYSICAL SCIEN
Start Date : August 16,  1999
Expires    : June 30,  2001       (Estimated)
```

3. The `seq2sparse` command is another useful utility that creates vectors from the supplied sequence files. There are two kinds of vectors that are output by this command. The first is a sequence file with the document ID and a vector of tokenized document terms. The second is a sequence file containing the document ID and a vector of Tf-idf scores. The `seq2sparse` command eliminates the need for calculating the Tf-idf scores separately. The command has many options such as `-namedVector` that creates a named vector, `-maxDFPercent` that sets a limit on the maximum percentage of documents that should considered for document frequency measurements, and `-minDF` that sets the minimum document frequency for a term. In the following example, we create vectorized representations of the grants files using named vectors and a `maxDFPercent` value of `85`. The following is a listing of the grants-seqdir-sparse directory in HDFS:

```
Found 2 items
-rw-r--r--   3 sandeepkaranth supergroup          0 2014-09-09
15:14 grants-seqdir-sparse/df-count/_SUCCESS
-rw-r--r--   3 sandeepkaranth supergroup     159253 2014-09-09
15:14 grants-seqdir-sparse/df-count/part-r-00000

Found 1 items
-rw-r--r--   3 sandeepkaranth supergroup     162107 2014-09-09
15:14 grants-seqdir-sparse/dictionary.file-0

Found 1 items
-rw-r--r--   3 sandeepkaranth supergroup     159233 2014-09-09
15:14 grants-seqdir-sparse/frequency.file-0

Found 2 items
-rw-r--r--   3 sandeepkaranth supergroup          0 2014-09-09
15:14 grants-seqdir-sparse/tf-vectors/_SUCCESS
-rw-r--r--   3 sandeepkaranth supergroup     646642 2014-09-09
15:14 grants-seqdir-sparse/tf-vectors/part-r-00000

Found 2 items
-rw-r--r--   3 sandeepkaranth supergroup          0 2014-09-09
15:14 grants-seqdir-sparse/tfidf-vectors/_SUCCESS

-rw-r--r--   3 sandeepkaranth supergroup     646642 2014-09-09
15:14 grants-seqdir-sparse/tfidf-vectors/part-r-00000
Found 2 items
-rw-r--r--   3 sandeepkaranth supergroup          0 2014-09-09
15:14 grants-seqdir-sparse/tokenized-documents/_SUCCESS
-rw-r--r--   3 sandeepkaranth supergroup     884092 2014-09-09
15:14 grants-seqdir-sparse/tokenized-documents/part-m-00000

Found 2 items
-rw-r--r--   3 sandeepkaranth supergroup          0 2014-09-09
15:14 grants-seqdir-sparse/wordcount/_SUCCESS
-rw-r--r--   3 sandeepkaranth supergroup     193944 2014-09-09
15:14 grants-seqdir-sparse/wordcount/part-r-00000
```

4. We examine the created files using the `seqdumper` command. Both the Tf-idf vectors and the dictionary file that contains the term ID for terms mapping are examined using the `seqdumper` command. The following outputs give the Tf-idf vectors for a single file and a sample dictionary file snippet:

```
Key: /a9996454.txt: Value: /a9996454.txt:{3050:4.144606113433838,2
77:2.0784096717834473,501:3.9535505771636963,190:1.200166940689087
,6974:2.745239496231079,998:3.8460910320281982,6977:1.971051096916
1987,2819:2.483874797821045,2496:1.2779039144515991,1185:4.5240955
3527832,2039:1.704549789428711,4493:2.9781711101531982,4418:3.8701
69162750244,4868:3.5626842975616455,5574:4.786459922790527,5556:6.
918078899383545,5802:4.449987411499023,779:5.297285556793213,1037:
3.028601884841919,5024:3.655057668685913,6496:2.589235305786133,12
46:5.009603500366211,7356:3.793208122253418,4662:3.541300296783447
3,6829:3.756840467453003,4325:2.8123786449432373,2121:4.4499874114
99023,6497:5.292787075042725,2640:3.2604033946990967,1045:4.316456
317901611,1542:5.075188636779785,643:5.143134593963623,2411:4.3164
56317901611,5123:7.907101154327393,5565:6.330745697021484,4773:2.5
56445360183716,7500:3.1770219802856445,6687:5.080615043640137,2683
:4.211770057678223,321:5.143134593963623,850:3.451458692550659,580
7:3.1000609397888184,7750:5.479607105255127,6370:3.157219171524048
,2868:5.9904327392578125,5561:2.276860475540161,3510:4.95756196975
708,7066:4.691149711608887,5721:3.655057668685913,2673:4.786459922
790527,2397:4.604138374328613,5208:2.784979820251465,195:1.6337237
358093262,7737:3.3048553466796875,1856:8.246277809143066,1854:5.47
9607105255127,3564:4.449987411499023,1402:3.451458692550659,7533:2
.2746293544769287,1881:5.297285556793213,5236:2.493925094604492,55
95:3.756840467453003,4947:2.589235305786133,5707:3.081711769104004
,6532:5.9904327392578125,4031:4.144606113433838,7249:2.84054970741
27197,4208:2.252763032913208,1902:4.997402191162109,5624:4.8918204
30755615,4676:1.9650808572769165,7765:2.4770045280456543,1638:12.7
9179573059082,1637:4.604138374328613,2995:2.930161714553833,4099:3
.157219171524048,2778:5.143134593963623,5874:2.930161714553833,248
3:8.76198959350586,574:5.143134593963623,3847:3.2199668884277344,6
704:4.786459922790527,3485:2.9146575927734375,3529:7.0053181648254
395,7574:5.143134593963623,7608:3.4781270027160645,2697:4.19867324
8291016,3597:2.84804368019104,5083:1.8686890602111816,2435:3.91099
09534454346,2896:3.756840467453003,7386:5.479607105255127,6678:5.9
904327392578125,4613:4.255831718444824,1526:4.691149711608887,4517
:5.26334810256958,4218:7.273904289245605,2561:2.5044660568237305,
2425:2.611708164215088,7065:4.255831718444824,387:5.14313459396362
3,6800:3.687847375869751,6244:2.635207414627075,3846:3.68784737586
9751,5904:2.352846384048462,3954:4.144606113433838,197:2.406913757
3242188,6774:4.604138374328613,3235:3.756840467453003,7205:5.14313
4593963623,1224:4.38099479675293,6898:2.473924398422241,32:1.26304
47149276733,601:5.143134593963623,3943:5.9904327392578125,2509:4.8
91820430755615,7181:3.4781270027160645,3337:4.188774108886719,3860
:2.6702041625976562,6963:4.198673248291016,7216:3.5336968898773193
,3925:4.152933120727539,1863:5.7027506828308105}
```

```
Input Path: /user/sandeepkaranth/grants-seqdir-sparse/dictionary.
file-0

......

Key: zirconia: Value: 7871

Key: znati: Value: 7872

Key: zoe: Value: 7873

Key: zone: Value: 7874

Key: zones: Value: 7875

Key: zooplankton: Value: 7876

Key: zygotes: Value: 7877

Key: zygotic: Value: 7878
```

5. Once we have the vectorized representations of our grants files, we then run k-means clustering. The Mahout binary has the `kmeans` command that is used to run this clustering algorithm. The distance metric we choose is the cosine distance measure and can be specified by the `-dm` option. It is implemented by the `org.apache.mahout.common.distance.CosineDistanceMeasure` class. In the following example, we specify the number of clusters as `3` with the `-k` switch. The `-x` switch can be used to specify the maximum number of iterations. In our case, we have set it to `10`.

6. We can view the cluster output by the k-means clustering using the `clusterdump` command supported by Mahout. The `clusterdump` command has some elaborate options such as the `-b` option that allows the user to choose the number of characters in the file to be displayed, the `-n` option that shows the topmost *n* terms based on the Tf-idf scores, and an `-evaluate` option to evaluate the input. The following snippet shows the output of the `clusterdump` command:

```
14/09/09 15:45:51 INFO evaluation.ClusterEvaluator: Scaled
Inter-Cluster Density = 0.6053257638783347

14/09/09 15:45:51 INFO evaluation.ClusterEvaluator: Intra-
Cluster Density[277] = 0.6828160148795702

14/09/09 15:45:51 INFO evaluation.ClusterEvaluator: Intra-
Cluster Density[423] = 0.6729720492208191

14/09/09 15:45:51 INFO evaluation.ClusterEvaluator: Intra-
Cluster Density[97] = 0.6610114589088609

14/09/09 15:45:51 INFO evaluation.ClusterEvaluator: Average
Intra-Cluster Density = 0.6722665076697502

14/09/09 15:45:51 INFO clustering.ClusterDumper: Wrote 3
clusters
```

RHadoop

R is a programming language used for statistics, data science, and visualization. It has a number of packages that can be imported to perform some specialized or custom tasks. It has more than 5,000 data analysis algorithms implemented as libraries. These algorithms can be used to facilitate a wide variety of data analysis tasks, much more than those supported by Apache Mahout. The community using R as a language is very big and vibrant.

However, R has two drawbacks: it executes in memory and its support for multithreading is minimal. These drawbacks make R unsuitable for big data crunching where disk-based analysis and distribution are mandatory. One alternative would be using R programs by using Hadoop Streaming. But this is a tedious proposition, and RHadoop had to be envisioned. RHadoop also uses Hadoop Streaming as its underlying mechanism to run R scripts in Hadoop, but alleviates some of the pain points that native streaming has. Some of the advantages of RHadoop are as follows:

- It eliminates the need to script R functions manually in the MapReduce paradigm. In-built library functions do this automatically for the user.

- It allows access—both reading and writing data from and to HDFS.

- It allows the same R script to run locally and on cluster environments.

RHadoop is a set of five R packages that can be used to analyze data in Hadoop. The following are the constituents of RHadoop:

- `ravro`: This is the R package that helps in serializing and deserializing data that is present in the Avro data format.

- `rmr`: This is the R package that provides Hadoop MapReduce functionality within R.

- `rhdfs`: This is the R package that provides functions to manage the data resident in HDFS from within R.

- `rhbase`: This is the R package that provides functions to manage an HBase database from within R.

- `plyrmr`: This is the R package used for structured data processing similar to `plyr`. This package uses `rmr` as the underlying framework.

Summary

Hadoop is a very useful tool for big data transformation and processing. It can come in handy at almost all the stages of the data analytics workflow. Data analytics is not about the algorithms but more about the data. Larger data can yield almost two-fold improvements in prediction. A data scientist should worry more about the cleansing, transformation, feature engineering, and validation of results rather than the actual algorithm that will be used to do the analysis. This does not mean that the analysis algorithm choice is not important. Instead, it means that there are other players that are equally important and vital for healthy decision making.

In this chapter, the key takeaways are as follows:

- Hadoop is generally used for analytics on data sizes of 1 TB and above. However, the ease of use brought about by functional programming concepts in Hadoop tempts people to use it for smaller data sizes. There is nothing wrong with this approach as long as they are cognizant of the fact about higher latency in doing so.

- Data mining is the branch that deals with discovering patterns and knowledge from data. Machine learning provides the tools for data mining.

- Machine learning algorithms are of the supervised, unsupervised, and the semi-supervised kind. Supervised learning requires labeling from domain experts and can be expensive. There are newer crowd-sourced methods that can gather labeled data. One such approach is to use Mechanical Turk by Amazon.

- Apache Mahout and RHadoop are popular data analysis libraries that have extensive support on Hadoop. Apache Mahout has stopped accepting algorithms in the MapReduce paradigm since April 2014. However, the older entries in the library still support Hadoop. It is important for the individual using these algorithms to check whether the implementation is parallelized or not as these libraries accept non-parallelized single-machine implementations as well.

- Tf-Idf is a popular metric used in text analytics. It takes into account both the popularity of a term in a document and penalizes non-differentiating terms by looking at the corpus that the documents come from. Cosine distance is used to measure similarity between documents. Euclidean distances fail because of variations in document lengths.

Hadoop for
Microsoft Windows

Traditionally, Hadoop has been supported on Unix-based operating systems. Installation on Microsoft Windows was tedious and not consistent. It involved installing Unix-based emulators such as Cygwin and carrying out installation steps similar to Hadoop installations on Unix systems. Other alternatives were to run a Linux virtual machine on Windows hosts and install Hadoop on them. But Hadoop was still not natively available on the Microsoft Windows operating system until Hadoop 2.0 arrived.

With all major players moving into the cloud, the **Hadoop as a Service (HaaS)** offering is becoming popular. It offers an easy and cost-efficient way of analyzing big data on the cloud. Microsoft also joined the cloud bandwagon with the Azure suite of services on the cloud. The Microsoft Azure cloud not only supports Linux Virtual Machines, but also provides Hadoop as a service. Players such as Hortonworks collaborated with Microsoft to bring Hadoop to Windows.

Hadoop's native support on Microsoft Windows becomes immensely important because:

- Microsoft Windows is known for having excellent tooling for business intelligence. Microsoft Excel, PowerPivot for Excel, and PowerView are a few examples of tools that can facilitate powerful decision making by analyzing and visualizing data from enterprise data sources. The power of these native Windows tools can be unleashed on big data stored and processed by Hadoop.

- SQL Server and related technologies are native Windows database solutions that are widely deployed in many enterprises. They cater to the enterprise needs of storing and managing structured data. With Hadoop on Windows natively, unstructured data can also be added into the mix for insightful decision making. This involves almost zero migration and learning costs for the enterprise.

In this chapter, we will look at single-node deployment of Hadoop on Microsoft Windows.

Deploying Hadoop on Microsoft Windows

In this section, we will look in detail as to how we can build and install Hadoop natively on a Windows system. We will be using Windows 8 to install Hadoop. The same steps can be employed to install Hadoop on Windows Server 2008 or Windows 7. We will be installing Hadoop on a 64-bit Windows OS running on 64-bit hardware.

Prerequisites

Installing Hadoop on Windows requires the following platforms, software, and tools installed:

- **Java JDK**: Java is the soul of Hadoop and requires it to be installed on the machine. Java from Oracle comes with the **Java Runtime Environment** (JRE) and the **Java Development Kit** (JDK). Hadoop installation requires the JDK. The JDK can be obtained from Oracle's website. To reiterate, it is very important to choose the JDK that is higher than 1.6. We will choose the latest— JDK 1.8. The following screenshot shows the page from where the JDK can be downloaded. In this example, we choose the **Windows x64** product. A 32-bit user can choose the **Windows x86** product. The download is about 170 MB in size. Once downloaded, it can be installed using the installer in the package. It is very important to choose the right processor architecture and OS for the JDK. Otherwise, there could be undesirable results.

Java SE Development Kit 8u20

You must accept the Oracle Binary Code License Agreement for Java SE to download this software.

Thank you for accepting the Oracle Binary Code License Agreement for Java SE; you may now download this software.

Product / File Description	File Size	Download
Linux x86	135.24 MB	jdk-8u20-linux-i586.rpm
Linux x86	154.87 MB	jdk-8u20-linux-i586.tar.gz
Linux x64	135.6 MB	jdk-8u20-linux-x64.rpm
Linux x64	153.42 MB	jdk-8u20-linux-x64.tar.gz
Mac OS X x64	209.11 MB	jdk-8u20-macosx-x64.dmg
Solaris SPARC 64-bit (SVR4 package)	137.02 MB	jdk-8u20-solaris-sparcv9.tar.Z
Solaris SPARC 64-bit	97.09 MB	jdk-8u20-solaris-sparcv9.tar.gz
Solaris x64 (SVR4 package)	137.16 MB	jdk-8u20-solaris-x64.tar.Z
Solaris x64	94.22 MB	jdk-8u20-solaris-x64.tar.gz
Windows x86	161.08 MB	jdk-8u20-windows-i586.exe
Windows x64	173.08 MB	jdk-8u20-windows-x64.exe

Java SE Development Kit 8u20 Demos and Samples Downloads

Java SE Development Kit 8u20 Demos and Samples Downloads are released under the Oracle BSD License.

Product / File Description	File Size	Download
Linux x86	58.65 MB	jdk-8u20-linux-i586-demos.rpm
Linux x86	58.49 MB	jdk-8u20-linux-i586-demos.tar.gz
Linux x64	58.71 MB	jdk-8u20-linux-x64-demos.rpm
Linux x64	58.56 MB	jdk-8u20-linux-x64-demos.tar.gz
Mac OS X	59.22 MB	jdk-8u20-macosx-x86_64-demos.zip
Solaris SPARC 64-bit	13.57 MB	jdk-8u20-solaris-sparcv9-demos.tar.Z
Solaris SPARC 64-bit	9.28 MB	jdk-8u20-solaris-sparcv9-demos.tar.gz
Solaris x64	13.5 MB	jdk-8u20-solaris-x64-demos.tar.Z
Solaris x64	9.22 MB	jdk-8u20-solaris-x64-demos.tar.gz

- **Setting the Path variable**: Now the Windows `Path` environment variable has to be set so that the command-line tools can directly pick the Java executable from the path. In the Windows **Control Panel**, under **System Properties**, a button is provided for **Environment Variables**. Clicking on this button opens up the **Environment Variables** dialog. The appropriate environment variable can be chosen for editing if it is already present, or a new one can be created. We use the existing `Path` variable and add the `bin` folder for the Java binaries. In the preceding example, it is `C:\Program Files\Java\jdk1.8.0_20\bin\`. It is very important to separate the paths using a semicolon. The path can be tested by opening the command prompt and typing `java -version`. This should give the version number of the installed Java software. The following screenshot shows the setting of the `Path` environment variable:

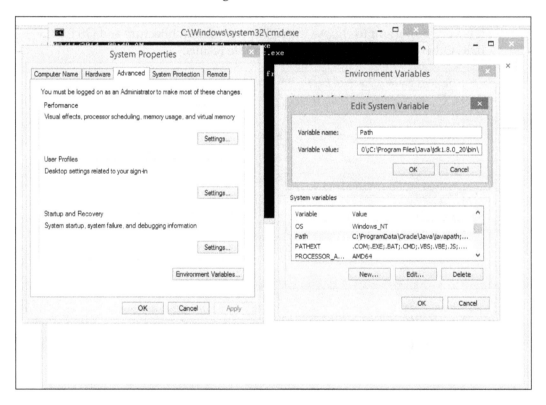

- **Setting the JAVA_HOME environment variable**: All Hadoop binaries choose the version of Java by looking up the JAVA_HOME directory. It is important to set this variable before starting off with Hadoop deployment and usage. Again, we use the **Environment Variables** dialog to do this. This time, instead of editing, we click on the **New** button to add a variable. In the following example, we set JAVA_HOME as C:\Progra~1\Java\jdk1.8.0_20. It is important to note that the Program Files folder has been shortened to a 8-letter path called Progra~1. This is because Hadoop does not handle spaces in the paths. Windows OS understands this 8-letter scheme, as it is a legacy feature.

  The following screenshot shows the actual setting of the JAVA_HOME environment variable:

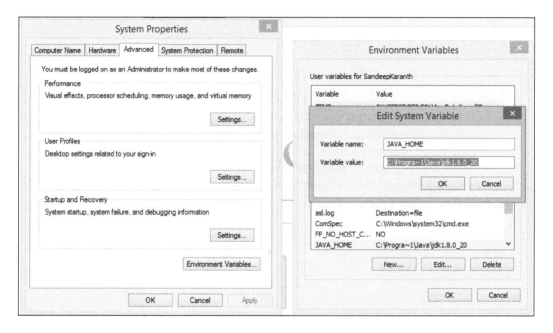

- **Downloading Hadoop sources**: We download the Hadoop sources from the nearest mirror site. It is important to download the sources, compile them, and then deploy Hadoop on Windows for native support. Using the binaries as is throws an error when deploying Hadoop on Windows. At a later point of time, there could be support to install Hadoop from binaries. We choose the latest version of Hadoop to install, Hadoop 2.5.0. As in the following screenshot, we download only the source tar file, hadoop-2.5.0-src.tar.gz. The sources can then be extracted into a local folder. The download is about 15 MB in size.

In the example, we download and extract the sources to the `C:\hdp\hdp` directory. It will save you a lot of pain if the directory names are short. Windows has some restrictions on the maximum number of characters in the directory name.

- **Protobuf compiler**: Protobuf is a serialization format and the Hadoop build requires this compiler to be available during the build process. The Windows version of the compiler binary needs to be downloaded. In this example, we choose `protoc-2.5.0-win32.zip` and download it as shown in the following screenshot. Once we download and extract it, we use the **Environment Variables** dialog to add the `bin` directory of the protobuf compiler to the `Path`.

- **Maven Build System**: Hadoop is built using the Maven build system. The build system uses specifications specified in the `pom.xml` file, which is found in the `root` directory of the Hadoop sources. To install Maven on the Windows machine, we can go to the Maven project page and download the latest Apache Maven binaries. We choose the version 3.2.3. Once downloaded, the ZIP file is extracted and the `bin` folder is again appended in the `Path` environment variable for ease of use.

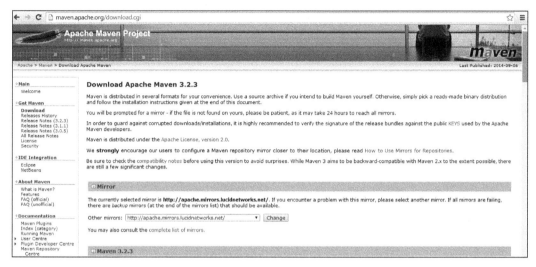

Download page for Apache Maven 3.2.3

- The next important thing is to download the Windows SDK. If you are using an x86 machine, it is important to get the x86 build tools. Otherwise, the user needs to get the x64 build tools. Installing a high SKU of Visual Studio may install all the necessary tools. In this example, we will install Visual Studio Express for C++ 2010, which is a free Visual Studio download. This Visual Studio SKU does not come with the Windows SDK. We must separately install the Windows SDK. The version of the Windows SDK installed is 7.1. To verify that the SDK is installed, you can navigate to `C:\Program Files\ Microsoft SDKs\Windows` on your computer. For x86 machines, it will be present in `C:\Program Files(x86)\Microsoft SDKs\Windows`. Also, it is important to include the SDKs `bin` folder in the `Path` environment so that the build process can automatically pick it up. An alternative to using the Windows build tools is installing CMake, but this requires the user to change a few configurations within the `pom.xml` files in the Hadoop sources.

Building Hadoop

Once all the pre-requisites are in place, Hadoop can be built and packaged. To do the build, you can open the Microsoft Visual Studio command prompt. It sets some of the necessary environment settings. Additionally:

1. It is important to set the `Platform` environment variable to `x64` or `Win32` depending on the Hadoop deployment desired. This can be done using the following command:

   ```
   set Platform=x64
   ```

   For Win32, use the following command:

   ```
   set Platform=Win32
   ```

2. It is very important to ensure that the environment variable has the right name. This variable is case sensitive and instructs the Visual Studio project files to use the appropriate build configuration.

3. The next step is to actually issue the Maven build command. The command `mvn package -Pdist,native-win -DskipTests -Dtar` is used to start the build. Using the newer JDK can cause some parse issues when generating Javadocs. This can be solved by either using an older JDK such as 1.7 or skipping Javadocs generation. The latter is done by adding the `-Dmaven.javadocs.skip=true` option in the Maven package command.

   The following screenshot shows the end of the build process. The summary of the standard output shows the status of each build step. Once a failure is encountered, the rest of the steps are skipped. It is also important to have the computer connected to the Internet during the build process. Maven automatically downloads dependencies from configured binary repositories during the build process:

```
Visual Studio Command Prompt (2010)                              _  □  ×

[INFO] Apache Hadoop HDFS ............................... SUCCESS [02:07 min]
[INFO] Apache Hadoop HttpFS ............................. SUCCESS [ 29.920 s]
[INFO] Apache Hadoop HDFS BookKeeper Journal ............ SUCCESS [  8.066 s]
[INFO] Apache Hadoop HDFS-NFS .......................... SUCCESS [  0.778 s]
[INFO] Apache Hadoop HDFS Project ...................... SUCCESS [  0.055 s]
[INFO] hadoop-yarn ..................................... SUCCESS [  0.052 s]
[INFO] hadoop-yarn-api ................................. SUCCESS [ 37.205 s]
[INFO] hadoop-yarn-common .............................. SUCCESS [  8.169 s]
[INFO] hadoop-yarn-server .............................. SUCCESS [  0.061 s]
[INFO] hadoop-yarn-server-common ....................... SUCCESS [  2.124 s]
[INFO] hadoop-yarn-server-nodemanager .................. SUCCESS [ 10.652 s]
[INFO] hadoop-yarn-server-web-proxy .................... SUCCESS [  0.284 s]
[INFO] hadoop-yarn-server-applicationhistoryservice .... SUCCESS [  0.496 s]
[INFO] hadoop-yarn-server-resourcemanager .............. SUCCESS [  4.664 s]
[INFO] hadoop-yarn-server-tests ........................ SUCCESS [  0.335 s]
[INFO] hadoop-yarn-client .............................. SUCCESS [  0.409 s]
[INFO] hadoop-yarn-applications ........................ SUCCESS [  0.054 s]
[INFO] hadoop-yarn-applications-distributedshell ....... SUCCESS [  3.552 s]
[INFO] hadoop-yarn-applications-unmanaged-am-launcher .. SUCCESS [  0.174 s]
[INFO] hadoop-yarn-site ................................ SUCCESS [  3.439 s]
[INFO] hadoop-yarn-project ............................. SUCCESS [  5.835 s]
[INFO] hadoop-mapreduce-client ......................... SUCCESS [  0.173 s]
[INFO] hadoop-mapreduce-client-core .................... SUCCESS [  9.365 s]
[INFO] hadoop-mapreduce-client-common .................. SUCCESS [ 15.497 s]
[INFO] hadoop-mapreduce-client-shuffle ................. SUCCESS [  4.117 s]
[INFO] hadoop-mapreduce-client-app ..................... SUCCESS [  1.249 s]
[INFO] hadoop-mapreduce-client-hs ...................... SUCCESS [  8.073 s]
[INFO] hadoop-mapreduce-client-jobclient ............... SUCCESS [  1.917 s]
[INFO] hadoop-mapreduce-client-hs-plugins .............. SUCCESS [  0.147 s]
[INFO] Apache Hadoop MapReduce Examples ................ SUCCESS [  2.223 s]
[INFO] hadoop-mapreduce ................................ SUCCESS [  5.418 s]
[INFO] Apache Hadoop MapReduce Streaming ............... SUCCESS [  0.526 s]
[INFO] Apache Hadoop Distributed Copy .................. SUCCESS [  8.463 s]
[INFO] Apache Hadoop Archives .......................... SUCCESS [  0.168 s]
[INFO] Apache Hadoop Rumen ............................. SUCCESS [  3.711 s]
[INFO] Apache Hadoop Gridmix ........................... SUCCESS [  3.811 s]
[INFO] Apache Hadoop Data Join ......................... SUCCESS [  0.232 s]
[INFO] Apache Hadoop Extras ............................ SUCCESS [  3.550 s]
[INFO] Apache Hadoop Pipes ............................. SUCCESS [  0.046 s]
[INFO] Apache Hadoop OpenStack support ................. SUCCESS [  4.067 s]
[INFO] Apache Hadoop Client ............................ SUCCESS [ 14.406 s]
[INFO] Apache Hadoop Mini-Cluster ...................... SUCCESS [  0.135 s]
[INFO] Apache Hadoop Scheduler Load Simulator .......... SUCCESS [  3.873 s]
[INFO] Apache Hadoop Tools Dist ........................ SUCCESS [ 13.643 s]
[INFO] Apache Hadoop Tools ............................. SUCCESS [  0.064 s]
[INFO] Apache Hadoop Distribution ...................... SUCCESS [ 59.012 s]
[INFO] ------------------------------------------------------------------------
[INFO] BUILD SUCCESS
[INFO] ------------------------------------------------------------------------
[INFO] Total time: 09:33 min
[INFO] Finished at: 2014-09-13T00:00:36-07:00
[INFO] Final Memory: 91M/482M
[INFO] ------------------------------------------------------------------------
C:\hdp\hadoop>_
```

4. The build yields a target directory. Inside the target directory, Hadoop binaries, samples, and configuration files are bundled in a zipped TAR file. In this example, a `hadoop-2.5.0.tar.gz` file is generated. We extract the contents of the file to the `C:\hdp\hdp` path.

Configuring Hadoop

In this section, we will see the different configuration settings for single-node deployment of Hadoop on Windows:

1. The `Hadoop-env.cmd` file is present in the `etc\hadoop` directory at the root of the Hadoop installation. This is the configuration directory for Hadoop. The `hadoop-env.cmd` command file needs to be modified to set the right environment to execute the Hadoop daemons correctly. The most important configuration is the setting of the `JAVA_HOME` environment variable. We also set `HADOOP_HOME` to the root of the Hadoop installation, that is, the path from where we extracted the Hadoop binaries and configuration files. The `HADOOP_CONF_DIR` and `YARN_CONF_DIR` environment variables are set to the configuration directories of Hadoop and YARN respectively. The YARN configuration directory is the same as the Hadoop configuration directory in our example. We also add the Hadoop directories to the `Path` variable. The following script snippet is a sample `hadoop-env.cmd` script file:

```
@rem The java implementation to use.  Required.
set JAVA_HOME=%JAVA_HOME%


set HADOOP_HOME=c:\hdp\hdp


@rem The jsvc implementation to use. Jsvc is required to run
secure datanodes.
@rem set JSVC_HOME=%JSVC_HOME%


set HADOOP_CONF_DIR=%HADOOP_HOME%\etc\hadoop


set YARN_CONF_DIR=%HADOOP_CONF_DIR%
set PATH=%PATH%;%HADOOP_HOME%\bin


@rem Extra Java CLASSPATH elements.  Automatically insert
capacity-scheduler.
if exist %HADOOP_HOME%\contrib\capacity-scheduler (
  if not defined HADOOP_CLASSPATH (
    set HADOOP_CLASSPATH=%HADOOP_HOME%\contrib\capacity-
      scheduler\*.jar
  ) else (
    set HADOOP_CLASSPATH=%HADOOP_CLASSPATH%;%HADOOP_HOME%
      \contrib\capacity-scheduler\*.jar
  )
```

```
)

@rem The maximum amount of heap to use, in MB. Default is
1000.
@rem set HADOOP_HEAPSIZE=
@rem set HADOOP_NAMENODE_INIT_HEAPSIZE=""

@rem Extra Java runtime options.  Empty by default.
@rem set HADOOP_OPTS=%HADOOP_OPTS% -
Djava.net.preferIPv4Stack=true

@rem Command specific options appended to HADOOP_OPTS when
specified
if not defined HADOOP_SECURITY_LOGGER (
  set HADOOP_SECURITY_LOGGER=INFO,RFAS
)

if not defined HDFS_AUDIT_LOGGER (
  set HDFS_AUDIT_LOGGER=INFO,NullAppender
)

set HADOOP_NAMENODE_OPTS=-
Dhadoop.security.logger=%HADOOP_SECURITY_LOGGER% -
Dhdfs.audit.logger=%HDFS_AUDIT_LOGGER% %HADOOP_NAMENODE_OPTS%
set HADOOP_DATANODE_OPTS=-Dhadoop.security.logger=ERROR,RFAS
  %HADOOP_DATANODE_OPTS%
set HADOOP_SECONDARYNAMENODE_OPTS=-
  Dhadoop.security.logger=%HADOOP_SECURITY_LOGGER% -
    Dhdfs.audit.logger=%HDFS_AUDIT_LOGGER%
      %HADOOP_SECONDARYNAMENODE_OPTS%

@rem The following applies to multiple commands (fs, dfs,
  fsck, distcp etc)
set HADOOP_CLIENT_OPTS=-Xmx512m %HADOOP_CLIENT_OPTS%
@rem set HADOOP_JAVA_PLATFORM_OPTS="-XX:-UsePerfData
  %HADOOP_JAVA_PLATFORM_OPTS%"

@rem On secure datanodes, user to run the datanode as after
  dropping privileges
set HADOOP_SECURE_DN_USER=%HADOOP_SECURE_DN_USER%

@rem Where log files are stored.  %HADOOP_HOME%/logs by
  default.
```

```
@rem set HADOOP_LOG_DIR=%HADOOP_LOG_DIR%\%USERNAME%


@rem Where log files are stored in the secure data environment.
set
HADOOP_SECURE_DN_LOG_DIR=%HADOOP_LOG_DIR%\%HADOOP_HDFS_USER%


@rem The directory where pid files are stored. /tmp by
  default.
@rem NOTE: this should be set to a directory that can only be
  written to by
@rem        the user that will run the hadoop daemons.
  Otherwise there is the
@rem        potential for a symlink attack.
set HADOOP_PID_DIR=%HADOOP_PID_DIR%
set HADOOP_SECURE_DN_PID_DIR=%HADOOP_PID_DIR%


@rem A string representing this instance of hadoop. %USERNAME%
  by default.
set HADOOP_IDENT_STRING=%USERNAME%
```

2. Next we configure the `core-site.xml` file. The most important configuration is setting the `fs.default.name` property to the HDFS NameNode host and port. In our case, since it is a single node deployment, it points to `localhost` on port `19000`. The following configuration snippet illustrates this setting:

```
<configuration>
    <property>
        <name>fs.default.name</name>
        <value>hdfs://0.0.0.0:19000</value>
    </property>
 </configuration>
```

3. We then configure the `hdfs-site.xml` file. Here we set the replication factor to 1 as we are doing a single-node deployment of Hadoop. The following configuration snippet illustrates this setting:

```
<configuration>
    <property>
        <name>dfs.replication</name>
        <value>1</value>
    </property>
</configuration>
```

4. The `mapred-site.xml` file needs to be configured and pointed to YARN in Hadoop 2.X. The `%USERNAME%` element can be replaced by the username of the entity submitting the jobs. The following configuration snippet illustrates a sample `mapred-site.xml` file. If the file is not present, it can be copied from the `mapred-site.xml.template` file present in the configuration directory:

```
<configuration>
    <property>
        <name>mapreduce.job.user.name</name>
        <value>%USERNAME%</value>
    </property>
    <property>
        <name>mapreduce.framework.name</name>
        <value>yarn</value>
    </property>
    <property>
        <name>yarn.apps.stagingDir</name>
        <value>/user/%USERNAME%/staging</value>
    </property>
    <property>
        <name>mapreduce.jobtracker.address</name>
        <value>local</value>
    </property>
</configuration>
```

5. The `yarn-site.xml` file is configured for the settings on the ResourceManager and NodeManager daemons. The configurations include setting the daemon endpoints and the log directories, and specifying the shuffle handlers. The following configuration snippet illustrates a sample configuration for the YARN daemons:

```
<configuration>
    <property>
        <name>yarn.server.resourcemanager.address</name>
        <value>0.0.0.0:8020</value>
    </property>
    <property>
        <name>yarn.server.resourcemanager.application
            .expiry.interval</name>
        <value>60000</value>
    </property>
     <property>
        <name>yarn.server.nodemanager.address</name>
        <value>0.0.0.0:45454</value>
    </property>
     <property>
        <name>yarn.nodemanager.aux-services</name>
```

```xml
          <value>mapreduce_shuffle</value>
      </property>
      <property>
          <name>yarn.nodemanager.aux-
              services.mapreduce.shuffle.class</name>
          <value>org.apache.hadoop.mapred
              .ShuffleHandler</value>
      </property>
      <property>
          <name>yarn.server.nodemanager.remote-app-log-
              dir</name>
       <value>/app-logs</value>
      </property>
      <property>
          <name>yarn.nodemanager.log-dirs</name>
          <value>/dep/logs/userlogs</value>
      </property>
      <property>
          <name>yarn.server.mapreduce-appmanager.attempt-
              listener.bindAddress</name>
          <value>0.0.0.0</value>
      </property>
      <property>
          <name>yarn.server.mapreduce-appmanager.client-
              service.bindAddress</name>
          <value>0.0.0.0</value>
      </property>
      <property>
          <name>yarn.log-aggregation-enable</name>
          <value>true</value>
      </property>
      <property>
          <name>yarn.log-aggregation.retain-seconds</name>
          <value>-1</value>    </property>
      <property>
          <name>yarn.application.classpath</name>
          <value>%HADOOP_CONF_DIR%,%HADOOP_COMMON_HOME%/share/
hadoop/
common/*,%HADOOP_COMMON_HOME%/share/hadoop/common/lib/*,%HA
DOOP_HDFS_HOME%/share/hadoop/hdfs/*,%HADOOP_HDFS_HOME%/shar
e/hadoop/hdfs/lib/*,%HADOOP_MAPRED_HOME%/share/hadoop/mapre
duce/*,%HADOOP_MAPRED_HOME%/share/hadoop/mapreduce/lib/*,%H
ADOOP_YARN_HOME%/share/hadoop/yarn/*,%HADOOP_YARN_HOME%/sha
re/hadoop/yarn/lib/*</value>
      </property>
</configuration>
```

Deploying Hadoop

Once the configurations are complete, it is time to start the Hadoop daemons. This is done by performing the following steps:

1. Before starting the daemons, we can format the NameNode by issuing the following command:

```
hdfs namenode -format
```

The following screenshot shows the output of the format command. Now the HDFS is formatted and ready to use. Since we have not specified a particular directory name, the NameNode uses the `C:\tmp` directory to store all of the metadata.

2. We then start the HDFS daemons, the NameNode, and the DataNode. This is done by issuing `start-dfs.cmd`. This command script is present in the `%HADOOP_HOME%\sbin` folder. The Windows firewall may pop up a notification asking the user to allow the daemons to open a listening port in the firewall. It is important to allow the firewall to be reconfigured so that the DataNode and NameNode can communicate with each other. The following screenshot shows the Windows Firewall screen offering to allow access:

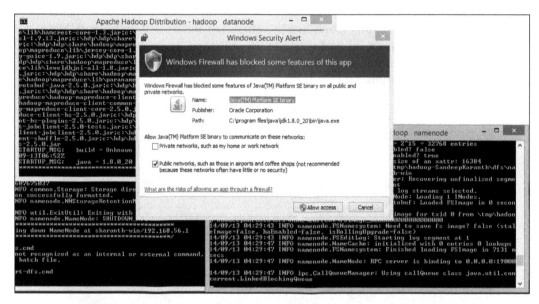

Once access has been granted, the NameNode and DataNode start in two separate command windows, as shown in the following screenshot. The standard output of each HDFS operation can be examined in these two windows. Issuing HDFS commands on the filesystem once both the daemons are up and running can conduct tests to validate HDFS. You might have to create the user directories using the `mkdir` command before starting off though.

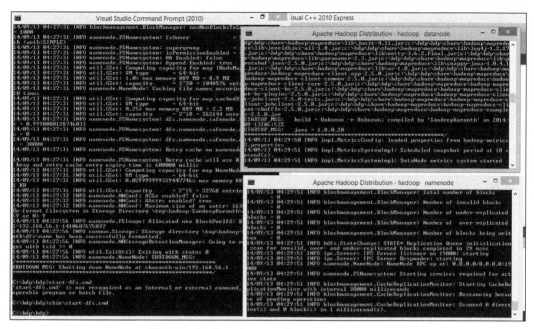

The NameNode and DataNode command windows

3. Next we need to start the YARN to run MapReduce jobs. This can be done by the `start-yarn.cmd` file present in the `sbin` folder. Again, the ResourceManager and the NodeManager start off in two separate command windows as illustrated in the following screenshot. The standard output can be examined to see the trace on the ResourceManager and NodeManager.

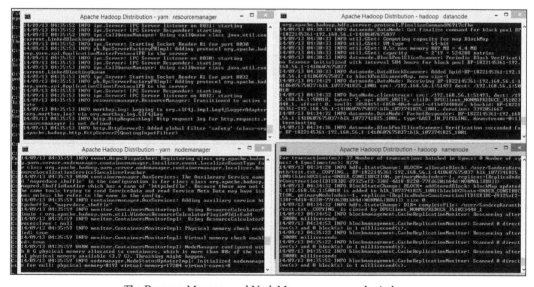

The ResourceManager and NodeManager command windows

4. By navigating to `localhost:50070` on the browser, the user should now be able to see the web endpoint for HDFS. The home page is shown in the following screenshot. It gives an overview of the health of HDFS and the different parameters that were used to configure it.

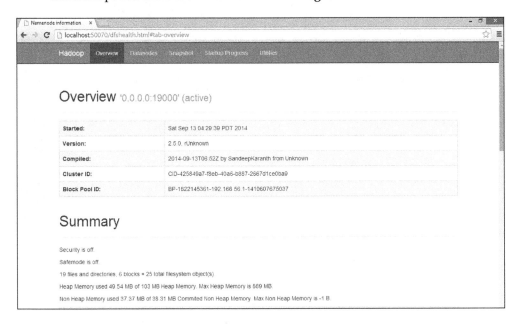

5. Selecting the **Datanodes** link on the top bar gives the different DataNodes present in HDFS and the health of each DataNode, as shown in the following screenshot:

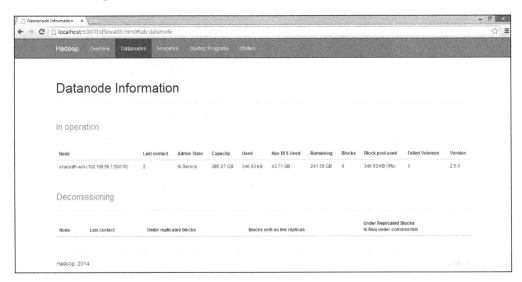

6. The startup progress link in the top bar shows the health of HDFS during startup. This includes statistics about the `fsimage` and `edits` file during NameNode startup. It also indicates whether HDFS went into safe mode or not.

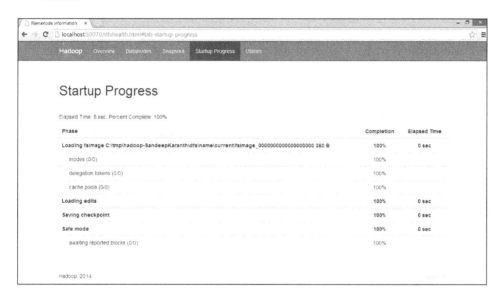

7. The utilities link gives two options: one to browse HDFS and the other to view the logfiles. The browse functionality is based on a search box that can be used to search the HDFS directory structure. Each listing for a file is similar to executing the `hdfs dfs -ls` command on the directory. It also gives statistics about the block size and a deep link to peek into the contents of the file.

Summary

With cloud computing becoming a focus for its elasticity and cost-effectiveness, Microsoft has moved into the arena to compete with existing players. To maintain parity with competition, Microsoft Azure not only offers Linux-based Virtual Machines, but has also embraced open source big data systems such as Hadoop. HDInsight offers HaaS on Microsoft Azure.

The key takeaways from this chapter are as follows:

- Hadoop is now natively available on Windows. Installing Unix emulators or Linux VMs on Windows OS is no longer necessary.

- Hadoop support on Windows natively has two missing features: Security features and short-circuit HDFS reads are not yet integrated with this system.

- Hadoop on Windows requires building the Hadoop distribution from scratch. Direct download of Hadoop binaries for Windows is not yet available.

- HDInsight, Hadoop as a service offering on Microsoft Azure, provides seamless Excel integration and integration with platforms such as the Hortonworks Data Platform.

Index

LZO compression format 154

M

machine learning
  about 299
  process, steps 300, 301
machine learning, types
  semi-supervised learning 300
  supervised learning 299
  unsupervised learning 300
manual failover 266
Map data type, Pig 72
MapFile format 150, 151
MapR 29
MapReduce
  about 31, 192
  and Avro 139-141
  Map 31
  Reduce 31
MapReduce input
  about 32
  filtering 41-44
  Hadoop's small files, dealing 35-40
  InputFormat class 32
  InputSplit class 33
  RecordReader class 34
mapreduce mode 71
MapReduce output
  optimizing 52
  speculative execution, of tasks 52
MapReduce plan, Pig scripts compilation 75
MAPS, complex types 108
Map-side aggregation for GROUP BY 120
Map-side joins
  about 64-67, 121
  considerations 64
Map task
  about 31, 44
  Combiners 48, 49
  dfs.blocksize attribute 45
  intermediate outputs, fetching 49
  intermediate outputs, sorting 46-48
  intermediate outputs, spilling 46-48
Master node, Apache Storm
  about 194
  key functions 194

MasterServer 211
Maven Build System 325
merge() function 125
Merge join 85
Merge-sparse join 85
metastore, Hive 106
Microsoft Azure HDInsight. *See* HDInsight
Multi-Group-By Inserts 120
multiquery mode, Pig 100

N

name quotas 284
NameServiceId 262
Namespace, HDFS architecture 258
Namespace Volume 260
nested FOREACH operator 79, 80
nextTuple method 198
nimbus command 217
node command 188
node-local reducers. *See* Combiners
NodeManager (NM) 20, 158, 161, 169
none grouping 204
Nutch 13

O

Object-relational mapping (ORM) 106
open method 198
optimization rules, Pig
  AddForEach 98
  FilterLogicExpressionSimplifier 96
  GroupByConstParallelSetter 98
  LimitOptimizer 98
  MergeFilter 97
  MergeForEach 98
  PartitionFilterOptimizer 96
  PushDownForEachFlatten 98
  PushUpFilter 97
  SplitFilter 97
Optimized Row Columnar files
    (ORC files) 109
ORDER BY clause
  versus SORT BY clause 120
outputs, Map task
  fetching 49
  sorting 46-48

small files, Hadoop
  dealing with 35-40
snapshots, HDFS 22
Software as a Service (SaaS) 221
Sort Avoidance 48
SORT BY clause
  versus ORDER BY clause 120
Sort join 85
space quotas 284
Spark 162
specialized joins, Pig
  Merge join 85
  Replicated join 83
  Skewed join 84
  usage 103
speculative execution 52
split-brain scenario 266
splits
  and compressions 153
spout 196
SQL
  about 70, 105
  versus Pig 70, 71
ssl-client.xml file, properties
  ssl.client.keystore.location 291
  ssl.client.keystore.password 291
  ssl.client.keystore.type 291
  ssl.client.truststore.location 291
  ssl.client.truststore.password 291
  ssl.client.truststore.reload.interval 291
  ssl.client.truststore.type 291
SSL configuration
  modifying 287-289
ssl-server.xml file, properties
  ssl.server.keystore.location 290
  ssl.server.keystore.password 290
  ssl.server.keystore.type 290
  ssl.server.truststore.location 290
  ssl.server.truststore.password 290
  ssl.server.truststore.reload.interval 290
  ssl.server.truststore.type 290
stagglers 52
stemming 307
storage layer enhancements, Hadoop 2.X
  HDFS Federation 22
  HDFS snapshots 22
  high availability 20, 21

store functions 95
Storm 162
Storm-on-YARN
  building 207
  installation procedure 208-216
  installing 207
  prerequisites 207
Stream 196
streaming computation models 192
streaming paradigm 191
stream processing
  diagrammatic representation 193
STRUCTS, complex types 108
supervised learning 299
supervisor command 217
supporting components, Hive 107

T

table 111
term frequency 304, 305
Term Frequency - Inverse Document
      Frequency (Tf-idf)
  about 304-306
  calculating, in Pig 306-309
terminate() method 125
terminatePartial() method 125
three-layer network topology
  versus four-layer network topology 267
Thrift
  about 145
  versus Avro 145
throughput 25
Ticket Granting Server (TGS) 276
Ticket Granting Ticket (TGT) 277
timeline, Hadoop 16, 17
topologies 194, 196
training data 299
truststore
  about 289
  configuring 289-293
Tuple data type, Pig 72

U

UDTF 123-127
ui command 217
UNION operator 81, 82

Thank you for buying
Mastering Hadoop

About Packt Publishing

Packt, pronounced 'packed', published its first book, *Mastering phpMyAdmin for Effective MySQL Management*, in April 2004, and subsequently continued to specialize in publishing highly focused books on specific technologies and solutions.

Our books and publications share the experiences of your fellow IT professionals in adapting and customizing today's systems, applications, and frameworks. Our solution-based books give you the knowledge and power to customize the software and technologies you're using to get the job done. Packt books are more specific and less general than the IT books you have seen in the past. Our unique business model allows us to bring you more focused information, giving you more of what you need to know, and less of what you don't.

Packt is a modern yet unique publishing company that focuses on producing quality, cutting-edge books for communities of developers, administrators, and newbies alike. For more information, please visit our website at www.packtpub.com.

About Packt Open Source

In 2010, Packt launched two new brands, Packt Open Source and Packt Enterprise, in order to continue its focus on specialization. This book is part of the Packt Open Source brand, home to books published on software built around open source licenses, and offering information to anybody from advanced developers to budding web designers. The Open Source brand also runs Packt's Open Source Royalty Scheme, by which Packt gives a royalty to each open source project about whose software a book is sold.

Writing for Packt

We welcome all inquiries from people who are interested in authoring. Book proposals should be sent to author@packtpub.com. If your book idea is still at an early stage and you would like to discuss it first before writing a formal book proposal, then please contact us; one of our commissioning editors will get in touch with you.

We're not just looking for published authors; if you have strong technical skills but no writing experience, our experienced editors can help you develop a writing career, or simply get some additional reward for your expertise.

Big Data Analytics with R and Hadoop

ISBN: 978-1-78216-328-2   Paperback: 238 pages

Set up an integrated infrastructure of R and Hadoop to turn your data analytics into Big Data analytics

1. Write Hadoop MapReduce within R.

2. Learn data analytics with R and the Hadoop platform.

3. Handle HDFS data within R.

4. Understand Hadoop streaming with R.

5. Encode and enrich datasets into R.

Microsoft SQL Server 2012 with Hadoop

ISBN: 978-1-78217-798-2   Paperback: 96 pages

Integrate data between Apache Hadoop and SQL Server 2012 and provide business intelligence on the heterogeneous data

1. Integrate data from unstructured (Hadoop) and structured (SQL Server 2012) sources.

2. Configure and install connectors for a bi-directional transfer of data.

3. Full of illustrations, diagrams, and tips with clear, step-by-step instructions and practical examples.

Please check **www.PacktPub.com** for information on our titles

Hadoop MapReduce Cookbook

ISBN: 978-1-84951-728-7   Paperback: 300 pages

Recipes for analyzing large and complex datasets with Hadoop MapReduce

1. Learn to process large and complex data sets, starting simply, then diving in deep.

2. Solve complex big data problems such as classifications, finding relationships, online marketing and recommendations.

3. More than 50 Hadoop MapReduce recipes, presented in a simple and straightforward manner, with step-by-step instructions and real world examples.

Securing Hadoop

ISBN: 978-1-78328-525-9   Paperback: 116 pages

Implement robust end-to-end security for your Hadoop ecosystem

1. Master the key concepts behind Hadoop security as well as how to secure a Hadoop-based Big Data ecosystem.

2. Understand and deploy authentication, authorization, and data encryption in a Hadoop-based Big Data platform.

3. Administer the auditing and security event monitoring system.

Please check **www.PacktPub.com** for information on our titles

CPSIA information can be obtained
at www.ICGtesting.com
Printed in the USA
BVHW052306210221
600749BV00005B/77